EVEN SEAGULLS CRY

Agnes Rands

Linden Press • Sisters, Oregon

ISBN: 0-9675827-1-7

Linden Press
Sisters, Oregon

Rosanna Mattingly - Meta Writing and Education Services: Portland, OR
Mike Banner: Cover photos

Printed in the United States of America by
Maverick Publications • Bend, Oregon

DEDICATION

To Charles Warren,
my husband of four years,
who advised and encouraged me
in the writing of my book,
though at times I felt
that the story was not that important.
And perhaps it isn't.
But Chuck would remind me
that I was writing a personal chronicle
of an important time
in the history of our world,
and that this was justification
enough for the book.

WORDS OF APPRECIATION

To my sister Thelma Banner, Shelton, WA, and to my cousin Art Carlson and his wife Alice, Marietta, GA, for sharing their memories of our family and the world around us during my growing-up years. To my nephew, Mike Banner, for the untold hours he spent on Anacortes beaches, snapping pictures of seagulls in flight.

To my four daughters, Debbie Cullen, Lisa Wysel, Julie Mikula, and Shelley Jorgensen, for reading and reacting to sections of the book and encouraging me to keep on writing. And a special thanks to Shelley for arranging the family names that appear in the book into an organized chart that may be of help to the reader.

To my *småkusin* Ralf Häggqvist, Närpes, Finland, for telling me about his father, Birger, and uncle, Edvin, and their experiences in the Winter War and Continuation War, and to Ralf's wife, Elizabet Knip, who translated my father's letters to his mother, and to both for helping me understand Finnish history.

To my cousin, Nadine Sjöroos Flóijer of Overmalax, Finland, for describing in a letter the experiences of her brothers, Alarik, Mauritz, and Manne during the Finnish-Russian wars. And to my cousin Elli Sjöroos, Molpe, Finland, for her priceless gift to me of the letters my father wrote to his mother from 1906 to 1941.

To Margareta Pensar of Molpe, Finland, who discovered through my book *Where the Huckleberries Grow* that my father was from her village, and who became an invaluable source of information about the community, including her translated account of the influx of refugees in the fall of 1944.

To Marita Agnew, Olympia, WA, who told of her experiences as a young girl in Finland during the wars and who translated from the Swedish book, *Finland Swedes in America,* an account of starting Anacortes Veneer, Inc.

To Kiki Nakauchi of Morgan Hill, CA, who shared so generously her family's experiences as Japanese Americans during the Second World War.

To the Maricich and Lunsford families, and to Marijo Taylor of Eugene, OR, who loaned me the diary her mother, Frances Maricich, had written during her high school years in Anacortes, 1943 to 1947.

To Jack Kamps, Vancouver, WA, who wrote me in loving detail about the life of his sister, Joy, and her struggle with infantile paralysis.

To my high-school friends who helped me remember those years: Edna Haglund Dorothy, Kirkland, WA; Faith Charlot Rohrabaugh, Norfolk, VA; Ed Carlson, Camano Island, WA; Lois Persons Rancourt, Renton, WA; Marivonne Stover Whipple, Burlington, WA; Joyce Kilgore Webber, Oak Harbor, WA; Phyllis Luvera Ennes and Bonnie Cross Riley of Anacortes, as well as many other high-school friends.

To Rosanna Manningly, who painstakingly copy-read and advised me on my manuscript to make it the best it could be.

To the Anacortes Museum for making available copies of the *Anacortes American* from 1939 to 1946 (excepting 1945), and responding to e-mail requests for further information about subjects relevant to my story.

PREFACE

"We can never separate the remembered event from our imagination: They stick together."
(Murdock 2003 p.13 in Unreliable Truth: On Memoir and Memory.)

At a recent Class of '46 reunion in Anacortes, Washington, I told my classmates I was writing a book about our high-school years, and that I would, of course, create fictitious names. "Oh, no!" several protested. "We want our names in the book!" And so, with only a few exceptions, I have used real names. The happenings, to the best of my memory, are true, though sometimes rearranged or combined for the sake of story. Writing in the *genre* of Creative Nonfiction gives one that privilege. I have tried very hard not to abuse it.

My objective in writing this book is to relate what it was like to be a young girl going to high school during a time of war. Angie is challenged to put aside the usual teenage needs, to look at the larger needs of the world, and to accept "home front" responsibilities. This is also a coming-of-age story in which Angie deals with growing up in an immigrant family and being embarrassed by her parents' broken English and old-country ways.

The book would have been greatly enhanced if I could have communicated in writing the delightful accent of my parents and their Swedish friends, but this would have been tedious to read. For instance: *T for th, v for w, j* for *y* and *y for j*. Only in Chapter 2, where

Tilda talks to Angie's teacher, have I written Tilda's words phonetically, as the accent in this case was an integral part of the story.

I once learned at a writing workshop that when you do research on family background, expect the unexpected. In 2003, when I visited my father's home in Molpe, Finland, my cousin Elli brought out a shoebox full of letters that my dad had written his mother from the time he immigrated to America in 1906 until her death in 1943. Elli gave me the letters. It was a generous gift, a real treasure. I have included in this book translations of the last four letters he wrote to his mother.

As I associate *huckleberries* with life in the logging camps, so *seagulls* evoke memories of Anacortes. When I stood in my backyard, I heard them call to each other and imagined their swooping along the shore of Guemes Channel as they searched for food among the shells on the gravel beaches. Their cries seemed melancholic, and I sometimes wondered if they knew something I should know.

TABLE OF CONTENTS

PART I · 1939

CHARLIE'S LETTER

Potlatch Wash
Nov 27, 1939

Dear Mother,

I will now answer the letter that we got some time ago. I have waited for the madness in Europe to be over but instead it is just getting worse. I was going to send you a few dollars for Christmas but now it isn't possible to send anything to Finland. I hope that everything will get better.

I will now let you know that we all live and are well and wish you the same. Thelma has given up father and mother and lives with her beloved husband. She married a month ago. They work at the same place. Thelma will work until Christmas. He is an American. His name is Benny Banner. He is a good man.

Ya now we are through with work in Potlatch at last so I have been out of work for two months and that would be very good if all my clothes hadn't got too small. I must go out after Christmas and find myself some work.

We went to Portland last week so I went to see an acquaintance. Her husband died a while ago. She has much sorrow.

I will now close for this time with dear greetings to you, my mother.

Warmly, Chas Lind

P.S. Agnes sends many greetings to her grandmother. Many greetings to brother and his family from us all.

1

MOVING DAY
December 1939

Angie scrunched down between the packing boxes in the back seat. Maybe if she made herself smaller and smaller, she would finally disappear. Then the next time her mother turned around and asked her why she was so quiet and didn't she want to sit up and look out the car window at all the Christmas lights along the highway, she'd be gone. They'd probably stop the car and look for her between the boxes. Maybe they'd look inside the boxes between the folded towels and sheets, and, when they didn't find her, they'd be sorry and turn back to Potlatch....

"Angie, why so quiet?" Mama asked, just like Angie knew she would. "We're going through Everett now and all the stores are decorated with Christmas lights. Don't you want to sit up and look at all the lights?" Her mother reached into the back seat and touched Angie's knee. Angie guessed she hadn't disappeared after all.

"Stop fussing with her," Daddy said, keeping his eyes on the traffic ahead. "She's been moody all day. Time she snapped out of it."

"But, Charlie, I can't help worrying. She's only eleven and at that age, change is hard," Mama said in Swedish, like she thought Angie didn't understand. Mama knew better. They always talked Swedish at home to each other and to her. "She hasn't been herself all week," Mama went on, "ever since we started packing to move to Anacortes."

"She should be glad we're finally moving to a real town—with paved streets and sidewalks," Daddy added and turned to smile at Mama. Mama had a thing about sidewalks.

"You're right," Mama said, returning his smile. "And you say there's a fine Lutheran church in Anacortes? We haven't lived close to a church since we left Ballard. That was 1922. Seventeen years ago. We've gotten away from our upbringing. Angie doesn't even know what it is to go to church, to be Lutheran."

Angie could see the sides of their faces in the headlights of the oncoming cars. She decided she would sit up after all. Not to look at the Christmas lights, but to listen.

"And the three of us will sit together like families do when they go to church. Unless Angie sings in the choir. Then we can sit and watch her sing. I get excited when I think about it. You know, I can hardly believe we're on our way," Mama said.

"I can believe it!" Daddy said. "I been packing and hauling boxes to John's truck since six o'clock this morning. When did we get so much stuff? The move from Camp Two to Potlatch three years ago was nothing compared to this."

"Well, we didn't have much to move after living all those years in little camp houses," Mama said. "And, anyway, the company helped us with that move. Remember? Two boys from the bunkhouse loaded what we had into the box car and rode the train to Potlatch to unload it."

"*Ja*, that's true."

"Now that we're not with Phoenix Logging Company any more," Mama went on, "naturally we have to move ourselves."

Daddy didn't answer. It was starting to rain. Angie listened to the screech, screech of the windshield swipes and watched the raindrops slide sideways across the windows on both sides of the car. Cold was creeping into the back seat from around the edges of the doors. She pulled the car robe up to her chin.

"Charlie," Mama said, interrupting the silence, "you're not sorry you quit the logging business this time, are you? When we was first married, you quit the woods because I worried about logging accidents and living in a logging camp, away from everything. You quit logging for me, but then you went back to it."

Angie leaned forward to hear better over the noise of the car.

Daddy didn't answer right away. Mama was watching him. Waiting. Angie waited, too. "No," he said at last. "It's all right. I logged thirty-five years without accident. I didn't want to push my luck by staying with the company another day, even when I knew they was shutting down for good at the end of the year. When that log came rolling down the side hill at me and I saw I couldn't outrun it, I knew it was time to give up logging."

"*Ja*, I won't forget that day," Mama sighed. "When I heard your step on the porch and it wasn't quitting time, I knew that something was wrong. I still have nightmares when I think of what might have happened if that log hadn't caught on a snag."

"It was the snag that saved me, all right. Logging's for young guys that can move quick. I'm ready to work at something else." Then Daddy frowned at Mama and said, "I guess all I'm sorry about is that we didn't get an earlier start this morning. It's an all-day drive to Anacortes."

Mama smiled. "*Ja,* after being out of work for two months you were ready to listen to my brother-in-law."

"I guess I was," Daddy said. "We did the right thing when we followed his advice and bought stock in the Anacortes mill. I'm ready to work out of the weather, and I won't miss tramping through deep snow in the winter and mud in the spring. Even with caulk shoes, a man takes his life in his hands when he walks down a slippery log carrying a six-foot saw on his shoulder. I was there when Johnson fell on his saw and nearly bled to death before we could get him to a doctor."

"Life in camp was good in lots of ways, though, wasn't it," Mama said, not really asking. "The friends we made, the picnics and dances. But I'm glad we don't have to worry any more about forest fires or logging accidents. Or live in camp houses that was terrible hot in summer and freezing cold in winter."

"That's right," Daddy said. "Wait 'til you see the comfortable house I rented in Anacortes."

"Half a house, you mean," Mama laughed. "Isn't that what a duplex is?"

Angie heard her dad chuckle. She wondered what was funny about moving into half a house. And which half? Would they have half a kitchen? Maybe a refrigerator, but no stove. And what about the bathroom? She didn't understand "duplex," but mostly she didn't understand why they were moving away from all their friends in Potlatch in the middle of the school year! Angie tucked the car robe around her legs and leaned forward again to listen.

"It will be different to pay rent again," Daddy was saying. "We haven't paid rent since we moved from Ballard. That was one good thing about living in the logging camps. No rent for company houses."

"Will you make enough money at the mill to cover the rent and groceries and school clothes for Angie? She's growing so fast." Mama sounded worried.

"You bet I will! Salary at the mill will be good. By summer we should be able to build our own house on our lot across the street from the duplex."

"Our lot? Charlie, what are you saying? You didn't tell me you bought a lot!"

"It was going to be a surprise," Daddy said. "Anyway, I just put some money down to hold it and we'll pay a little each month. I know what you're thinking—that I've gone overboard taking on both rent and a mortgage, but it will be for just a few months. We'll get a loan to build our house and, when we move, we'll be through with the rent payments."

"I don't know, Charlie. We never gone in debt before," Mama said. "You know how it was in the Depression. People went into debt buying houses and cars and then, when they lost their jobs, they lost everything."

"*Ja*, but things are getting better now. And, as stockholder in this veneer plant, I'm guaranteed a job and good wages. Now, what else are you going to worry about?" Daddy asked in his teasing voice.

Mama looked out the window then, even though there were no more Christmas lights. "You know what else?" Mama asked. "You listen to the news and read the newspaper. I worry about what's happening to Finland. Russia is trying to take over again."

"*Ja*, but the Russians will back off when they see what they're in for, fighting the Finns. And, you know, the whole world is on the side of Finland. You saw that in the papers, too, didn't you?"

Mama nodded.

Angie wanted to ask her dad when they would get there, but knew he didn't like that question very much.

"You know something, Charlie?" Her mom sounded cheerful again. "I'm as excited about this move to Anacortes as I was about coming to America."

"*Ja*, and I know why," Daddy said, smiling at Mama. "For the first time in seventeen years, you won't have to look out the front-room window at oily railroad tracks or a dirt road."

The car slowed. They were driving through another town. "Mount Vernon," the sign said. Christmas lights covered the storefronts and filled the display windows. In one of the windows, Santa with a bulging pack sat next to a tinseled Christmas tree. Outside, people with arms full of packages were hurrying up and down the sidewalk. A bundled-up man in a red knit cap and black boots stood on the street corner ringing a bell. A big kettle hung from a wooden rack next to him and a lady handed her little boy money to drop into the kettle. As they left town, they saw another sign, "Anacortes 17 miles." Angie scrunched back down between the boxes.

"This move will be good for Angie, too," Daddy continued. "I saw her school when I was in Anacortes last week. The school and playground stretch across most of a city block."

Angie's stomach knotted.

"*Ja*, but going from a one-room school with seven kids to a big school like that—that's an awful big change."

"But a change for the better," Daddy said.

"I hope you're right," Mama said.

Charlie glanced down at the gas gauge. Looked like they'd make it to Anacortes without stopping to fill up. The trip had gone good. The rain was no problem. He'd replaced the rubber on the windshield swipes before they started. Now, just so it didn't start to snow. But he'd heard that Anacortes was in the shadow of the Olympic Mountains and didn't get much rain or snow. Anacortes, a town of 6,000, sat on Fidalgo Island, joined to the mainland by a bridge, and had the mild weather of a coast town. Not too hot in the summer or too cold in the winter.

Ja, this was a good move. It wasn't just the good weather. He'd bought working shares in a company that was going to make them comfortable, maybe even rich, for the rest of their lives. He wouldn't mind having some extra money for a change. Tilda could use a new coat, and she was always looking at dishes when they were in a department store.

"When we going to get there?" A barely audible voice from the back seat interrupted his thoughts.

"Twenty minutes," Charlie called over his shoulder and gave Tilda's knee a squeeze. He couldn't remember when he'd felt so good. Or so lucky. Fifty-one wasn't old. He'd started logging in the old country at fourteen and when he came to this country at eighteen, he'd kept right on logging. Except for a year in the mines in Montana and a couple years in the cedar mill in Ballard, he'd worked steady in the woods. He still had all his limbs and his health and was starting a new life as part owner of a plywood mill. He'd really come up in the world.

And he deserved to, he figured. He'd worked hard all his life. Over the years him and Tilda had scrimped and saved to make sure they had enough money to last 'til the end of the month, with some left over for a rainy day. And he wasn't one to jump head-first into new things. Before he drew the $2,000 out of his savings to buy a working share in the Anacortes mill, he talked to his brother-in-law, Charlie Carlson. The family called him "Ida's-Charlie" to keep the two Charlies straight.

While his brother-in-law was head millwright at the Vancouver Veneer Mill, he'd drawn the plans for the Anacortes plant. He'd been so sure about the future of plywood, he'd bought two shares in the Anacortes mill while it was still on the drawing board.

But Charlie hadn't taken just his brother-in-law's word for it, that it was a good investment. He wanted to know how other plywood mills were doing. He talked to some of the working stockholders in the Olympia Veneer Company, a mill that, he'd heard, was making money faster than they could count it. "You can't go wrong!" they'd said. "This country is growing, and plywood is what it needs for building."

He looked into the history of that mill. In 1920, two sawmill workers in Tacoma, J. J. Lucas and Ed Westman, both Swedish immigrants, were interested in this new plywood product and wanted to start a mill that they could own and operate. They didn't have a lot of cash, but Westman was head of Swedish fraternal lodges in Tacoma and Everett and talked some of his friends in those lodges into investing. Charlie read that Ed Westman sold about 85 per cent of the shares to Swedes and Swedish-speaking Finns like himself, and to other Scandinavians. In January 1921, 200 shareholders incorporated as Olympia Veneer Company. Charlie didn't know if it was true or not, but he'd heard that 15 years later, 1936, the 70 original stockholders voted themselves a Christmas dividend of a quarter of a million dollars each.

Two years before this, in 1934, J. J. Lucas had started pushing to build another co-op plywood company somewhere in the Northwest. Three of Charlie's Swede-Finn friends, Al Eriks from Lappfjärd, John Carlson from Molpe, no relation to Ida's-Charlie, and Ted Ness from Larsmo, headed a committee to find the best place for a mill. Port Angeles was a possibility, but they didn't get much community support. When a delegation of men from the Anacortes Chamber of Commerce led by its president Paul Luvera offered them the vacated Fidalgo Lumber and Box Company building on 35 acres of land next to the water for a good price, they grabbed it. Here Anacortes Plywood, Inc. was started.

Charlie took his handkerchief out of his pocket and leaned forward to wipe the moisture off the inside of the windshield. Must be getting cold outside the way the windows steamed up. He put his handkerchief away and settled back into his seat.

Things didn't go well at first for the Anacortes plant, he remembered. The board had overlooked incorporation laws like registering stocks with the Securities Exchange Commission. It took a long time to straighten that out. Because of this, they had trouble selling stocks, and some who bought stock wanted their money back. Machinery orders had to be cancelled. By the end of 1938, most of the money was used up and the plant still wasn't ready to start. Some partners wanted to sell the company for half the money they'd put into it. Early in 1939, shareholders met and worked out a plan to form a new company that would take over the old company's assets and start again. It was to be called Anacortes Veneer, Inc.

And then Charlie heard that the corporation still wasn't out of the woods. Banks refused to loan money to the new company. His friend, Gust Bonde, Swede Finn from Närpes, asked the bank if it would recommend buying stock in Anacortes Veneer, Inc. Word was that the bank told Gust, "You won't ever see smoke from the chimneys of those crazy Scandinavians' foolish undertaking." Gust told his friends that if this investment don't look good for the big banker, then it has to be good for us working-class people. Gust went ahead and bought shares. Others followed suit.

Because Ida's-Charlie had been the architect of the mill, the Anacortes board called on him for advice. The manager of the Vancouver plant excused him for six months to go to Anacortes to see what he could do. On November 27, Anacortes Veneer, Inc. started up with 250 stockholders. Charlie was told that with cash from investors and advice from Ida's-Charlie, the plant was bound to do good. They might never make it big like Olympia Plywood, Charlie knew, but, "By Gawd," he said aloud, hitting the steering wheel with the heel of his hand, "this Christmas, Tilda, we're starting down easy street."

PART II - 1940

2

WHITNEY GRADE SCHOOL
January

"Hold still now, Angie, while I tie this ribbon in your hair," Mama said. "You don't want to be late your first day in a new school."

"I don't want a ribbon," Angie protested. "That's babyish. Sixth-graders don't wear ribbons."

"How do you know that?"

"A girl that looked my age walked by the house and she wasn't wearing a ribbon."

"Can you decide on what sixth-grade girls wear by seeing one girl? This blue ribbon matches your dress and looks so nice, but okay. No ribbon. Get your coat and notebook. We have to hurry."

"Mama, you're not walking me to school! You registered me yesterday, so I know where to go. I can walk to school by myself."

"But I want to talk to your teacher."

"No, please no!" Angie pleaded.

"I haven't met your teacher yet, so I go with you. And when you come home, I'll have a snack waiting for you and you can tell me all about your day."

The low, white school building spread across the large, fenced-in yard like spilled milk. Next to the building, big kids jumped in and out of swings and ran to sit on the ends of the slides. Young children sat at the top of the slides calling for the teacher to come make the big kids get out of the way.

Angie hurried ahead of her mother toward the school entrance. Two big girls with ribbons in their hair leaned against the door. Angie tripped on the top step. The girls giggled behind their hands and moved aside. Angie tugged open the heavy door.

They stepped into the empty, brightly lit hallway and paused as the outside door wheezed shut behind them. Classroom doors stood open. The smell of freshly oiled floors reminded Angie of her schoolroom in Potlatch. Mama reached for the registration card in her pocketbook. "Room t'ree, Angie," she said. "Your teacher is Mrs. Elder."

"*Three*, Mom, not *t'ree*." Angie never noticed her parents' accent when they talked to their friends who talked the same way. But now her mother—in broken English—was about to talk to her teacher!

A bell clanged above their heads. Another moment and the outside doors flew open and play-mussed children scurried into their classrooms, banging doors behind them until the hall stood empty again. Angie clutched her notebook to her chest. "I can find my room myself. Please don't come with me," she begged and started down the hall.

Mama caught up with her at the door numbered "3" and tapped lightly. They listened for an answer but heard only the scraping of chairs and murmur of voices. Cautiously, Mama opened the door. The teacher and the children all turned to look at them.

"Mrs. Elder, I'm Mrs. Lind," Mama said, a slight quiver in her voice. "My girl Angie is supposed to be in this class. Vere should she sit?"

The class stared. It was Mama's Swedish accent. Why did she have to come to school with her!

"Why, yes, I see her name on the roll sheet," Mrs. Elder said. "I should have been watching for you. I guess I don't have everything together yet, the first day after Christmas vacation, you know." She smiled apologetically. "Angie, there's an empty desk in the middle of the row by the window. You may sit there."

Angie looked straight ahead as she hurried to her seat. She knew everyone was watching her.

"So, Mrs. Lind, would you like to sit in on the class for a little while?"

"*Nej*," Mama said, looking over at Angie, "I t'ink I should go now."

"Well, before you go, perhaps you could tell the class where you are from and what brought you to Anacortes," Mrs. Elder said.

Mama looked again at Angie. Angie stared at her desktop. "Ve're from Potlatch on Hood Canal. Angie's *pappa* logged in the hills above the canal."

Mrs. Elder smiled. The children smiled. They were waiting for her to go on.

"Ve been living in logging camps since before Angie vas born. Ve t'ink living in a town and vorking in a mill vill be a nice change."

The children giggled. Mrs. Elder shook her head at them. "Angie is a very pretty name," she said. "The hard 'g' makes it unusual."

"It's Svedish," Mama said. "Short for *Angnes*, which is the Svedish vay ve say 'Agnes.'"

"I thought you probably were Swedish," Mrs. Elder said.

Two girls in the front of the room whispered and turned to look at Angie. The teacher frowned at them over the top of her glasses.

"You immigrated from Sweden then," Mrs. Elder said.

"No," Mama answered. "From Finland."

Angie wanted this conversation to end, but now her mother would have to explain that she and Daddy were Swedes from Finland and no one would understand. She wished she could run out the door and never come back.

Mama went on. She told how Finland was a country with two official languages, Finnish and Swedish. She explained that Finland was under Swedish rule from 1323 to1809 when Russia took over. In 1917, after the first World War, Finland gave Russia some of its land in exchange for its freedom and Finland became an independent country. But people who live along its west and southwest coast still speak Swedish and practice Swedish customs, and that's where she and Charlie are from.

Angie slid down in her seat.

"Well, Mrs. Lind," Mrs. Elder said, "that was a real history lesson. Thank you so much. It reminds the class and me how much we have to learn about the world. Wasn't that interesting, boys and girls?"

The class nodded obediently but stared at Angie. She knew they were all thinking how strange she was. Mama thanked Mrs. Elder and the class for being so patient with her and her poor English and then excused herself and hurried to the door.

"Thank you again, Mrs. Lind. We feel so fortunate to have Angie in our class. Don't we, children?"

The class nodded again.

Angie wanted to die.

When the bell rang for recess, Mrs. Elder said, "Bundle up, boys and girls. The wind is a little sharp today."

Angie waited until the class had filed out and then peeked around at the empty room. It was a lot bigger than her classroom in Potlatch, but, like Potlatch, the alphabet in capital and small letters stretched along the top of the blackboard and the American flag stood in the corner at the front of the room—

"Angie," Mrs. Elder said, "you need to join the other children on the playground. Everyone goes outside for recess. Your coat is hanging on the hook by the door. Run along now."

Angie slipped into her coat as she walked down the deserted hall. She hesitated at the outside door and watched the children through the window. Finally, she pushed the door open and stepped out into the cool winter sun. A group of boys from her class stood at the bottom of the steps.

"Hey, Angie," one of the boys called, "Ve been vaiting for you! Tell us about the logging camp."

Angie figured they'd been waiting to tease her. She spun away from them and walked briskly toward the corner of the building. She knew as she stood there with her back to the wall that she looked like the sad, skinny little girl on the Ovaltine can Mama kept in the cupboard. Mama wanted her to be *skookum* like her big sister. But, even if she gained weight, she would never be as strong or brave as Thelma. If her sister had been here now, she would have challenged the boys and found out if they really wanted to know about logging camps.

Angie wished Thelma still lived at home instead of getting married. And now, since Angie had moved to Anacortes and Thelma still lived in Shelton, she'd never see her. She'd never be *skookum* either, no matter how much Ovaltine she drank!

Angie glanced back at the boys. They were sparring with each other, pushing and wrestling. The two girls with ribbons in their hair that had been on the school porch when she tripped on the top step were watching the boys and laughing. Angie thought one of them looked over at her. A larger group of girls stood next to the swing set. She could see they weren't waiting for an empty swing. They were talking and laughing, too. Could they be talking about her? Angie drew in her breath, slipped back along the wall to the school entrance and prayed for recess to be over.

When the bell rang signaling the end of the school day, Angie streaked out of the room, but when she reached home, she hesitated at the kitchen door. What would she say to her mother? That she hated her for taking her to school? For not knowing how to talk right? For going on and on about being Swedes from Finland? For telling that her dad was a logger? No wonder the girls with ribbons had looked at her and laughed behind their hands. Now Mama would be all cheerful and ask about her day.

She inched the kitchen door open. Late afternoon shadows grayed the room. Were her parents saving electricity by not turning on a light? That was another thing about her parents. They were always saving!

The room was still. Her parents were sitting at the kitchen table. They weren't talking.

"Mama?"

Mama raised her head and looked at her. "You still have boxes to unpack. Go to your room and do that now. Daddy and I are talking."

But they weren't talking. They were just sitting.

"Do as I say," Mama repeated.

Angie had things to say, too. And if they had things to talk about, why weren't they talking? Why were they just sitting across the kitchen table from each other? And why was Daddy slumped down in his chair, staring at his coffee cup?

Tilda sipped her coffee, the letter in her pocket momentarily forgotten as she watched Charlie. She hadn't seen him like this since the day in Potlatch when he came home early from work and told her he'd turned in his time. That day she had reminded him that Ida's-Charlie and John Carlson and others had talked to him about the veneer plant in Anacortes where he could buy a working share and have good income and job security for the rest of his life—

"Mama, why can't I talk to you?" Angie called from the bottom of the stairs.

Tilda got up from the kitchen table and walked to the dining room door. She could see both the dining room and the front room from where she stood. Gold-flowered wallpaper, hardwood floors, an open stairway the same rich, dark color as the floors. Even though they were only renting the duplex, Tilda had felt like a queen moving into such a fine place. And next summer they would build a house of their own on the lot across the street.

She looked at Angie without seeing her. Her life had been filled to overflowing until this morning when the letter came from Ester, her sister-in-law in Finland. She'd carried it in her apron pocket all day, waiting for Charlie to come home. But now, with Charlie in such a bad mood, she'd wait a little longer to show it to him.

"Mama?" Angie repeated.

Tilda sighed. "Go unpack your boxes. We talk later," she said and walked back into the kitchen. She picked the coffee pot up off the stove—the same copper pot she had brought to this country in 1912—and turned to Charlie. "Ready for a *på tår*?"

"*Nej*. Cup's still full," he said.

Tilda put the coffee pot back on the stove and sat down again. "I don't understand what's going on," she said, trying to control the tremor in her voice. "You haven't said a word since you got home from the stockholders' meeting. What happened?"

Charlie looked up then. His mouth was tight as he spoke.

"Six weeks ago, November 27, the mill started up. People from all over town came to help celebrate. Even the mayor. The newspaper called Anacortes a Lazarus town brought back from the dead.

Today," Charlie said, skidding his chair back from the table, "this afternoon at the stockholders' meeting, the damn board of directors said there wasn't enough money to pay our wages."

"I can't believe that!" Tilda exclaimed.

"Well, you can believe it. The most they can pay a man is thirty-five cents an hour, hardly enough to put food on the table. But they don't want to do even that. They want us to forego any salary until the company gets on its feet. Sure, they pay us back if the company makes it, but how long is it going to take?"

"Well, if the mill don't make it, we get our money back, don't we? Money we paid for stock?"

"Hell, no, we don't! There was no guarantee."

"But the Olympia mill is doing so good."

"It don't matter about the Olympia mill. It's this mill we have to worry about," Charlie said, spinning out of his chair and walking to the kitchen window. He stood silhouetted against the last light of the afternoon. Tilda saw the tension in his shoulders.

"Did you volunteer to work without pay?" Tilda asked tentatively, thinking about the upcoming rent and the payments on the lot.

Charlie hesitated. He spoke without turning around. "*Ja*, I felt I had to. There's men with bigger families and more debt than we have."

Tilda listened to the ticking of their alarm clock on the kitchen counter. She must have brought it downstairs this morning to keep track of the time when Angie was getting ready for school. She should have listened to Angie when she came home this afternoon, but with Charlie so upset and the bad news from Finland, she couldn't think straight.

"Ida's-Charlie was at the meeting, wasn't he?" Tilda pursued. "Ida wrote he planned to come back from Vancouver for the meeting."

"*Ja*, he was there," he said, turning to Tilda. "Had to be there as board member. Today they elected him board president. I figure he's got his work cut out for him."

Tilda thought of Angie and of the letter from Ester.

"Charlie," Tilda whispered, "I think we all do."

Tilda thought morning would never come. Charlie had tossed and turned all night and Angie had called out several times in her sleep. Even without those disturbances, Tilda would have lain awake thinking about the letter from her sister-in-law in Finland. Tilda's brother Ivar used to write often—long, interesting letters. In the two years since he died of blood poisoning, Ester had tried to keep in touch, but she didn't have as much schooling as Ivar, and it was an effort for her to write. Tilda knew when she saw Ester's letter in the mailbox that it would be about something serious.

She carried the coffee pot to the kitchen table and poured herself a *på tår*. She looked forward to her second cup of coffee in the morning. It meant that Charlie was off to work and Angie, off to school, that the breakfast dishes were done, the house was quiet, and she could pull her thoughts together. This morning she would reread the letter.

She removed Ester's carefully folded paper from its travel-stained envelope and laid it flat on the kitchen table where the morning light from the window would help her read the lightly penciled words. "Russia has invaded our peaceful country again," Ester wrote, "and both my boys, your nephews, are fighting on the front lines."

Tilda knew, of course, about the November 27 invasion. Through radio and newspapers, the whole world knew about the event and was shocked by it, but she hadn't wanted to think about how it would affect her family. The summer Ivar died, Ester's boys were already in the army and had nearly finished their required enlistment time. Tilda remembered Ester writing that Edvin was stationed near their home and was able to help her and his young brother Ture with the harvest. Birger, too, came home to help whenever the army gave him leave.

Tilda dropped her head into her hands. Her nephews were young—Birger, 23, and Edvin, 22. Ivar had been proud of his boys, their strength and willingness to work. They were good, honest young men and had their lives ahead of them. But she knew that, even if the boys had completed their required time in the army, they would have re-enlisted to defend the homeland they loved against this long-time enemy.

Soviet leaders tried to justify the invasion. They said they feared the growing power of Germany. Germany had invaded and conquered Poland, and Russia thought Germany might turn on them next. Russia, in order to protect Leningrad, which was only ten miles from Finland's border, wanted Finland to cede them some of its land as a buffer against Germany. Russia further wanted Finland to let them build air and navy bases in Finland and agree to defend these bases if attacked. Finland was determined to remain neutral and would not agree to any of this. As a result, four armies of Russians, 600,000 men, had marched across the border into Finland, planning, out of spite, to take over the entire country.

Tilda stood up from the table and walked to the window. The winter sun, pale and low in the gray sky, offered little heat. Even with a fire in the kitchen stove, the room was chilly. She hugged her sweater close and thought again of Ester's letter. She had written that never in anyone's memory had Finland known a winter as cold as this. Their young men were fighting on the snowfields and living in tents. When they were close to the enemy, they lived in holes they dug in the snow. They used evergreen branches for roofs and camouflaged them with more snow.

The Russians were concentrating their attacks on Finland's Karelian Isthmus, a narrow strip of land connecting Finland and Russia, bordered on the west by the Gulf of Finland and on the east by Lake Ladoga. Russians first bombed and then moved in with tanks and machine guns. Ester wrote that it was here, the Karelian Isthmus, where Birger and Edvin had been sent to fight.

How strange, Tilda thought, that November 27, a black day for their relatives in Finland, had been the day the veneer mill started up, a day of celebration. It was the day that opened the door to their new life in Anacortes. *Ja*, the mill was having trouble, but what was that compared to what Ester and her boys were facing, or what were Angie's problems at school compared to any of this!

3

SECOND DAY
January 1940

"Mom, today you can tie a ribbon in my hair, but you're not walking me to school," Angie said, handing her mother a blue cotton ribbon. She heard her mom sigh like she did sometimes. As quick as the bow was tied, Angie grabbed her books and rushed out the door.

Angie stepped into her classroom just as the starting bell rang. She had scuffed her way to school hoping that the kids would be in their seats when she got there so she wouldn't have to talk to anyone. As she started down the aisle toward her desk, the boy in the seat in front of hers stuck out his foot. Angie tripped, caught herself, and sat down.

"Children, we'll start the morning as usual with arithmetic," Mrs. Elder said. "Please turn to page 92." She caught Angie's eye and smiled at her. A girl across the aisle slipped out of her seat to help Angie find the right book in the cubbyhole under her desktop.

Angie worked the problems without much difficulty. They had covered those lessons before she left Potlatch. She finished just as the teacher asked them to hand in their papers, however much they'd completed, so she could see how they were doing. Angie watched the girl who'd helped her find her book. She folded her paper in half lengthwise, wrote her name at the top of the outside fold, and passed it down the row. Angie did the same. She watched her teacher collect the papers from each row, fasten them together with a rubber band, and set them in a basket on her desk. Mrs. Elder was very organized and her class was very orderly. Angie felt safe enough to lift her eyes and look around.

She noticed that the student desks were joined together in rows like in her school in Potlatch, the top of one desk fastened to the back of the next seat. Angie examined her own desk. The top was varnished shiny-smooth except for "Mary luves Billy" and "Girls are sisys" etched into its surface. The desktop had a hole in the upper right-hand corner for an ink bottle. Underneath was the shelf for books, but the top didn't lift up like it did on her desk in Potlatch. You probably wouldn't want a top that lifts if you had a bottle of ink in the hole.

"Take out your geography books now, children," Mrs. Elder said, "and read Chapter 15. I'm going to write five questions on the blackboard about the material in those pages. Remember to answer the questions in complete sentences."

Feet shuffled and desks squeaked as the students scrunched over to find their textbooks and tablets in the cubbyholes. Then, except for the tap, tap of the chalk on the blackboard, the room was quiet.

Angie opened her book, but her eyes wandered off the page and around the room. The two girls who wore ribbons in their hair yesterday weren't wearing any today. Angie worked her ribbon loose and stuffed it into her desk. She watched a pretty girl with very curly, light-brown hair and long, curly eyelashes lean forward and whisper something to the girl in front of her. They both turned around and then quickly turned back to their books. Others noticed their movements and one by one began looking toward the back of the room.

Angie wanted to turn around, too, but she saw that some of the kids were now looking at her. Some were grinning. Angie's arms began to feel prickly and her stomach tight. Her eyes sought out Mrs. Elder at the blackboard, willing her to turn around, but she kept tapping her way across the blackboard, her skirt swinging to the rhythm of her writing. Tap, tap. Was Angie hearing the sound of the chalk on the blackboard or was she hearing her own heartbeat?

The boy in the seat in front of her turned so his feet were again in the aisle. "Angie," he whispered, "turn around. Chet's trying to tell you something."

Angie felt eyes watching her. Tap, tap, tap, her heart in time with the chalk. She turned because she'd been told to and because she didn't know what else to do. Then she saw it. Heat burned its way up her neck and into her face. Her eyes blurred. A boy had poked his long, skinny, middle finger up through the hole in the top of his desk and was grinning at her.

"All right, class," Mrs. Elder said as she turned and blew the chalk dust off her hand, "do as much as you can before recess and finish it at home tonight. The paper is due at the beginning of the period tomorrow. Are there any questions?"

The bell for recess finally rang. "Hey, wait up," a girl called, but Angie didn't wait. She rushed out of the classroom and down the hall. She pushed open the outside door, turned and ran the full length of the long building, and ducked behind a tall shrub next to the schoolhouse wall. She had tried to concentrate on her geography assignment until recess, but the printing on the pages blurred and all she could think of was escaping.

"Angie, you sure can run fast," the girl from across the aisle exclaimed as she slid to a halt next to the shrub. Another girl, the one with the very curly hair, caught up and stood beside her. "We wanted to tell you to ignore Chet," the first girl went on. "He's a creep. He's always embarrassing somebody. Really."

"Really!" the other girl echoed.

Angie shook her head. She didn't know what the boy's gesture meant, except that it was something bad.

"My name is Phyllis," the first girl said. "Phyl for short. I wanted to talk to you yesterday, but you looked like you didn't want to talk to anybody."

"And I'm Faith," the other girl said. "I guess that's short for 'faith, hope and charity,'" she giggled. "They sing about me every Sunday in church. 'Faith of our fathers living still....'" She laughed and Phyllis laughed. "Mom's right. We're silly-willys," Faith said. "Your mom talks real cute. Can you talk Swedish? If you can—"

"Come on," Phyllis interrupted. "We can talk more at the swings. Last one there is a rotten egg."

"I have two brothers and a sister," Faith said to Angie after they settled into swings and began pumping. "What's your family like?"

"I have a sister that's married and I had a brother," Angie answered.

"You had a brother? What happened to your brother?" Faith asked, sailing higher with each pump.

"He got killed."

Both Faith and Phyllis dragged their feet in the dirt until their swings stopped. Dust flew up around them.

Phyllis stared at Angie. "He got killed? How?"

"He was run over on the railroad track in front of our house. Mom saw it all from the kitchen window."

Angie twirled her swing, unwound, and then twirled the other way. The girls were watching her, waiting for her to say more, but she didn't know what else to say. The playground sounds of screaming and laughing drifted around them like the disturbed dust.

"Do you miss him?" Faith whispered.

"I never knew him. He died before I was born."

"How old was he?" Phyllis asked.

"Almost five. My sister was six and she missed him a lot. So did my mom and dad, but I think now they're getting used to his being gone."

The girls began pumping again, seeing who could go highest.

"My mother's name's Mary," Phyllis told Angie as her swing zipped by. "And my brother's called Paul, like my dad," she said as the swing came back. On the next swing through she added, "I have a little sister named Anita—" Phyllis stopped the swing on her way back. "I don't know who she's named after."

Faith, too, timed her description of her family to the back-and-forth movement of the swing. "Margery's my big sister— Bill's my big brother— Bobby's my little brother— And we all live together— with our mom and dad— in a little white house."

All three girls laughed at themselves and their game.

"Do you have other relatives?" Phyllis asked Angie as she coasted to a stop.

"I have a *moster* and an uncle and a cousin Art."

"What's a *moster*?" Faith asked as her swing whizzed by.

"*Moster* means aunt in Swedish," Angie replied. She thought everyone knew that.

"Hey!" Faith said, her feet dragging her to a stop. "Maybe you could come to church and BYF with me Sunday night. After church the kids all go to someone's house for 'Fireside.' We sing songs and eat and have lots of fun."

"What's 'BYF' stand for?" Angie asked, and then wondered if she should know that.

"Baptist Youth Fellowship. You went by the church when you drove into town."

Angie sat without moving. "It was dark when we came," she mumbled, digging the toes of her shoes into the dirt.

"You really don't need to know where it is because my mom and I can pick you up. So, would you like to come?" Faith persisted.

Angie knew her dad would never let her go to a Baptist church. She remembered so well what he told Thelma when she invited the Baptist kids in Shelton to their house in Potlatch for a meeting. "What you want to get mixed up with those Baptists for!" he'd exclaimed. "Pastor in old country told us Baptists eat their young!" Mama had laughed and said she guessed their pastor didn't want them to listen to the Baptist missionaries that were trying to take them away from the Lutheran church.

"Or you could visit church with me," Phyllis said. "Lots of kids go to the Catholic church, too."

Angie swallowed hard and tried to smile at Phyllis, but she knew that her Lutheran parents would never let her go to a Catholic church. A cluster of girls stood nearby, waiting for a turn at the swings. She felt her new friends watching her, waiting for an answer. She wanted more than anything to be their friend, to do things with them. But how could she? Her toe dislodged a small rock under the swing.

"I have to stay home and finish unpacking," she said, kicking the stone as hard as she could.

4

CELEBRATION
February 1940

"Charlie, bring in some kindling. I need to start the fire so I can cook supper," Tilda said, scrunching up newspaper and poking it into the front of the firebox in the wood stove.

Charlie, about to sit down at the kitchen table, turned and strode across the kitchen and out the door. He was back in a minute with kindling and an armload of wood for the wood box. Tilda placed the kindling and two small pieces of wood on top of the paper, lit the paper, and shut the firebox door.

"I come home from work expecting coffee and what I get is orders," Charlie groused. "Why so excited? What's the hurry? Telma said they wouldn't get here 'til after six o'clock."

"I know, but this is their first visit since we moved to Anacortes, and I want everything to be just right. Where's Angie? We're eating in the dining room tonight and I need her to set the table."

"Looks like you need everyone's help. You've cooked company dinners before."

"*Ja*, but I'm out of practice with all the moving business." Tilda pulled a small sack of potatoes from the cupboard and set it on the sink board. "Anyway, I'm still catching my breath after the big party last night. Wasn't that something, Charlie? The whole town came out to welcome us plywood people."

Ida and her Charlie had come from Vancouver for the celebration. They joined hundreds of people for the tour of the mill in the afternoon, and then they all met at the community hall for the biggest *smörgåsbord* Tilda had ever seen. They heard Harley LaPlant, manager of the Anacortes Veneer, give a talk, and Mayor Teeter and other important people followed him. The high-school band played some numbers and then at nine o'clock a dance band started up. People could go to another room and play cards or they could stay in the big room and dance. Her and Charlie always liked to dance, and the band even played a schottische and a polka for the Scandinavians in the crowd. Just before the last dance, two members of the Chamber of Commerce, Paul Luvera and Gus Dalstead, thanked everyone for coming and announced that the evening was one of the finest community celebrations ever held in Anacortes.

Never had she felt so welcome, and she knew Charlie had a good time, too. Maybe that's why he was a little cranky today. He'd had too good a time!

"Artur is coming to supper tonight, too," Tilda said. "He'll be here as soon as he gets off work. He hasn't seen Telma since she was married and you know what a good time her and Artur had when they was kids. And I invited Ida and her Charlie for supper, too, of course."

Tilda set Charlie's coffee cup on the table and placed the weekly edition of the *Anacortes American* next to it. She always tried to make things comfortable for her husband when he came home from work.

Charlie sat down and studied the front page. "'Huge Crowd Attends Plywood Company's Open House Party,'" he read aloud. "That part's true, but all I can say is it might be a little early to celebrate. We still don't know if the mill will make it."

"I think they make it," Tilda said as she poured his coffee. "Ida's-Charlie says things are going better at the mill. You remember, he ordered some second-hand machinery that's more automatic and will speed up production."

"How can they pay for even second-hand machinery when they can't pay wages?" Charlie exclaimed, his face reddening like the lid on the firebox.

"Now you're getting too excited. Read the paper while I work on supper."

Art came by after his shift at the mill and sat talking with Charlie at the kitchen table. He was living with Al and Lydia Eriks, paying $8 a month room and board, but he often stopped in. Art turned out to be a fine young man, Tilda mused, taller than his father by far, good-looking, and still full of the dickens. Hard working, too. Charlie said he was doing good at the mill.

Steam from the cooking fogged the inside of the windows. Tilda watched Angie wipe a clear spot in the window of the door facing the street. A streetlight at the corner of the block cast the spidery shadow of a bare maple tree across the sidewalk and the parking strip that bordered the lawn next to the house.

"When will they get here?" Angie asked. "I've been waiting forever."

"Any time now," Tilda answered, turning back to the stove and lifting the lid on the kettle of boiling potatoes. She poked a fork into one of the potatoes and replaced the lid.

"I think they're here," Angie shouted. Art and Tilda joined her at the window and watched a car slow to a stop at the curb next to their house. Angie rushed out the door first, but Art, with his long strides, reached the car ahead of her. Tilda followed as far as the porch to watch, eager to catch sight of her grown-up daughter. It was still hard for Tilda to realize that Telma was married, but Bennie was a good man and it was clear they were good together.

"About time!" Tilda heard Art exclaim as he pulled open the door on the passenger side of the car.

"What do you mean, 'about time'!" Thelma retorted. "We made good time. We didn't miss supper, did we?"

"You did, but we left you some scraps," Art said.

"Art's fibbing," Angie said, reaching for Thelma's hand to pull her out of the car. "We wouldn't eat without you."

"I'd believe my little sister any time over my ugly cousin," Thelma said as she climbed out of the car. "Angie, I'll race you to the door," she challenged. Art grabbed Thelma's arm and held her back while Angie ran for the house. She got there first, but the others tumbled into the kitchen a second later, laughing at nothing more than the fun of being together.

Tilda followed them into the kitchen, smoothing her apron with her hands. She hugged Bennie and kissed and hugged Thelma. Then she held Thelma at arm's length and studied her. When her daughter at thirteen had reached her full five-foot-eight height, Anna Carlson, their neighbor in camp, would ask her why she didn't put a book on her head so she wouldn't grow any more. Thelma didn't mind the teasing. She liked being tall like her dad.

Tilda noticed that Telma's hair still curled a little around her face as it had as a child. Her glasses didn't spoil her good looks but instead made her look smart—which she was. Tilda gave her attractive daughter another hug. Charlie stood by the table waiting his turn to greet his daughter and son-in-law.

"Are you tired from the long drive?" "How was the traffic?" "Let me have your coats." "You must be terrible hungry." "Would you like some coffee before dinner?"

Everyone talking at once. The rich aroma of roast beef filled the room.

"Angie," Tilda said, "show them to your room so they know where they sleep."

"Where will Angie sleep?" Thelma asked.

"On the couch. She likes that fine. My, we're happy to see you. It's been only two months, but it seems much longer. Go get settled now while I mash potatoes and make gravy. *Moster* and Uncle will be here any minute."

Tilda waited until everyone was seated at the dining room table before she bowed her head. Her heart was full as she prayed.

I Jesu namn gå vi till bords
Äta och dricka på ditt ord
Gud till ära, oss till gagn
Så få vi mat I Jesu namn. Amen.

"It's nice, Mom, to hear you say the Swedish blessing," Thelma said. "When I try to say it, it doesn't sound right, so we say a Baptist blessing." She looked across the table and smiled at her dad.

"Food don't digest good with Baptist blessing," Charlie said. Tilda saw a smile flicker at the corners of his mouth when he looked back at his daughter. "God only hears Lutheran blessings. You know that."

Angie set her fork down and looked from one to the other. While others filled and refilled their plates, she picked at her food. Bennie finished his supper first.

"So, Art, how do you like working at the mill?" Bennie asked.

"I like it fine," Art said. "They've got me working green chain. I had a hard time at first pulling the sheets of veneer off the moving belts. Then someone told me to take hold of the end of the sheet and give it a shake to let air under the panel. No trouble moving it then."

"It's all in knowing how, I guess," Bennie said. "But what about school? Don't you plan to go on to school?"

"I sure do," Art said. "Last June when I graduated from high school, I decided to stay out a year and work and save up money for college. I had my 1934 Ford V8 and two jobs going when Dad called in December from Anacortes to tell me the mill was starting up and I could work his share. This sounded good to me. Mill wages would be better than the two jobs put together. Course I didn't know then I'd be making thirty-five cents an hour." He smiled at Charlie.

Charlie didn't smile. "That's thirty-five cents an hour more than I make," he grumbled.

"This coming year I'm going to Clark Community College," Art went on. "I'll live at home to save money and then transfer to the University of Washington to study engineering."

Bennie nodded. "Sounds like you have it all worked out."

"Who's ready for apple pie?" Tilda interrupted. All but Angie raised their hands.

It was late when Tilda brought out the blankets and helped Thelma make up Angie's bed on the front room sofa.

"How's school going, Angie?" Thelma asked, tucking a sheet under the edge of the sofa cushions and unfolding a blanket.

"Classes are okay, but I don't know about the rest."

"What do you mean?"

"I don't like being new. I don't think kids like me."

"You must have made some friends."

"A few. Well, two friends, but I only see them at school." Angie stretched out on the sofa. "Mostly they do stuff with kids that go to their churches."

"Well, can't you go with them?"

Angie shook her head and looked at Tilda. "Mom and Dad take me with them to the Lutheran church."

"Aren't there kids there you know?"

"Edwin Carlson from camp and a couple girls. Mostly it's old-country people."

Tilda was working a sofa pillow into a pillowcase, but felt Angie look at her.

"Well, the folks wouldn't care if you went where there were more kids," Thelma said. "I'm sure they wouldn't. I go to the Baptist church in Shelton, you know."

"Sure, you're married and can do what you want, but you know what Dad thinks about Baptists. God doesn't even hear Baptist table blessings!"

Angie pulled the tightly tucked blanket up to her chin and turned her face to the back of the sofa. Thelma leaned over and kissed her cheek. Tilda heard her whisper, "Dad and I will have a talk tomorrow."

CHARLIE'S SECOND LETTER

March 24, 1940

Dear Mother,

I will now send you a few lines to let you know that we all live and that we are in good health.

It worries me that I don't know how you all live at home after all that has been going on there lately. I guess they all went out [to the war]. I wonder how many from Molpe remained behind and if brother was one of them. I guess it has been a miserable winter in Finland. I did write you a letter before Christmas but I guess it didn't get through.

Ya, here it's spring again and fine weather. We have moved from the woods now. The forest was at an end in Potlatch so now we are living in town and I have bought a share in a cooperative veneer company, so I am working there now. Maybe you have heard about this before because John Carlson and William West are stockholders, too. We are 250 partners and everyone has put in 2000 dollars. It makes half a million dollars and everyone has work here so it is a big company.

In the last letter I did write that Thelma got married and she has been married for six months now. The time passes by and soon Agnes is grown-up and we are old and abandoned but that is the way of the world. Henry Sjoblom is in the hospital in Seattle and he has a bleeding from his heart so I guess his time will soon be over.

I will stop now for this time with a dear greeting from all of us to you my mother who I will never forget. Warmly,

Chas Lind
1419 9th Street
Anacortes, Wash

Give our regards to brother and his family from us. Write when you can, brother, if you can let us know what happened to Stina's son [Johan]. You were all there [in the war] weren't you, all of you? Also your son.

Warmly, brother Karl [Chas]

5

BOXES
April 1940

Tilda pulled the kitchen table from the wall and lifted the drop leaf. For everyday purposes, they extended just one leaf, but today she wanted both leaves up to give her more working space. To think they'd bought this oak table second-hand for a dollar in Ballard in 1917 when they were first married. It had traveled with them from logging camp to logging camp. Every once in a while, Charlie would repaint it or fix one of the braces that supported the leaves, and then the table would be as good as new. Tilda wondered how many meals they'd eaten at this table. Her and Charlie, Telma and Angie, Leonard.... A sigh escaped her. Enough wondering. She had work to do.

Tilda set two empty cardboard boxes and a paper sack full of groceries on the table and turned to the cupboard for scissors and her ball of string. Telma used to make fun of her for adding even little pieces of string to the ball. She wouldn't laugh today if she could see how handy it was to have that string. It takes a lot of string to go around boxes that are traveling all the way to Finland.

The kitchen door flew open. "Hi, Mom, I'm home," Angie announced.

"Is school out already?" Tilda exclaimed. "Where does the time go? I'm glad you're home. Run change your clothes and then come help me fill these boxes."

Angie didn't move. Tilda looked up.

"I've got a box to fill, too," Angie said and held out a heavily shellacked, wooden pencil box.

"What's this?" Tilda asked. "Somebody giving you presents?"

Angie nodded, her face reddening. "The boy who sits in front of me made this in shop class. He gave it to me."

"Why did he do that? Isn't he the boy who teases you and tries to trip you when you go by his desk? Why—?"

"I don't know why. He set it on my desk at the end of school and then ran out the door."

"Well," Tilda said, taking the box and running her hand over its smooth surface. She handed it back to Angie. "Well," she repeated, turning back to the groceries to hide a smile, "these things happen."

Angie stood on her toes to look into the tall grocery sack. "Coffee, sugar, flour, canned meat," she recited. "What's all this for?"

"For our relatives in Finland. Your daddy's brother Vilhelm and his family and my sister-in-law Ester and her boys. You've heard Daddy and me worrying about them."

"Because they're fighting a war, I know. But are they going to fight the war with coffee and sugar and cans of meat?" Angie asked, half smiling.

"You know better, Angie! It's nothing to joke about. The war is over but—"

"That was a short war," Angie interrupted, walking toward the cookie jar on the counter.

"You're right. The war lasted only three-and-a-half months, but cities and villages were bombed and farmhouses, blown to pieces. People are starving to death!" Tilda's voice broke.

Angie lifted the lid on the cookie jar, but replaced it without taking a cookie and returned to the table. "Did a lot of people die?" Angie asked, serious now.

Tilda sat down. "Thousands of people died in the bombings."

"Kids, too?"

"In war, children die, too. But many escaped because their mothers put them on trains and sent them to families in Sweden who offered to take care of them. Mothers who could, went with them, but mostly the children traveled without family. Russian planes dropped bombs on one of the trains. The train stopped and children and helpers ran into the woods until the planes left."

"Will they get to go home now that the war is over?"

"Some will have no home to go to. No village. The government will try to help them find their mothers."

Angie sat down and rested her chin in her hands. "What about their dads?"

"Some of the dads will come home, but many died on the battlefields. The Finnish soldiers were terrible out-numbered." Tilda took a deep breath. "You know we got a letter from your Uncle Vilhelm a few days ago. Daddy had asked him if he was in the war, too. Vilhelm wrote he wasn't called up because of his age. The best news, his son Alarik made it home. Also your dad's half-sister Stina's son came home. We got a letter from Ester, too, and she said Birger and Edvin made it through the war. We thank God every day that our nephews lived through all that fighting."

"They're my cousins, aren't they? Like Art?" Angie asked.

Tilda knew that Angie knew the answer, but their families in Finland were just names to her. Remembering they were cousins made them more real.

"*Ja*, Angie, they are your cousins like Art. If your *moster* and uncle had stayed in Finland when they moved back there in 1931, Art would have been fighting in this war, too."

Angie twisted the hem of her skirt around her finger. "But Art won't have to fight in a war, will he? Our country won't get into war, will it?"

"No, Angie. No one would attack a big country like America. We are so lucky to be safe. That's why we have to help our Finland relatives. Now, go change your clothes and hurry back. I need your finger on the string when I'm ready to knot it."

Angie ran upstairs as Charlie came in the kitchen door. He was through work at three o'clock, so he came home the same time as Angie.

"So, where's my coffee? I don't smell the coffee?"

"Oh, my!" Tilda said. "You caught me this time." Charlie always acted grumpy when his coffee wasn't ready. She would drop what she was doing and make the coffee in a hurry. It was a game they played. "I've been so busy getting these boxes ready for Finland that time ran away from me. Coffee will be ready in a minute."

Charlie sat down and pulled off his work shoes. He leaned back stiffly in the straight-backed kitchen chair and studied the boxes on the table. "You think two boxes will be any use?"

"I don't know, but I feel like we have to do something. You read Ester's last letter. They haven't been able to buy coffee since before the war. Most of the food they stored from last summer's crops went to the army, and now, what's left, they share with the refugees."

"*Ja*, it's bad there," Charlie said. "I read in the paper that thousands of people left their homes along Finland's border because they didn't want to live under Russian rule. The Russians told them that if they left, they'd have to walk out and take only what they could carry."

"So we do what we can," Tilda said. "I'm packing Angie's outgrown clothes for Vilhelm's daughters Nadine and Elli," she explained as she folded pajamas and a dress and then another dress. "Nadine's just two years younger than Angie, you know, and Elli can wear the clothes when Nadine outgrows them."

Charlie nodded.

"Hey, Mom," Angie said, running into the room, "I forgot to tell you. Faith invited me to a BYF roller skating party tonight in Burlington. Faith's mom is taking a carload of kids and invited me to ride with them. Can I go?"

"What's BYF?" Charlie asked.

"Baptist Youth Fellowship. All the kids are going. Can I go? Please? Please can I go?"

Tilda looked at Charlie. He shrugged his shoulders. "I guess so," Tilda said. Let children enjoy life while they can, she thought. Soon enough they grow up and learn its hardships.

Tilda adjusted her crocheted doilies on the arms of the sofa and over-stuffed chair. She liked having people in. They saw John and Anna Carlson often because they were friends from camp, but Al and Lydia Eriks were new acquaintances. Tilda had been looking forward all day to their coming for coffee this evening. She hurried back to the kitchen when she heard footsteps and talking on the back porch. Their company had arrived and Charlie had gone to the door to greet them.

"So where's Angie tonight?" Anna Carlson asked as Charlie took their coats and hung them in the hall closet. "Edvin and Roy came along and thought they could play some games."

"I'm sorry," Tilda said. "Angie's friend Faith and her mother stopped in this afternoon with some clothes for Finland, and they invited Angie to a skating party tonight with the Baptist young people. I didn't think about the boys coming with you tonight when I said she could go."

"Baptist party? Is she going to be a Baptist now? Us Lutherans aren't good enough for her?" Mrs. Carlson said, laughing good-naturedly. "Don't worry about the boys. They like to listen to old folks talk."

"Who are you calling 'old folks'?" Mrs. Eriks asked, setting her pocketbook on the kitchen table and sitting down in one of the chairs. "We're as young as we feel. Isn't that right, Mrs. Lind?"

"*Ja*, that's right. Now let's go sit in the front room. I don't know why people always come in the back door and settle in the kitchen."

"Because that's where we're most at home," John Carlson said. "And that's where the food is!"

Charlie laughed. "That might be so, but we have more places to sit in the front room."

"We're in fine company tonight, Tilda," Charlie said when he'd settled into his wide-armed, wooden rocking chair. "It was Al and John that helped get the mill started, you know, and talked me into buying a share. Course I haven't decided yet if I should thank them." He turned to Al. "Think the mill's going to make it?"

"Things are looking better," Al said. "Your brother-in-law Charlie Carlson knows how to get a plant going, and now we have access to more timber. We'll make it unless we just decide to give up."

"Say, we can take a lesson from the Finns," John said. "They didn't give up. Not 'til they had to. I read somewhere that there were forty-four Russian soldiers for every Finn. Russia had twice the number of machine guns and cannons and artillery. They had up to fifty tanks in each division and the Finns had no tanks. You wonder how the hell they held off the Russians as long as they did."

"They were fighting for their homeland," Al said. "And they were clever. Damn clever! That's how. Did you read how the Finns planted mines with ropes attached under the ice in the lakes? When the Russian tanks rolled onto the frozen lake, the Finns pulled the rope and blew up the whole company. Soldiers and equipment sank to the bottom of the lake."

"*Ja*, and when the Russians came after them in tanks on land," John said, leaning forward in his chair, "the Finns were ready for them. They piled a wall of rocks across the road and dug ditches where they hid and waited. When the tanks had to stop, the Finns threw Molotov cocktails, bottles filled with gasoline, into the air intakes of the tanks, blowing them up, or they tied dynamite sticks together, stuck them into the treads of the tank, and lit them. Whoom! That was it!"

John looked around the room and saw that everyone was listening. "And if they didn't have dynamite, they pushed a log or crowbar into the treads of the moving tank, putting it out of commission."

Al said, "That's what I was saying. Our Finn boys were clever."

"*Ja*, and they had smart, experienced leaders," John said. "Marshall Mannerheim fought the Germans and Austrians in World War I. He's the one that thought of using ski troops in this war. He set up ninety miles of defenses along the border—machine gun nests, barbed wire, boulders, and tree trunks to stop the Russian tanks. The newspapers tell us that the Mannerheim Line held off the Russian army until finally the number of Russian troops was too much."

"I guess you all know how the Finnish border troops tried to even the odds," Charlie said. "Their ski patrol wore white uniforms and circled the Russian troops, shooting them from the side. The Russians couldn't see the skiers against the snow. Same thing at night. The Finnish sharpshooters skied through the woods and fired on the Russians where they were camped, and then they disappeared like ghosts, back into the woods. The Russians never knew where the bullets were coming from."

"*Ja*," Al Eriks put in, "Stalin bragged at the beginning of the war that the Russian tanks would be in the streets of Helsinki within a few days. They bombed hell out of the city, but the tanks never got there—

thanks to the ski troops, Molotov cocktails, and the hunting rifles the soldiers carried.

Tilda listened to the men talk, but then she thought of the other enemy, that terrible cold. The coldest winter in one hundred years, the Swedish newspaper reported. Ester wrote that her sons fought in temperatures forty degrees below zero. Their food froze before they got it to their mouths and their guns froze up, so they were useless. Even with the heavy, hand-knitted head warmers and scarves, gloves, and stockings the wives and mothers sent them, they were in danger of freezing. Birger wrote his mother that the men sewed vests for themselves out of newspaper to keep the wind out. But, he said, they were better off than the Russian troops. They froze to death on the battle line because they weren't outfitted with the right clothes.

Birger wrote that when they were near Summa village, fifty tanks broke through their lines. They fought day and night for five days before they drove the mass of well-equipped Russians back. They learned later that the Russian troops were sick from the cold, short of food, and tired of fighting a war that even their commanders had trouble justifying.

Tilda spoke up. "My nephew Edvin spent the four months of the war in field artillery, most of the time firing cannons. He lost most of his hearing in one ear." She sighed deeply before going on. "He said that during the last weeks of the war, the Finnish soldiers were almost out of ammunition, and they were short of men—"

"By Gawd," Charlie exploded, "There's the problem! If they'd had one more Finn, they'd have won the war."

Tilda was glad Charlie said that because, in spite of the seriousness of the conversation, everyone had to laugh.

"You could be right, Charlie," Al said. "Finland lost the war and gave up ten percent of its land, but, you know, Finland kept its independence. So maybe they won the war after all."

Everyone seemed to be thinking about that. Anna interrupted the silence. "So where do we go from here?"

"I say we go to the table for some coffee and cake," Charlie said, jumping to his feet.

"Best idea yet," John said.

6

COMPANY PICNIC
August 1940

"Tilda, pass your potato salad down this way," John Carlson called from the other end of the picnic table.

"I think we keep it here," Charlie called back. "I plan to eat the rest myself."

John slid off the bench and strode around to where Charlie and Tilda sat across the table from each other. "This isn't the logging camp," John said. "You're not 'Bull-of-the-woods' here!" He picked up the bowl of potato salad and returned to his place.

"*Ja*, guess that's so," Charlie said, shaking his head. "Maybe I could be 'Bull-of-the-green-chain' at the mill."

Everyone laughed.

Ted Ness said, "There's no 'Bull' in a co-op. That's what makes it a good place to work."

Charlie had to admit the corporation was running a good business now. In January, because of the trouble in Europe, President Roosevelt asked Congress for $1.8 billion for defense, and then, in May, for more money to start building 50,000 planes a year. In July, Congress appropriated $4 billion for a two-ocean navy. All that building meant orders for plywood. The mill was running two shifts to keep up with the orders. Everyone was getting full wages now and had been paid back for the days they worked without salary. It had given him and Tilda the courage to plan their house on the lot across the street from the duplex.

Charlie felt good. It wasn't just the food. It was the day. Sunday afternoon at Rosario Beach. Blue sky, full sun, a breeze from the salt water cooling the air. Old and new friends seated around picnic tables loaded with food. More families coming from the parking lot with their covered dishes and walking toward the empty tables in the area marked, "Reserved for Anacortes Veneer Co. Picnic." The sign should read, "Reserved for the First Annual Anacortes Veneer Co. Picnic."

He and Tilda knew all the Scandinavian people at the picnic. Many they'd met before they moved to Anacortes because of their years together in logging camps, and through Runeberg doings in Olympia and Portland. And now, through the mill, they were getting acquainted with some people of other national backgrounds. Good people, too, even if they weren't Swede Finns.

Charlie looked around the long picnic table. The Bill Wests were friends from camp. Mrs. West, already too fleshy, was busy filling her plate again while West was talking to anyone who'd listen. Their son, Big Leonard, worked in Seattle but was home for the weekend and the picnic. Charlie's stomach twisted as he remembered his own son had been called "Little Leonard" in camp because he was the younger of the two boys.

Ed and Tillie Frantz sat next to Bill West with their son Carl. Ted and Elsie Ness and their daughter Patty were sitting with the John Carlsons at the far end of the table. Their boy Glen and Edwin Carlson had already left the table to play horseshoes. Ida sat on one side of Tilda. Ida's-Charlie and Art sat on the other side with their heads together—talking about the mill, Charlie figured.

It was not a surprise that Ida and her Charlie drove all the way from Vancouver for the picnic. Ida's-Charlie was still president of the board even though he'd gone back to his job at the mill in Vancouver. Better reason than that, he'd been asked by the planning committee to play his fiddle at the picnic. He, along with two other fiddlers and Gust on the accordion, were to provide the afternoon entertainment. There was no place to dance at Rosario Beach Park, but people liked to listen and tap their feet to good music.

Art planned to show his dad some new machinery at the plant in the morning, and then he'd be leaving for Vancouver to start junior college. Angie would miss him, Charlie knew. They'd all miss him.

Charlie looked across the table at Tilda. Pretty as the day he married her. Blue eyes, fine skin, pink cheeks—with the help of a little rouge, but that was all right. He was a lucky man to have had her for a wife all these years. They'd lost Little Leonard in the accident on the railroad track, but him and Tilda had learned to live with this. They'd raised one daughter and married her off, and the other one was coming along fine. She was moody sometimes and didn't think the kids at school liked her, but mostly she was doing all right.

"*Hej, och goddag,*" a tall fair-haired man said, striding up to the picnic table with a big smile and an outstretched hand. "I'm Vic Haglund and would like to get acquainted with some of the mill folk."

"*Ja, goddag,*" Charlie said and stood to shake his hand.

"I'm bringing my family to Anacortes in October, but I'm in town now to find a house to rent. As long as I was here, I thought I'd come to the picnic and meet some of the other stockholders."

"*Välkommen!* I'm Charlie Lind. This is my wife, Tilda, her sister Ida and her *man,* Charlie Carlson. Down the table—Wests, Frantzes, Nesses, John Carlsons. So where you from, Vic?"

"Camp Five. Simpson Logging Company out of Shelton. If you mean before that, it was Larsmo, Finland." He grinned good-naturedly. "Bought stock in the Anacortes Veneer not too long ago. Thought it was time to retire," he said laughing.

"*Ja,* mill work looks like retirement when you've been a logger," Charlie agreed. "We still have lots of food on the table. *Var så god.*"

"*Tack så mycket.* I can eat all right."

Tilda found a paper plate and a fork and table knife in the picnic box and set another place. Angie had left the table for the beach as soon as she had eaten, so there was plenty of room for Vic to sit down. Charlie started to ask Vic more about his plans when Angie ran up to the table and skidded to a stop in a whoosh of dust.

"Mom," Angie said, breathless from her run, "I met the swellest girl! They moved to Anacortes just a little before we did, only she's been going to Nelson Grade School. She's my age and will be starting junior high, too. Her name is Joyce Kilgore and she's real cute and her dad is a saw filer in the mill—"

"Whoa. Slow down and catch your breath," Tilda said.

"Are they Scandinavian?" Charlie asked.

"I don't know. It doesn't matter, does it?"

"Of course not," Tilda said.

"She goes to the Lutheran church. Maybe that counts!" Angie said, tossing her head.

"Maybe you could bring her over to the table so we could meet her," Tilda said, reaching for her hand.

"Not now," Angie said, stepping back. "Someone brought extra inner tubes so I'm going to change into my bathing suit. Joyce already has her suit on, but she said she'd wait for me before going in the water." Angie pulled the bag with her swim suit and towel out of their picnic box and ran to the building marked "Rest Rooms."

"That your little girl?" Vic asked.

"*Ja*," Tilda said, "but not so little any more. Angie turned twelve this month. August 4."

"My girl Edna was twelve August 7. She's going to be happy when I tell her I met someone almost exactly her age." He stabbed a slice of ham on the serving platter with his fork and added it to his plate.

"So," Elsie Ness greeted Vic, "welcome to Anacortes." She walked around the table and sat down. Vic nodded, his mouth too full to answer. "You come at a good time," Elsie went on. "The mill is on its feet and paying good wages. We can all make plans—"

"Time for the three-legged race," someone shouted into a megaphone. "Everyone, grab a partner and get your gunny sack. This race is for everybody. Young and old!"

Art called to Leonard West to join him, and they ran to the pile of gunnysacks.

"Come on, Charlie," Al Eriks hollered from the next table. "Let's show those young whippersnappers a thing or two."

"You bet!" Charlie answered. "John, Ness, let's show them what us old loggers can do."

Soon all the available gunnysacks were taken. Everyone who had a sack knew what to do next. The right leg of one partner and the left leg of the other went into the sack. The partners then pulled the sack up as far as it would go and gripped it hard. Some partners practiced taking a few steps. One pair tipped over but quickly scrambled to their feet.

"Racers, on your mark," the man with the megaphone commanded. The pairs of runners hobbled over to the starting line. Men,

women, and children lined up along the roped-off corridor and prepared to cheer for their teams.

"Get set, but wait for the starting whistle," the megaphone instructed.

Charlie was set. He listened for the whistle, but as he waited, he
heard much more: the hollering and shouting of young children chasing each other around the picnic tables, the screeching of fiddles as
amateur musicians tuned up to entertain the crowd, and the laughing
and cheering of the spectators along the sidelines in anticipation of
the race of the day.

The sun had dropped low in the sky, spreading color on the water
off Rosario Beach. The tide was in and lapped at the rocky beach
where the children had been playing. Women sitting around the picnic tables pulled on their sweaters against the breeze stirring the
early evening air. A few of the men had moved to a separate table to
smoke and talk over the day.

"Charlie, you and Al could have won that race if you hadn't
tangled with Leonard West and Art Carlson," Ted Ness said, grinning widely.

"The damn guys cut in front of us," Charlie said. "Hard to get
back on your feet with one leg in a sack."

"Leonard and Art had no problem. They rolled back onto their
feet and crossed the finish line before you got your feet under you."

Everyone grinned.

"Well, I guess there's something to be said for being young,"
Charlie admitted. "Anyway, we all got a piece of pie for trying.
Worse things can happen to a man than losing a three-legged race."

"Like what?" Al said, flinching as he reached up and rubbed his
dirt-streaked shoulder.

Everyone laughed.

The music stopped and the accordionist announced that the last
number for the day would be "*Lördagsvals.*" Charlie remembered
how he and Tilda used to waltz to that at the Blue Ox on Hood Canal
when they lived in Potlatch. That seemed a long time ago, but it had
been only eight months. So much had happened in that time. They'd

started a mill and drawn plans for a house. And Finland had fought and lost a war.

"I'll tell you what's worse than losing a three-legged race," Charlie said. "Living in Finland right now."

No one spoke. Someone cleared his throat. A large, black beetle made its way down the length of the table. It stopped when it reached the end, seeming to look around and wonder which way to go next. Vic Haglund broke the silence.

"The Finns should never have signed the Peace of Moscow in March. The French and British told them they'd send men to help them fight. Maybe by mid-April—"

"Mannerheim knew the troops couldn't hold out that long," Al said. "They had no choice but to sign when they did."

Charlie said, "Remember what Churchill said on radio when the war was at its worst? He said the whole world admires the courage of the fighting Finns—that Finland shows what free men can do."

John Westbloom, a friend from camp days, nodded his head and ground out his cigarette in the dust of the picnic grounds with the toe of his shoe. Al cleared his throat.

"*Ja*, but the treaty demanded too much!" Vic exclaimed. "A large part of Karelia, the Karelian Isthmus including Lake Ladoga and the city of Viborg, part of the Petsamo area in the north—altogether ten per cent of their land, some of Finland's best land."

Charlie knew most of the rest of the demands. The Finns agreed to construct a railway line linking the new Soviet border to Kemi at the head of the Bothnia Sea, and to lease the Hanko Peninsula to Russia for thirty years. The Soviets also expected Finland to agree that neither country would form an alliance against the other.

"And think of the refugees from Karelia," Vic went on. "The newspaper reports an estimate of 400,000 people!"

"*Ja*, that's bad," Charlie agreed, "but we can be glad that Finland takes care of its own. We all know that in June the government passed the Rapid Emergency Resettlement Act giving over 1200 square miles of land to farmers from Karelia."

"The Finns helped the displaced people build shelters on that land and find jobs," Westbloom added. "We can be proud of our countrymen."

Everyone nodded in agreement, but the mood of the men was still somber. Things in Europe had gotten worse since March 12 when the peace treaty was signed. Germany now occupied Norway, Denmark, Belgium, and France. Russia was afraid of Germany and, as a buffer zone, took over the Baltic Republics. Some were afraid that Russia would try to take over all of Finland for the same reason.

Now, according to the papers, the Soviets demanded the right to use the Finnish railway system to carry troops and military supplies across Finland to their base at Hango. Further, Molotov was demanding access to Finland's nickel mines near Petsamo.

"By the way," John Westbloom said, "have you heard that Congress passed a law in June that says, if we don't have citizenship papers, we have to register as aliens and be fingerprinted?"

"Haven't read anything about that," Al said. "Criminals get fingerprinted, or enemies of the state. Not law-abiding people in a free country."

Charlie had read about it. It was called the Alien Registration Act. He and Tilda had planned to get their citizenship papers someday, but to get your papers, you had to take classes and there were no classes in the logging camps. Lately they'd had too much on their minds to think about it, but, when he read about this law, he'd felt uneasy. Like him and Tilda couldn't be trusted.

"The trouble in Europe gives the whole world the jitters," John said.

"Look over there," Al said. "The ladies are packing up the picnic boxes. That gives me the jitters. I think the party's over."

"Well, it was a good one," John said, and they all agreed.

7

JUNIOR HIGH
September 1940

"**M**om," Angie cried, "I have to go! Faith is meeting me at the corner and I can't keep her waiting."

"I know, Angie, but you can't go to junior high with jam on the front of your new sweater. Come to the sink and I see if I can wash it out."

Angie danced on one foot and then the other while her mother dabbed at the front of her sweater with the wet dishrag.

"This is what happens," her mother scolded, "when you take so long to dress and comb your hair that you have no time to eat. You eat in such a hurry—"

"It's worse, Mom. Look! Now it's a big spot!" Angie wailed as she looked down at her sweater. Angie wanted something new to wear the first day of school, but her mom said she'd have to wait for new clothes. Daddy's salary was good now, but expenses had built up when he wasn't making any wages. Angie had coaxed and coaxed until finally they went to Penney's and found a sweater on sale. And now it was ruined!

"It's just a wet spot," Mama said. "It will be dry by the time you walk to school. Here's your notebook and lunch. Now, on your way." Mama smiled and pushed her gently toward the door. Mama wouldn't be so cheerful if she knew how hard it was starting junior high school. Even though Angie knew most of the kids from Whitney, there'd be kids from Nelson Grade School, too, and what if they didn't like her? Angie remembered her first day at Whitney last winter and shuddered in spite of the warm fall day.

"Hey, Angie, hurry up," Faith called from down the block. "I'm starting out."

"I'm coming," Angie answered and ran to catch up.

The girls walked and skipped and ran and then walked again. They fell in step with Annette and Beverly on the next corner. Angie didn't know them well, but they were always nice. The early morning sun warmed the air and, like Mama promised, dried the wet spot on Angie's sweater. This could be a beautiful day after all.

The girls were out of breath when they reached the bottom of the steps to Columbia Junior High. The old, three-story, stone building sat firm and square in the center of a wide summer-dried lawn. Two girls and a boy ran ahead of them up the cement steps. Another girl Angie didn't know by name said "Hi" and walked with them on up to the big double doors. Some boys and girls came out of the building with envelopes in their hands and sat down on the steps to read what was inside.

"Those must be the class schedules," Faith said. "Students are assigned a room according to their ability. This is called 'tracking.' You move with the same group of kids to the different classes. I remember when my sister Margie started junior high. She was so happy when she was assigned to a room with her friends."

"I sure hope we're in the same room," Angie said, a new worry.

"I'm sure we will be," Faith said. "They number the classes, 7-1 to 7-4. 7-1 is for the best students and 7-4, for those who don't get good grades. You and I get mostly good grades, so we'll be together. Come on. Let's pick up our envelopes."

The girls pulled open the heavy doors and stepped into the noisy, crowded entrance hall. A big boy pushed them aside as he darted past them out the door. Discarded envelopes littered the floor. Students were talking and laughing and playfully jostling each other as they waited in line at a room labeled "Office." The door stood open and Angie could see a young woman behind a desk handing out envelopes.

"Let's get our schedules," Faith said, raising her voice to be heard over the talking around them and the clanging of locker doors down the hall. A man's voice interrupted the chatter with instructions for the boys and girls who already had their letters to step out of the office area so students waiting in line could pick up their envelopes. And to please use the wastepaper basket next to the office for their discarded envelopes.

"Come on, Angie," Faith said, grabbing her by the hand and pulling her toward the end of the line of students. "There's Phyllis, and there's Joyce! She went to Nelson last year. You'll like her. She's fun."

"I know. I met her last month at the plywood picnic."

The girls hugged each other and then compared their new notebooks and new school clothes. Angie didn't have saddle shoes like the other three, but the girls said they liked her new sweater and, in no time at all, they were at the office.

"I'm Faith Charlot and this is my friend, Angie Lind. We need our envelopes." Angie admired the way Faith spoke up and talked to people she didn't even know.

The pretty young woman smiled and leafed through the remaining envelopes in the box, her long, bright-red fingernails flashing. "I find 'Faith Charlot,'" she said, handing the envelope to Faith, "but no 'Angie Lind'. There's an 'Agnes Lind.' Maybe there's a typing error."

"No, that's me," Angie said, hoping she wouldn't have to explain.

The pretty woman with lips as red as her fingernails studied the name and then handed Angie her envelope. "Your assigned room and locker number are in this envelope," the lady said, "as well as the day's schedule and directions to the cafeteria. This is the seventh-grade hall and the room number is over each door. Locate your room number, and, when the bell rings in a few minutes, you may go to your room."

Faith had already torn open her envelope. "7-1," she screamed, jumping up and down. "Just what I wanted."

"I'm in 7-1, too!" Phyllis exclaimed, waving her letter in the air.

Joyce opened her envelope and grabbed Faith, spinning her around. "Me, too! Me, too! Won't it be fun! Angie, quick! Open your envelope."

Angie tore the envelope apart. She pulled out the paper and unfolded it. She looked at it and then looked again. The number blurred in front of her eyes. Her face suddenly felt hot. "It says 7-4," she choked.

"Angie? Home already?" Mom exclaimed. "Where did the day go! There's milk and fresh cookies. Sit down and tell me about your first day in junior high. Did you like your teachers? Did you—Angie! What—?"

Angie didn't stop but ran up the stairs to her room. She threw herself on her bed and shut her eyes, but she couldn't shut out her day. Chet sat in the row next to hers. Behind him sat the boy from Whitney who was always late to class and the girl who never combed her hair. Before class started, a boy shot a spit-wad at this girl and, when she looked around, he stuck out his tongue.

The teacher had asked the class to please settle down and then called roll without smiling. They'd spent the period going over work Angie had studied clear back in Potlatch and then, as a group, they'd moved on to the next class. Finally, the day ended.

Angie pushed her food around on her supper plate with her fork. Her parents had finished eating and Mom was picking up their dishes.

"Well," her mother said, sighing deeply, "if you're not going to eat, leave the table and help me with the dishes. Here, take this dishtowel and start drying."

Angie took the dishtowel and picked up a plate from the sink board.

"I don't know what to do with you," Mama went on, rattling the dishes in the metal dishpan. "You come in the house after school like a tornado and go straight to your room when I'm standing in the kitchen with a plate of fresh-baked cookies in my hand. You don't come downstairs 'til I tell you that you have to eat some supper. Then you sit at the table like a stone. How can Daddy and I help when you don't tell us what's troubling you?"

What was the use of telling them anything, Angie thought. They wouldn't understand. Faith and Phyllis and Joyce were sorry she wouldn't be in 7-1 with them, but, when the bell rang, they grabbed each other's hands and ran to their room.

"It's hard to be patient with you," Mama said. "I guess you'll talk to us when you're ready."

Angie stared out the window as she dried the plate. She hoped none of her new friends ever found out her mother bleached and hemmed flour sacks for dishtowels.

"Stop dreaming now or you be drying dishes all night," her mom scolded. Angie picked up a cup from the sink board and dried it carefully. Then she wrapped the cup loosely in the dishtowel and set it back on the sink board.

"I don't feel good," Angie said, and walked slowly out of the kitchen and up the stairs to her room. She left the door open, sat down on her bed, and listened.

Mama's heels clicked across the kitchen floor and a cupboard door opened and closed. Her dad cleared his throat. She heard the newspaper rustle as he turned a page. The dishpan clunked as Mama turned it upside down in the sink. Quiet. Angie thought Mama was probably drying her hands on her apron. Next she would pick up the dishtowel—

CRASH. Just what Angie was waiting for.

"Oh!" Mama cried. "My best cup!"

Suddenly Angie knew how wrong she'd been. "Mama," she cried, running out of her room and down the stairs. "I'm so sorry."

Her mom stood over the pieces of shattered cup. Angie grabbed her around the waist and sobbed. "I'm so sorry," she repeated over and over, wiping her tears on her mother's apron. She sat down on the floor next to the pieces of glass and buried her face in her hands. The school had placed her in the lowest seventh grade class, her friends had run to their room and left her standing in the hall, and she'd broken her mom's special coffee cup....

"I guess you were pretty mad at somebody," Mama said. "Go get the broom and sweep up the pieces and you feel better. Then we sit down and talk."

Angie dressed slowly the next morning and poked at her breakfast. The first bell had already rung when she got to school. She found her seat in her 7-4 classroom. Her teacher had introduced herself yesterday when she first welcomed them to class, but Angie couldn't remember her name.

"Agnes. Agnes Lind." Her teacher was talking to her. "Agnes, please come up to my desk. There's a note here for you from the office."

Angie slid out of her desk and hurried to the front of the room. Was this more trouble, she wondered, as she took the note from her teacher's hand.

"I received a note, too," her teacher said. "Evidently the office made a mistake in registering you. You need to pick up your books and hurry along to room 7-1." Her teacher smiled and patted her on the shoulder. "I'm sorry you won't be in my class, but you'll do fine wherever you are."

Angie wanted to thank her teacher, maybe give her a hug even if she couldn't remember her name. She'd find out what her name was and drop by to see her sometime, after she was settled in her new room.

Angie picked up her notebook and ran down the hall. She was breathless when she arrived at room 7-1.

"You must be Agnes Lind," the tall woman with light brown, bobbed hair said. "I'm Miss Barnard. My class was full yesterday before they added your name to my roll sheet," she said, shaking her head. "You'll have to sit in a chair until the custodian brings in another desk."

Angie hesitated, not sure where to go.

"Over here, by my desk," Miss Barnard said, turning the chair so it faced the front of the room. "Now sit down, please. As you can see, class has already started."

Angie hurried to the empty chair.

"As I told you yesterday, boys and girls, my expectations are high. You must get to class on time and be in your seat when the bell rings."

She glanced down at Angie, her dark-rimmed glasses slipping down on her nose. Angie wondered if she was already in trouble, even though it wasn't her fault she was late.

"Now, did everyone remember my instructions from yesterday? Did you all bring a three-ring notebook, a pencil and pen and notebook paper?"

Students nodded their heads. Miss Barnard noticed Angie's notebook and other supplies, and nodded her approval.

"Your assignment for today was to write a page on what you hoped to learn in junior high, and you were to write the correct heading in the upper right-hand corner of your paper." Miss Barnard pointed to the blackboard where she'd written a sample heading. "Does your heading include your name, last name first, English 7-1, and date?"

More nodding.

"Is the title of your composition centered on the first line of the paper?" This time she didn't wait for a response. "If so, you may pass your paper forward." She turned to Angie. "I'll expect this paper from you tomorrow."

Notebook rings snapped as papers were released and passed down the rows. Miss Barnard picked up the papers and leafed through them, examining the tops of each page. The only sound in the room now was the hum of the electric clock on the back wall.

Someone giggled nervously.

Miss Barnard's head snapped up. Angie heard a locker door slam shut somewhere down the hall. Then all was again quiet. Finally, Miss Barnard set the papers on her desk and addressed the class.

"As I told you yesterday," she said, "we will be studying English grammar the first semester of this year, and literature the second semester. We will do a great deal of writing both semesters. I will read the compositions you just handed in very carefully to see what your writing needs are. You will, as you probably know, be expected to keep up with your assignments if you want to remain in this class. We will begin our work today—"

The door opened and a man in coveralls carried in a desk. Miss Barnard sighed and pointed to the back of the room. Then she nodded at Angie. Angie followed him and slipped into the desk as soon as he set it down. She was relieved to be in the back of the room where everyone wasn't looking at her and she could look around and see where her friends were sitting. Faith and Phyllis were in one row. Joyce sat across from them. Their attention, along with everyone else's in the class, was on Miss Barnard who was now demonstrating on the blackboard how to diagram a sentence. When the bell rang, the class filed out quietly.

Faith waited at the classroom door. "I couldn't believe my eyes when I saw you walk in," she said. "What happened?"

"Someone in the office made a mistake. I'm glad I'm in room 7-1 with you, but Miss Barnard scares me."

"I know. She scares me, too, but my sister had her when she was in seventh grade and said she really learned a lot from her. She teaches girls' P.E., too, and that's today. All the seventh-grade girls take the same P.E. class from her second period, Monday, Wednesday, and Friday."

Angie pulled her schedule out of her pocket to check. They didn't have school Monday because of Labor Day, and they didn't have gym yesterday because it was Tuesday so Faith was right. Today they had physical education.

They stopped at Faith's locker for a minute and then hurried to the small gym that was part of the junior high. Angie already knew that the large, stone building that stood between the junior high and the high school was called the "Big Gym" and was used mostly by the high school.

When they got to the small gym, the room was full of girls sitting on the floor facing Miss Barnard who was standing in the front of the room holding a red attendance book in one hand and a pencil in the other. She called for attention just as Faith and Angie sat down.

Miss Barnard stared at the class over the top of her glasses until everyone was quiet. She introduced herself and called roll. "Girls," she then said, "we have certain dress requirements in P.E. classes. In order to participate, you must wear red shorts and white blouses. J.C. Penney store downtown has stocked a variety of sizes. You have until next Monday to buy your uniform."

Angie dropped her head. What if her parents didn't have enough money to buy her uniform? She'd heard them talk about how expensive it was to build a house, and where would they get the money to buy an electric stove! If she didn't earn a P.E. credit, she wouldn't be able to go on to high school.

Faith elbowed her to pay attention.

"You will take a shower each day after P.E. class," Miss Barnard went on. "There are two large shower areas next to the locker room with a number of showerheads in each. There are no shower dividers. Modesty will not be an excuse for not showering. Is that clear?"

Angie and Faith looked at each other. It was clear that showering with dozens of other girls would be difficult to do.

Miss Barnard lowered her voice slightly and cleared her throat as she said, "You will, however, be excused from P.E. two days a month to allow for your sick days. On those days, you will go to the library to work on homework. Are there any questions?"

Angie wanted to be sure she understood. She gathered her courage and raised her hand.

"Yes, Agnes, what is it?"

"I was wondering," Angie started.

"Speak up, Agnes. Voices don't carry well in this gymnasium."

"I was just wondering," Angie began again, louder. "I hardly ever get sick. Could I save up those sick days and be excused from P.E. class the last month of school?"

Angie waited for a reply, but Miss Barnard just looked at her. The girls in the class were looking at her, too. She heard giggles. Angie felt her face get hot.

"Miss Lind," her teacher said, "please see me after class. I'd like to talk to you a minute." More giggles. Miss Barnard quieted the girls with a look.

"Now, girls, everyone stand and spread out across the room. I'm going to teach you the warm-up exercises we will be doing at the start of each P.E. class."

Angie tried to follow the instructions for the exercises, but felt awkward, like her arms and legs didn't want to obey. When class was over, she waited in place. Miss Barnard came to her.

"Agnes, I'll be brief," Miss Barnard said, studying her red attendance book. "You need to have a talk with your mother." She paused and cleared her throat. Her face was suddenly red like her attendance book. "See that you do. That's all." She turned and walked out.

Faith was waiting in the hall. "What'd she say?"

"She said I had to talk to my mother."

"Are you going to?"

"I don't know what I'm supposed to talk about," Angie said. She couldn't keep her chin from quivering.

"I think I know," Faith whispered. "My mom is good at talking about that stuff if you want to talk to her."

Angie studied her friend, not knowing what to say or think. Finally, "I'll talk to my big sister. She knows a lot."

"Come on, then," Faith said, grabbing her by the hand. "If we don't run, we'll be late for our next class.

CHARLIE'S THIRD LETTER

Anacortes, October 7, 1940

Dear Mother,

I will now send you a few lines as an answer to your letter, that we received some time ago and in which we find you in good life and health which is nice to hear and the same good things we are able to send back to you, that we all live and are in good health and we hope that these lines will reach you still living and healthy. I work every day and everything goes on nice and smoothly as usual.

Agnes is back in school again. It is her seventh year in school so soon she will also be grown up and married. Ya, time passes by. Thelma has been married for a year already. They were here two weeks ago and now on Sunday we will go there. It is 160 miles to go from here but that is not a long way now a days.

I guess that times are miserable in Europe now a days and everything gets worse all the time so I guess it is the end of the world soon.

I had planned to send you a few dollars last summer but it was impossible to send money here, but now the post department has opened up for sending money in letters to Finland again so I sent you ten dollars one week ago or the post sent them. I hope that you will get them in your hands for there is a big need for money now.

As for news Henrik Sjoblom is in poor health. He has lack of blood, so I don't think he has a long time left here on earth. He has a heart failure. Alfred West if you remember him he suddenly died one month ago from heart failure.

I will stop now with many dear greetings to you my mother who I will never forget.

Warmly, Chas Lind

Dear brother and family,

We all greet you so much and thank you for what you wrote again. It was nice to hear from you after all that has been going on at home, but I guess it is not so nice to have the rheumatism either. I hope you will get rid of it in some way. I will stop now with a warm greeting to all of you.

8

"ARSENAL OF DEMOCRACY"
December 29, 1940

"Angie, hurry and finish your supper and come to the front room," Mama said again. "President Roosevelt is going to start his radio talk any minute."

Her parents were always telling her to hurry up when she ate. Sometimes she didn't feel like hurrying, but tonight she guessed she'd better take her plate to the sink and join them. Angie's social science teacher said they should always listen when the President talks on the radio. Not only because he was a very important President—the first to be elected to a third term—but also because of the war in Europe. Angie would listen and try to forget what was really bothering her— that Edna had beat her again in the weekly spelling bee!

Angie had been excited in October when the Haglund family found a house to rent catty-corner from them. Mom must have been happy, too, because she invited the whole family over for coffee before they even unpacked. Edna's parents were younger than Angie's parents, but they talked with a Swedish accent like her own mom and dad, so they felt comfortable together.

Edna's mother, Helga, was a little woman, but had lots of fire. She told Angie's mom that when she took Edna to junior high to register, Edna asked the principal to put her in the same room as Angie. The principal wasn't sure he should do that. He told Edna that the 7-1 class was advanced and, with school having already started, she'd have to work very hard to catch up and keep up. Keep up? Edna's mom told him that Edna was so smart, kids would have to work hard to keep up with her!

Angie told her mom that not only was Edna smart, but she had the most beautiful hair in the class. It was a bright, shiny blonde, not mousy-blonde like her own. Mama said she'd rinse Angie's hair in lemon juice every time she washed it to make it lighter, but the lemon juice hadn't worked yet. Another thing about Edna. She was quick to raise her hand when Miss Barnard asked a question. Edna wasn't at all scared of Miss Barnard.

"Angie, leave your supper now and come listen," Mama called. "This is supposed to be an important speech."

"It doesn't have anything to do with me," Angie protested, dragging her feet as she walked into the front room and flopped down onto the floor in front of the radio.

Chee Chee stepped into Angie's lap and started up his motor. That's what Dad called it when the kitty purred. He really wasn't a kitty. He was a full-grown cat, but Angie felt lucky he'd chosen to meow at their back door. Mama said someone must have taken good care of him because his black-and-brown striped coat was thick and shiny. They would read the Lost and Found ads in the *Daily Mercury* and the *Anacortes American*, but, if no one was looking for him, they could keep him. Angie named him Chee Chee because he had such fat cheeks.

Chee Chee had fun with their Christmas tree. He climbed into the lower branches and batted at the tinsel until it hung in tangles or dropped onto the rug. Mama said that even though the tree looked a little messy, they'd keep it up until New Year's Day. Christmas needed to be stretched out as long as possible, especially now with so much trouble in the world.

"This is not a fireside chat on war," the President began.

Good, Angie thought. Everyone was always talking about the war in Europe and that was a long way from Anacortes. She decided to listen.

> This is a talk on national security because the nub of the whole purpose of your President is to keep you now, and your children later, and your grandchildren much later, out of a last-ditch war for the preservation of American independence and the things that American independence means to you and to me and to ours....

Never before since Jamestown and Plymouth Rock has our American civilization been in such danger as now.... The Nazi masters of Germany have made it clear that they intend not only to dominate all life and thought in their own country, but also to enslave the whole of Europe, and then to use the resources of Europe to dominate the rest of the world.

Angie looked at her mom. There was something in her face that scared Angie. Her dad's face was tight, too. She pushed Chee Chee off her lap and went to sit between them on the sofa. Mama took Angie's hand and held it tight. The speech went on.

Thinking in terms of today and tomorrow, I make the direct statement to the American people that there is far less chance of the United States getting into war, if we do all we can now to support the nations defending themselves against attack by the Axis than if we acquiesce in their defeat, submit tamely to an Axis victory, and wait our turn to be the object of attack in another war later on.... Our national policy is not directed toward war. Its sole purpose is to keep war away from our country and our people....

We must be the great arsenal of democracy. For us this is an emergency as serious as war itself.

The President called upon the country to manufacture as much arms and munitions as possible in the shortest time possible.

I call for it in the name of this nation which we love and honor and which we are privileged and proud to serve. I call upon our people with absolute confidence that our common cause will greatly succeed.

The announcer came on then and said the President had completed his speech. Anyone who wished to respond could do so by sending a wire to the White House.

Daddy walked across the room and turned off the radio. Mama stood up and looked out the window. Angie joined her. It was snowing a little, a quiet, fluffy snow that had already hidden the cracks in the sidewalk. Angie couldn't see the broken spots, so maybe they weren't really there. Like the far-off war. She couldn't see the fighting, so maybe there wasn't a war. But she knew better. Not seeing it didn't mean it wasn't so.

"Yoo Hoo," someone called from the back door.

"It's Helga," Mama said, hurrying into the kitchen. "Come in! Come in!"

"*Ja*, I'm in," Helga answered, "and so is the rest of the family."

Helga, Edna, and her younger brother Vic and little sister Mildred followed Mama into the front room. Vic, the dad, came last with his hand outstretched. Daddy stood up and shook his hand. It seemed old-country people shook hands more than they needed to.

"Sit down," Mama said, pointing to the sofa and chairs. "I go put on the coffee."

"So, Charlie, you heard the President speak, too, I guess," Vic said, still standing. "What do you make of it? Are we going to war?"

"We will if Roosevelt has anything to do with it," Daddy answered.

"You think so? I think Roosevelt is trying to keep us out of the war. If we help England lick the Germans, the war might end right there. If England falls, Germany will be looking at us next."

"We don't know that!" Daddy said, his face reddening, like it always did when he talked politics. "If we send guns to England now, next thing we'll be sending them our boys. You remember in September Roosevelt put through a Selective Service Act and men from twenty-one to thirty-five had to register for the Army. Secretary of War Stimson started drawing draft numbers in October. This country is building an army to fight in someone else's war. I say what's going on between Germany and England is none of our damn business."

"It is our business!" Vic exclaimed. "There's less chance of getting into this war if we support the countries that are being attacked." He sat down then and shook his head. Daddy did the same.

"What do you think?" Angie whispered to Edna.

"I think we should do like the President says. Manufacture war stuff and send it to England. He said he needs all of us to help."

"How can we help? We're not old enough to work in a factory."

"Maybe someone will tell us what to do," Edna said. "You know, when I think about war, I get goose-bump scared. Like when I'm in Miss Barnard's English class and she moves around in front of her desk and looks at us."

Angie looked at Edna to see if she was joking. "You mean Miss Barnard scares you, too?"

"Yes! I'm always scared she'll call on me when I don't know the answer, so, when I do know the answer, I raise my hand quick."

Suddenly Angie felt good about her new friend. What did it matter that Edna was a better speller? She, too, was scared of Miss Barnard, and now, after hearing the President speak, they could be scared together about what could happen to their world.

PART III - 1941

9

BARK BREAD
March 20

Charlie finished his breakfast and sipped his *på tår*. One good thing about working swing shift was it gave him a chance to relax in the morning, drink a second cup of coffee, and read the newspaper. He was glad they'd subscribed to the *Seattle Star*. The *Anacortes American* was a weekly and reported mostly local news. He was interested in what was going in the rest of the world.

Looked like Congress passed the Lend-Lease Bill, he noted. The U.S. would be loaning England arms and munitions. England would pay America back in kind after the war. Maybe Roosevelt was right. Maybe that would keep the fighting in Europe. If it kept America out of the war, it would be worth it, he had to admit.

Here it was on the third page. News about Finland. America needs to be alert to an alliance taking place between Finland and Germany, it said. In the fall of 1940, Finland agreed to allow German military personnel to pass through their country and to establish military bases in Lapland. In return, Germany promised military aid to the Finnish army. Mannerheim declared in January of this year that, because of Russia's continual intimidation, Finland's security depended on accepting Germany's help.

Another article. A year ago this month, March 12, 1940, Finland and Russia signed the "Peace of Moscow" treaty, and yet there was little peace in Finland. Russia continued to harass the small country with demands that were difficult to meet. Meanwhile, people were suffering from a shortage of food for themselves and for the 400,000 refugees who fled their homes when the Russians took over the Karelian Isthmus.

Charlie shook his head and handed Tilda the newspaper. "Tilda, read these articles. People won't know what to think about Finland."

He watched Tilda as she read. Finally Tilda looked up. "Charlie," she said, "when was the last time you wrote to your mother?"

Charlie took another sip of his coffee. *Ja*, his mother would be among those struggling. He'd sent her $10 before Christmas and included a short letter. He sent another $10 a couple weeks ago, but they'd been so busy moving into their new house, he didn't write anything. He needed to get a letter off to her, all right.

"Get me pencil and tablet, Tilda. I'll write a letter right now."

Work at the mill was going fine, he wrote his mother. Lots of orders for plywood because of the war in Europe. He and Tilda built a house across the street from where they were renting and were now moved in. It was the first house they had ever owned. The house wasn't real big, but it had two bedrooms with a bathroom between, a living room and dining room, and a kitchen, of course. From the far corner of the breakfast nook you could see Guemes Channel, which looked a little like the Bothnia Sea.

Chee Chee was under the table playing with Charlie's shoelaces. Charlie ignored him.

He wrote that the house had a full basement where Angie and her friends roller skated around the furnace. There was space for the car on one side of the basement and for a laundry room on the other. The house even had a laundry chute. You drop dirty clothes down a hole in the broom closet in the kitchen and it lands in a laundry basket below.

Charlie wrote that they had a new electric stove in the kitchen, with a trash burner on one end because they were used to the feel of a wood fire first thing in the morning. Tilda kept her woodstove though—put it in the basement so she'd have it when she cooked for company. Also, in the kitchen, a built-in ironing board folded out when Tilda needed to iron. He wrote his mother she couldn't imagine how warm and convenient—

"Gawdalmighty! What am I doing!" Charlie shouted.

Tilda came running. "Charlie, what's the matter?"

Charlie threw down his pencil. It bounced once and rolled off the table onto the floor. Chee Chee caromed the pencil between his paws through the chair legs until it hit the wall. Then he lay down beside the pencil and rested his chin on it.

"You know what I'm doing?" Charlie exclaimed. "I'm telling my mother how good we have it here in America when I know how bad things are in Finland." Charlie picked up the letter and tore it in half and in half again. He retrieved the pencil and began a new letter.

[CHARLIE'S FOURTH LETTER]

Anacortes, Wash
March 20, 1941

Dear Mother,

I will briefly send you some lines as an answer to your letter, that was nice to receive after such a long time.

It was nice to hear that you live and are healthy even though the conditions are bad there in poor Finland I can guess, for you as for many others. I really hope that you don't have to start eating bark bread on your old days like when you were young.

We sent you some coffee and sugar and little sweets about six months ago. I just wonder if you got it. We would like to send you some more but we have been waiting to hear if you got the package first.

I sent you $10. a couple of weeks ago and I hope you will get them in your hands. If you get this money I want you to give one *dollar to Nadine Sjöroos. I got a real good letter from her sometime ago in which she told about her sisters and brothers which was nice to hear.*

I am so lazy and poor to write so she will have to be contented with a friendly greeting and many thanks for the letter. She says that they sent us two Christmas cards a year ago but we did not get them. We moved from Potlatch before Christmas so they were lost. Hope she will write soon again.

Warmly, Chas Lind

"Tilda, come read this letter and see if I left anything out," Charlie called.

Tilda ran back into the kitchen and sat down at the table. Charlie handed her the letter and waited. He watched as she read.

"Oh, Charlie," she said, "do you think they have to eat bark bread now?"

"What's 'bark bread'?" Angie asked, coming out of her room. "That's not bread made from tree bark, is it?"

Charlie looked at his daughter. Her face was flushed from sleep and she stretched her arms above her head long and hard, a little like Chee Chee after a nap. She slid into a chair opposite her dad and waited for an answer.

"That's exactly what it is, Angie. When your grandmother was a girl, there was a terrible famine in Finland. Farmers had no wheat or rye to harvest, so women made bread from bark flour."

Angie nodded. "But what's bark flour?"

"Tilda, tell Angie about bark bread."

"Well," Tilda said, "in spring, starving people in Finland peeled bark from the trunks of pine trees. With sharp knives they cut loose a very thin, light-colored layer between the outside bark and an inside green layer. They stored this thin layer out-of-doors until it got as hard as cardboard. Then the women roasted the layers in ovens until they were light brown. Finally they ground the layers into fine meal-like flour and made the bread."

Charlie watched Angie as she listened. She'd quit stretching and yawning. "What happens to the trees?" she asked.

Tilda and Charlie both laughed. Charlie explained. "The bark is cut loose in a kind of flap. After the farmer cuts out the between layer, he puts the flap back in place—probably ties it to the tree trunk in some way—and the tree heals."

Tilda, still smiling, asked Angie if she didn't want to know what happened to the people who ate the bark bread.

"Yeh, of course. Didn't they get terrible stomach aches?"

"'Bread is bread,' they'd say. 'It will help us survive.' What we know now is that bark meal has lots of vitamins and minerals in it. And roughage," Tilda said and smiled again. "If they had any other flour—wheat or rye—they would add bark meal to the flour to make the flour go farther."

Charlie couldn't resist commenting. "Bears eat the bark from trees and see how big and strong they are!"

Angie looked at him now, like she didn't know what to believe. "Dad," she said, "I know bears eat bark, but I don't like to think about my grandma eating bark."

"There's a lot going on now in Finland—and the rest of the world—that I don't like to think about either," Charlie said, shaking his head.

10

SECRETS
May 1941

Miss Barnard had given her class the rest of the period to work on a reading assignment, but Angie couldn't concentrate. It wasn't spring fever. She knew what that felt like. It was because Laura Elliot, a girl she hardly knew, had come up to her in the hall before school and said she had a secret and it had something to do with Angie. If Angie would sit with her in the awards assembly at the end of the day, Laura would tell her the secret.

Angie rested her chin in her hands and stared out the window. When school had started in the fall, the maple tree outside the window had been covered with giant, green leaves. She'd watched the leaves turn orange and yellow and finally brown. When they dropped to the ground, bare limbs crisscrossed the gray, winter sky. Then one warm spring day, she looked out and saw that the limbs had been spatter-painted with tiny, apple-green leaves. The next time Angie noticed, the tiny leaves had broadened and darkened, and the school year was about to end.

Maple trees grew in Potlatch, too. She and her friends used to climb into the crotches of those trees and imagine they were hiding from kidnappers. Once she'd jumped from a high branch to a lower branch, to swing back and forth like Tarzan, before dropping to the ground. The force of the jump caused her hands to slip from the limb, and she landed on her back instead of her feet. Ainley Remple, a boy three grades ahead of her in school, had helped her up and offered to walk her home. Ainley was handsome in spite of being tall and skinny, but Angie had been embarrassed and told him, "No."

Angie wasn't in Potlatch now, but it was all right. She'd made a few friends and liked Columbia Junior High. She was still a little afraid of Miss Barnard because she was so strict, but Angie respected her and had learned a lot. Miss Barnard read poetry to the class and assigned exciting short stories for them to read. Miss Barnard started a "Scribblers' Club" and invited anyone who wanted to write to join the club. Angie liked to write, so Miss Barnard said she could become one of the charter members. Angie didn't even mind diagramming sentences, but now, this morning, she couldn't concentrate on her work. Laura Elliot had a secret and it had something to do with Angie.

Angie had admired Laura from a distance. She was tall for seventh grade and very slim and blonde, and pretty in a grown-up way. Angie thought Laura could be a model when she graduated. She was always friendly when they passed in the hall, but they had never sat together, even at lunch. Now Laura had asked her to sit with her at the assembly.

At the end of every school year, awards were given out at a student body assembly to those who had excelled in such things as athletics or music or art. Angie hadn't taken part in any of the extra-curricular activities, so she knew she wouldn't be eligible for an award, but she was anxious for this assembly to begin.

Students moved in chattering clusters toward the open door of the gym. They pushed their way down the aisles left open between the rows of folding chairs. Angie slipped through the press of excited schoolmates until she spotted Laura saving her a place near the front of the room. Student body officers were seated on the stage between large baskets of flowers. It was clear this was a very special occasion.

Mr. Hall, the principal, walked up to the microphone at the front of the stage and asked the students several times to please be quiet so the program could begin. Everyone stopped talking only after he said the program was long and they might have to run past dismissal time if they didn't get started.

"We will begin today's assembly as always with the flag salute and the singing of 'The Star Spangled Banner.' We will be accompanied by our school band," Mr. Hall said. "Will everyone please stand?"

Tilda liked it when Charlie worked day shift and came home in time for them to sit together in the kitchen and drink afternoon coffee. She always set the table with coffee bread or *scorpa* for him to dip in his coffee, and sometimes she had cake or cookies on hand. But today she made something special. *Feele bunk.* Angie turned up her nose at it. She said it was like eating a bowl of sour milk with a spoon. In a way, Angie was right. Its "starter" was a special kind of sour milk. But Charlie liked it and said it always made him think of his mother in Finland.

"Is this a special occasion?" Charlie asked.

"Maybe," Tilda said, and smiled behind her cup.

Charlie finished his bowl of *feele bunk* and set down his spoon. "Read this, Tilda," he said, and handed her the newspaper. Angie slipped into the chair next to her mother and read over her shoulder.

The United States had been building concrete and steel air-raid shelters since the first of the year, Tilda knew, but now, she read, the National Housing Authority was considering adding shelters to its federal housing projects. Also, 12,000 civilian spotters had been stationed at 685 observation posts between New York and Boston to warn the country if they saw enemy ships or planes. Hitler had promised to "deal Britain a knockout blow in the spring," and to torpedo ships of any nation that got in his way.

Tilda got up and walked to the window. She stared out at their peaceful street. Was it really possible that Germany would bomb America?

"Angie, come look," Tilda said, interrupting her own thoughts and pulling the kitchen curtain aside. "Here comes Faith and her mother with another armload of clothes. Charlie, quick! Put the newspaper away and get your work hat off the table. Maybe Mrs. Charlot will sit down and have a cup of coffee."

Charlie folded up the newspaper, placed his hat on the floor by his chair and brushed wood dust off the tablecloth with his hand as Angie opened the door.

"Come in," Tilda said. "More of Faith's outgrown clothes?"

"That's right," Mrs. Charlot answered. "These winter things won't fit her next year the way she's growing. We thought Angie's cousins in Finland could use the warm sweaters, and, if they don't need them, they can pass them along to other girls."

"*Ja*, everyone there needs clothes," Tilda said. "My sister-in-law wrote that when we sent them sugar and flour in cloth sacks, they sewed clothes out of the sacks. Everyone's terrible poor since the Winter War."

Angie stayed at the window. Tilda knew Angie was embarrassed about her mother's accent around regular Americans.

"They can't get coffee," Tilda went on, "and their ration of butter and fats is six ounces a week. They don't have coal so they cut down their forests for fuel. Their grain warehouses are almost empty. Four months ago Finland's Minister to America, Hjalmar Procope, said, if they didn't get help soon, they would starve or freeze to death."

"Didn't this country promise to help?" Mrs. Charlot asked.

"*Ja*, they were sympathetic, but—wait. Excuse me," Tilda said. "We don't have to stand up and talk. Charlie is just home from work and we're having a cup of coffee. Please join us."

"*Ja*," Charlie said, and pulled out the chair next to him at the table.

"Thank you," Mrs. Charlot said, "but we're on our way to the store to pick up something for supper." She started for the door and stopped. "Wait a minute. I almost forgot. Angie, Faith tells me you won second place in a popularity contest. Congratulations! I think that is quite an honor." She smiled at Angie and patted her on the shoulder. Angie pulled back and ducked her head.

"Angie!" Tilda exclaimed. "Is that how you act when someone says something nice to you?"

"That's all right," Mrs. Charlot said and smiled.

"Don't forget BYF Sunday night," Faith said. "Right after church we're going to Alexander Beach. We plan to build a campfire and sing and roast marshmallows. Can you come?"

"*Ja*, she can come," Tilda said, and thanked them again for the clothes as she followed them to the door.

Charlie picked his hat up off the floor and absently brushed the mill dust off the brim. "Tilda, you follow the news. You know the

U.S. turned Finland down when it asked for a loan to buy food," Charlie said.

"I read that, too, and I don't understand why," Tilda said, going to the stove and picking up the coffee pot. "America has always been sympathetic to Finland!"

"The U.S. was afraid the food would be passed on to the Germans. When Finland let German troops pass through their country last fall, America began to mistrust them. It's hard to know what's going on."

"Well, I don't know what's going on there," Tilda said, "but I know what's going on here." She poured Charlie a *på tår* and sat down. "It's been a secret until now."

She waited, putting on a serious face. She knew Angie would be curious and join them again at the table. Charlie set down his newspaper and looked at her.

"Well," Charlie said, a little impatient, "what bad news are you hiding in your apron pocket this time?"

"This news was too important for a letter. This news came by telephone. Long distance, and you know how much that costs."

"And long distance is usually bad news. So out with it! No more games."

Tilda took a deep breath. "Telma's going to have a baby!"

Angie sprang from her chair and hugged her mother.

Charlie was quiet. Tilda watched him. He fingered his coffee cup. Finally he looked at Tilda and grinned. "That means I'll be grandpa—young fellow like me! Can't imagine it."

"When?" Angie asked. "How soon?"

"Sometime in September," Tilda answered. "Telma kept it a secret so she could keep working at the gas company, but she said she'd started to show, so she had to tell Charlie Cole, her boss. He was happy for her and Bennie, but he had to let her go. He couldn't have her working right out in the front office when she was in a family way, you know."

"I hope they have enough savings to start a family," Charlie said. "You know how young people are. They don't plan ahead."

"I know," Tilda said. "That's a worry, but Telma is one to manage." She looked at Charlie. He couldn't be too worried the way he was smiling behind his coffee cup.

11

SHIFTS
July 1941

C hanging shifts every two weeks was hard. That's why Charlie liked Sundays. It was always the same. Him and Tilda went to church in the morning, had their big dinner after church, and maybe a nap. Then on sunny afternoons, they might drive to one of the beaches or maybe Deception Pass. There they could park the car, walk out on the concrete bridge, and look over the railing at the churning water 182 feet below.

On some Sunday afternoons after their naps, they might drop in on friends for a visit and a cup of coffee. Sometimes they had to drive around a while to find someone home because they were out driving around, too, looking for afternoon coffee and a visit. If they decided to stay home in the afternoon, the doorbell would be sure to ring and Tilda would be the one putting on the coffee.

Tilda told Charlie she liked Sundays as much as he did, but sometimes she wished the Scandinavian custom of entertaining was more like the American custom where all you did was serve a piece of pie or cake with coffee. She and her Swedish friends loaded their tables with all kinds of food—rye bread, coffee breads, pies, and cakes. A person baked all day Saturday just in case someone stopped by on Sunday!

This Sunday they knew where they were going. The Haglunds had invited them and the John Carlsons, Nesses, and Eriks for coffee in the afternoon. Charlie looked forward to going to their house because Helga always fixed a regular *smörgåsbord*. The last time Haglunds invited people in, Helga put out two kinds of pickled herring, smoked salmon, and different cheeses with hardtack and rye bread. After they'd filled up on that, she brought out fresh-baked coffee bread with cardamom seeds, sponge cake, and apple pie. Cookies, too. Charlie knew Angie didn't think much of the pickled fish, but she liked the cookies and she liked spending the afternoon with Edna.

"Helga, that was a fine spread," Anna Carlson said. "We ate like we hadn't seen food for a week."

Everyone agreed.

"You shouldn't have gone to so much trouble," Elsie Ness said.

Charlie didn't agree with that!

"No trouble," Helga said. "I like doing it. Now, you men are excused to go to the front room and talk politics while the ladies and I take care of the dishes."

"*Ja, tack så mycket*," one man after another said as he pushed away from the table. The women picked up the plates and coffee cups, and followed Helga into the kitchen.

"So, Charlie," Vic said as he led the men into the front room, "six months ago we heard the President talk about sending arms to England to help them fight off the Germans. I guess you were right when you said this country would be sending its boys next."

"*Ja*," Charlie answered, "that's what Roosevelt said in his radio speech in May. He said he'd send America's boys anywhere this country was threatened."

"And he announced an 'unlimited national emergency,'" Vic added, "and this country was going to build up its defenses to the limit of its powers."

Charlie nodded. "He's talking tough."

"He has to let this country and Congress know what they're up against with the damn Nazis," Vic said, motioning the men to sit down.

Vic had brought in the seats from their 1937 Plymouth and set them on the floor for them to sit on. Helga had apologized earlier for the inconvenience, but told them they were waiting until they moved into their new house on 36th Street before buying front-room furniture. Vic was building the house himself so it would be a while before they could move, but they'd make do. Like Helga said, living in logging camps had taught them that.

"I've said all along," Charlie said, "that the President should stay out of Europe's business—"

"That's true," Ted Ness interrupted, "but what's he to do when Germany sinks an American merchant ship in international waters?"

"*Ja*," Al Eriks said, "we all read about the German sub sinking the *Robin Moor*. And now two weeks ago Germany invaded Russia. Roosevelt's tough talk didn't slow the Germans."

"So now Roosevelt promises aid to Russia!" Charlie said, his voice rising, his face reddening. "What do you think about that?"

No one spoke, but Charlie knew what they were thinking. Russia had bullied Finland as long as any of them could remember, and maybe Russia was getting back a little of its own medicine and didn't deserve America's help.

The men all knew that the U.S. had its differences with Russia and condemned Russia's invasion of Finland. And America didn't think much of Russia's form of government. Still, the President explained to the press after his speech, he considered Communism less of a threat than Fascism, so this country was siding with Russia.

"I'll tell you what's got me worried," Ted said, finally breaking the silence. "We're going to see a big shift in how people feel about Finns. America is helping Russia and Finland is Russia's enemy, so now, suddenly, Finland is America's enemy!"

"You're right," Al said. "But, you know, the Finns gave people reason to think this. Last fall Marshall Mannerheim told the Germans they could pass north through Finland to set up supply bases in Lapland. When he did this, he was allying with Germany."

"But for a good reason!" John said. "Germany promised, in exchange for this, they would supply the Finns with military supplies to defend themselves against another Russian invasion. The Germans also promised to send food to Finland where the people were on the verge of starvation. Naturally that sounded like a good deal to the Finns."

Charlie, too, felt that Finland should not have tied in with Germany, but Russia had been making demands of Finland ever since the Peace of Moscow agreement a year ago—demands not in the peace treaty. The Winter War had cost Finland its best land and 25,000 men, but, in spite of these terrible losses, Mannerheim had succeeded in preserving Finland's independence. If he decided now that Finland's security depended on bargaining with Germany, then that's what Finland should do.

"What choice does Finland have anyway?" Charlie asked the men who sat silent, heads down, studying their shoes. "Finland's caught between two giant powers and, between the two, it trusts Russia least."

Straightening up and giving his knee a slap, Vic exclaimed, "All I can say is, if Finland keeps siding with Germany and this war keeps spreading, I can be damn glad Helga and I got our citizenship papers. Finlanders will be judged by the world as America's enemies. Think about that!"

Charlie didn't want to think about that. America was their home with or without citizenship papers. What difference would a piece of paper from the courthouse make!"

It had been two weeks since they'd been to Haglund's for Sunday afternoon coffee—two weeks of no sleep! "I tell you, Tilda, this graveyard shift is doing me in," Charlie exclaimed as he walked into the kitchen. He ran his fingers through his hair and scrubbed his scalp with the heels of his hands. "It's eleven o'clock in the morning. I've been in bed for three hours, and I haven't slept a wink."

"Oh, you slept some," Tilda said, humming as she wiped the toast crumbs off the breakfast-nook table. Even if there wasn't any crumbs, she'd be wiping the table, just to admire it. Tilda had found the red plastic-cushioned chrome set at Sears Roebuck and told Charlie she had to have it for their new house.

"You didn't give yourself enough time. Go back to bed now," she said and resumed her humming.

"It's no use," he said. He sat down in the breakfast nook and pulled the venetian blind slats apart to look out. "Tilda, that's why I can't sleep! Kids hollering! Cars speeding by! Why ain't they in school where they belong so a man can sleep when he's worked all night?"

"Charlie, it's summer vacation. You know that!"

Charlie tipped back in the chrome-framed chair. It could slide out from under him, he knew. Maybe the fall would knock him out and he could finally sleep. He knew he was cranky, but the graveyard shift did that to him. Two weeks out of every six weeks he worked from eleven at night until seven in the morning and went through this. He guessed he should be happy. The mill was running twenty-four hours a day now, six days a week, and paying full salary—so Tilda could buy chrome table sets!

At the first of the year, when Congress voted almost $11 billion for defense, the mill stepped up production and started running three shifts a day, just to keep up with the orders. Charlie liked the day shift when he could be home at three in the afternoon and sit down with Tilda for a cup of coffee and a piece of coffee bread. Swing shift wasn't too bad. You worked from three in the afternoon until eleven at night, and you could sleep in the next morning. But this graveyard shift was the tough one.

At eleven at night, when a man should be able to go to bed, he has to put on his working clothes and go to work. When he gets home at seven in the morning and everyone is getting up to go about their business, he's supposed to go to bed and sleep. Instead, he lies there listening to kids screaming and dogs barking and Tilda in the kitchen shushing Angie.

If a man worked graveyard shift all the time, he might learn to sleep during the day, but the board decided that, in order to be fair, everyone should work all shifts, two weeks at each. Just when Charlie got used to one shift, it was time to work a different one. Well, he'd be starting his two weeks of day shift Monday. Thinking about that cheered him up.

"Tilda, are we all out of coffee?"

Charlie sat back in his chair and sipped his coffee through a sugar lump. He'd had breakfast and coffee at seven when he came home from graveyard shift, but he hadn't had his *på tår*. Tilda had gone downstairs to wash clothes. He was alone with his thoughts.

In spite of the problem of changing shifts, Charlie had to admit he really was proud of the mill. From nothing, under good management, the mill was producing plywood for homes and airplane hangers and army barracks and anything else the country needed. Charlie liked taking friends from out of town through the mill to show them a first-class operation.

He'd start the tour at the farthest point of the veneer plant where the salt water from Fidalgo Bay floated gigantic Douglas-fir logs into the barnlike holding shed. "Watch this," he'd say to his guests and point to the tall crane lifting a log four feet in diameter out of the water and positioning it in the teeth of the barker. "Watch!" The giant machine would chew the bark off the revolving log and spit the bark into the water. Fresh, green moss would still be hanging on to some pieces of bark.

"Makes you think of someone eating corn on the cob, doesn't it?" Charlie would say. Instead of being amused, people would shake their heads in wonder at the size of the logs and the voracious appetite of the machine.

Without pause, the crane would next swing the log to the peeler where it again rotated, this time against long, steel blades that shaved off one-eighth or one-sixteenth inch plies and sent them down wide conveyer belts to the clipper.

"There's where I sit," Charlie would tell his friends, pointing to a seat mounted high above the conveyer belt. "That's the clipper. All I need for my job is a quick thumb! As the sheets move by on the belt, I watch for knots or tears in the wood and press a button that drops a steel blade and cuts out the bad spot. It's a hell of a lot easier than setting choker in the woods, I'll tell you, but it's not as easy as it looks either. I have to keep my eyes fixed on the sheet so I don't miss a spot. But smell the air! I sit up there and think I'm back in the woods."

Next Charlie would point to the green chain where the plies are fed into the dryer before they're glued together. Then there are trimmers and patchers and edge gluers and sanders—but that would be another tour.

Charlie never tired of showing people through the mill. Three-hundred men worked in the mill now, all shareholders. Co-owners. And now, with the country's demand for more and more plywood, the mill could hardly keep up with the orders.

Charlie was glad to be back at work Monday and starting two weeks of day shift. Now he listened for the noon whistle. He looked forward to eating his lunch outside with his friends. The warm sun and the smell of fresh salt air would make the sandwich Tilda packed for him taste even better.

Small groups of men sat on benches on the sunny side of the mill where a breeze from the bay and an occasional salt spray cooled the air. Black, metal lunchboxes lay open on the men's laps or at their feet. Charlie shaded his eyes against the sun as he looked around for a place to sit and eat.

"Yo, Charlie," Axel Anderson called out. "There's a place over here."

Charlie strode across the plank deck that abutted the mill to join the men sitting on a bench overlooking the water. From there, he would probably see Pete Rasmussen working on the log pond and, with a little luck, he might see Pete's friend, a one-legged seagull named Bill.

Charlie sat down, snapped open his lunch bucket, and nodded at the other men. All Swede Finns. Good company. But why so serious today? "No jokes about the Norwegians to liven up our lunch?" Charlie asked as he unwrapped the wax paper from his sandwich.

Axel spoke first. "You haven't heard the news?"

Charlie looked from one to the other. No one was smiling.

"Finland's back at war."

Charlie set down his sandwich. His stomach tightened.

John spoke next. "The Finns along with the Germans invaded Russia this morning."

"It was on the radio," Al Eriks said. "Mannerheim told his troops that, with the help of Germany, they'd take back the territory they lost in the Winter War and free the people of Karelia."

When Charlie drove home after day shift, he always wrestled with the traffic on Commercial Avenue. People driving on this two-lane arterial into town were going either too slow or too fast. He was quick to use the horn if drivers passed when they had no business passing. That was the only problem with driving home at three in the afternoon when traffic was heavy.

But today Charlie's mind wasn't on the traffic. A little more than a year ago, after months of bombings and hand-to-hand fighting in the coldest winter on record, Finland had made peace with the

Russians. It was hard to believe that now Finland was stepping right back into it.

Charlie was not a man of deep thought, but he couldn't help noticing how much of life was like shifts at the mill. You just got used to one thing, and then everything changed.

When he grew up in Finland, they had nothing. When he got married and they moved to the logging camps, they had to count every penny. Now in Anacortes, they could afford to build their own house and buy a chrome breakfast set and whatever else they fancied. Same with their friends. They were all making good wages and living high. The whole country was moving out of the Depression into good times. A shift for the better and easy to get used to.

But Finland's going to war on the side of Germany was something else. The whole world had been on Finland's side when the Russian bear jumped their little country. England and France promised them help. All of Scandinavia, Belgium, Switzerland, Italy, Spain, Central and South America, everyone had spoken out for Finland. Former President Hoover and some American celebrities organized a Finnish Relief Fund and a Senate committee recommended that the Finns be offered $20 million in credit. Now, suddenly, the U.S. and Finland, long-time friends, were on opposite sides.

Charlie wound up the car window to keep out the exhaust fumes from the traffic, but he still smelled something bad. He smelled danger, even a personal danger in this political shift.

12

CURRENT EVENTS
September 1941

"*Gud i himlen!*" Tilda exclaimed. "Here she comes again, running like a bear was after her."

"Poor Edna," Angie said, joining her mother at the break-fast-nook window. "I'll let her in. She likes to hide here when her mom starts up their washing machine."

Angie knew the story. Without electricity in Camp Five, people had to use noisy, gasoline-run washing machines or wash clothes by hand on a scrub board. When they used the gas machine, they couldn't keep the noise inside because they had to run a big exhaust hose out the door. That was okay in camp, Edna had told her, because some other families had the same kind of machine, but, in a real town like Anacortes, it was embarrassing. Kids from around the neighborhood came and watched, like there was a monster in Edna's house sticking its tail out the door.

Edna burst into the kitchen before Angie could open the door all the way. She stood in the middle of the room with her hands over her ears. "Why does my mother have to wash clothes every day of the week!" she exclaimed.

"Now, Edna," Mom said, patting her on the shoulder. "Your mom does wash clothes more often than most people, but I don't think it's every day."

"It seems like it!" Edna retorted. "Even today, Labor Day, a holiday. When I try to talk to her, all she says is she likes washing clothes and don't I like everything clean?"

"Well, today is Monday and Monday is always wash day," Mom said with half a smile.

"That doesn't explain the other days of the week," Edna wailed, dropping into a chair in the breakfast nook and peering out the window. "Look at that! Kids are starting to come."

"Well," Mama said, "when you move into your new house on 36th Street, your *pappa* will probably buy a washing machine that runs on electricity."

Angie retrieved her cat from where he was cowering under the table. "Your washing machine scares Chee Chee, too," she said. "You can hold him if you want, and you'll both feel better."

Angie placed the cat on Edna's lap. Chee Chee buried his head under his front paws until Edna began petting him. Then he stretched his back against her hand and started up his motor. "Listen to him purr," Edna said. "Chee Chee likes me, even if it is my mother causing all that racket."

"So, you've both had birthdays and are thirteen now," Mama said, probably trying to get Edna's mind off the monster washing machine.

"I'm three days older," Angie stated and grinned at her friend.

"In old country we were grown up when we were thirteen," Mama said, ignoring Angie's interruption. "So maybe I should pour you ladies some coffee while you're sitting at the table?"

Edna shook her head, still peering out the window at her house. Angie didn't like coffee and being thirteen didn't feel grown up. Tomorrow school was starting and she was worried. She had her class schedule and knew that she and Edna and Phyllis and Joyce and Faith were all in 8-1, so that was no problem. What she didn't know was how the other kids would act toward her. Being chosen last spring by a professional women's club as the second-most-popular girl in the seventh grade should give her confidence, but, for some reason she couldn't explain even to herself, it made her uneasy.

The next morning, Angie was out of bed before her mom knocked on her door. She put on her same navy-blue skirt from last year, but then stood back from her closet and admired her new school blouses.

Since she was thirteen now and almost grown up, she'd insisted on doing her own shopping for school clothes. Her mother had given her $20 with instructions to go to Penney's and shop wisely. Angie had been immediately attracted to a rack of bright-colored, short-sleeve, cotton blouses that sold for $5 each. When she brought home four identical blouses in four colors—red, yellow, blue, and green—her mom had shaken her head, but Angie wasn't sorry.

Eenie, meenie, miney, moe. She'd pick the yellow one to go! She slipped on her yellow blouse, bobby socks, and saddle shoes and hurried to the breakfast table.

"You're quick this morning, Angie," her mother said, turning from the stove. "Your mush is still cooking. But stand up and let me see how you look on your first day in eighth grade."

Angie did as her mother asked, looking down at herself to be sure everything was right.

"Nice," her mom said, "but the shoes. Your shoes need polishing. You can't go to school with dirty shoes."

"Gee, Mom, don't you know anything! No one wears clean saddle shoes. They're supposed to look like this!"

"Well, I don't understand, but, if that's the way they're supposed to look, I guess it's okay. Sit down now and I dish up your mush."

Angie poked down her mush fast, which wasn't easy, and ran to meet Edna on the street between their houses. They stopped on their walk to school to pick up Annette and then crossed catty-corner for Beverly. Beverly was still eating her breakfast. Angie and Edna looked at each other when they saw she was eating a bowl of graham crackers soaked in milk. It seemed like a very strange breakfast, but Angie thought it probably tasted better than the mush she had to eat every morning.

Annette waited for Beverly, but Edna and Angie hurried on to school. They found their room and settled into seats close to Faith, Joyce, and Phyllis. Even though she saw her friends a lot during the summer, it felt good to sit near them the first day of school. Everyone in the room was chatting—happy to see each other. Angie had forgotten her earlier uneasiness in the excitement, but then she noticed a group of girls sitting next to the blackboard looking at her and whispering. Angie was relieved when the teacher walked into the room, wrote his name on the board, and asked for everyone's attention.

"Social Sciences, a very important subject," Mr. Ellis, the teacher began. "Can anyone tell us why it's important?" No hands went up, so he continued. "It's important because so much is happening in our country right now, events that may change the course of your lives—of all our lives—and perhaps even the course of history."

He looked away from the class then and walked to the window. From where Angie sat, she could see the row of fir trees that bordered the back of the school and the blue sky beyond, but she didn't see anything that could have caught their teacher's attention. The class waited quietly. Someone coughed and someone else giggled. Then Mr. Ellis turned and walked to the blackboard and began writing. Everyone sat quietly until he set the chalk down in the blackboard tray and turned to the class.

"President Roosevelt in his speech to the nation in January of this year named what he considered four essential human freedoms," Mr. Ellis said. He pointed to the board as he continued. "These are freedom of speech, freedom to worship, freedom from want, and freedom from fear. We'll be talking about these freedoms and what they mean because, according to our President, we are living in a very critical time, a time when these freedoms could be challenged."

Mr. Ellis picked up a book from his desk and opened it at a marker. "I want to read a statement from the President's speech to Congress that day." He cleared his throat and looked around the classroom to be sure everyone was listening. He read, "'At no previous time has American security been as seriously threatened from without as it is today.' Boys and girls, this speech was delivered nine months ago and the possibility that this country will be involved in a war to protect these freedoms is more real today than when the speech was delivered."

Angie thought about the letters from Finland, about her cousins fighting to keep their freedom, about their suffering from hunger and cold and seeing friends die right in front of them. About children being sent to Sweden for their safety and then not finding their families after the war.

Mr. Ellis pointed at the blackboard again. "Class, I want you to copy the four freedoms and keep them in your notebook. I'm asking you to remember them because much of what we study in this class will revolve around our country's struggle to secure these freedoms."

Notebooks flipped open. Students fumbled in pockets and zipper bags for writing tools. Then the room became quiet except for the soft sound of pencils moving across wide-lined notebook paper.

When everyone had finished writing, Mr. Ellis said, "We will use our social science texts during the first four days of the week and set Fridays aside for current events. Read your newspapers, boys and girls, and talk with your parents about what's going on in the world."

This would be easy, Angie figured, because her parents and their friends talked current events whenever they got together.

"Cut articles out of the newspaper," Mr. Ellis went on, "and bring them to class with you on Fridays to share with other students."

Angie remembered Current Events when she was in the sixth grade in Potlatch. Once Edwin reported that his cat had five kittens and two died. Don Reader said he saw a picture in the Seattle paper of boys at the University of Washington swallowing goldfish whole. But Mark Hussman, the oldest of the seven kids in school, reported that Germany invaded Czechoslovakia. Probably this was the kind of current event Mr. Ellis was looking for.

Mr. Ellis passed out the social science texts and asked students to sign their names on the white label inside the front cover, and to take good care of their books as they would have to pay for any damage. They had the rest of the period to begin reading Chapter 1.

When the bell rang, books slammed shut. Students skidded their chairs away from their desks and burst out of the room. They hurried to claim seats close to their friends in the next classroom. As Angie walked out the door, two of the girls who had been whispering caught up with her.

"You're not wearing your prize-winning sweater," one said. "Have you worn it out already?" the other said. Then they giggled and ran down the hall.

Morning went fast. Social Science class was followed by English and Home Economics. The teacher told the girls their first sewing project would be to make a cotton slip, an essential garment for every young lady. Then the bell rang for lunch. Angie deposited her books in her locker, grabbed her lunch bag and ran to the cafeteria. She spotted Joyce and Faith at a table near the door and joined them. The two girls who'd asked about her sweater were sitting two tables away.

"I heard what those girls said to you," Faith whispered to Angie. "They're just jealous."

"I'm not sure," Angie said. "Maybe there was a mistake. Maybe the award was meant for someone else."

"I don't think that was the mistake," Joyce said, unwrapping her sandwich.

Angie studied her friend. "What do you mean?"

Joyce took a bite of her sandwich before she answered. "Well, my mom knows Laura's mom, and Laura's mom is worried. She said Laura sometimes makes things up."

"Over here!" Faith called and signaled to Edna and Phyllis to join them. The conversation turned to who was in their classes—a cute new boy in Faith's science class—followed by giggles, an appraisal of the new health teacher, the sock hop in the Big Gym that was planned for Friday night after the football game. Angie listened. She studied her friends around the table. Real friends. Being the second-most-popular girl in the seventh grade was not nearly as important as these friendships.

13

BABY LINDA
October 1941

"When we gonna get there?" Angie asked, leaning over the front seat of the car.

"*Tyst, nu,*" Tilda said. "Don't keep asking. We get there when we get there." Tilda tried to be patient because she knew how excited Angie was, how excited they both were. Even Charlie had hurried them into the car this morning before they finished the breakfast dishes.

"What I don't understand," Angie persisted, "is why we had to wait so long before we could see the baby! She was born September 24—"

"I told you why," Tilda said. "We wanted to be there when Telma came home from the hospital, so we could help her with the baby. We can't make two long trips to Shelton in a week."

"Now, both of you, be quiet," Charlie ordered, turning on the car radio. "I think we get some news."

"Let's not listen to news today," Tilda said. "The news is always bad."

At the first of the month a German submarine had attacked an American destroyer off the coast of Iceland. The President told the world it would protect shipping between America and Iceland, and ordered navy planes and ships to fire at any German vessel that sailed into these shipping lanes. Tilda didn't want to think about what might happen next. She only wanted to think about the baby girl she would soon be holding in her arms.

"Charlie, you know why they named the baby 'Linda'?"

"Sure I know," Charlie said and snapped off the radio. "You're right! We have better things to talk about than the news."

"Why did they name her 'Linda'?" Angie asked.

"They named her 'Linda' after 'Lind'," Charlie answered, and smiled at Angie in the rear-view mirror.

"So, when we gonna get there?" Angie asked.

Shelton sat in a hollow between steep hills with Hammersly Inlet, a long slender arm of Puget Sound, bordering one edge. Simpson Lumber Mill spread itself across most of the waterfront. Stacks of lumber filled the acreage around the mill. Smoke belched from the mill's chimneys. Rayonier Pulp and Paper and McCleary's Fir Mill filled the rest of the waterfront space.

Each day the log train dumped its load into a large pond. There, men balanced themselves on floating logs and used their long pike poles to guide the logs onto a moving chain that carried the logs up into the mill. A tall smokestack and a round hog-burner stood side-by-side, like a wedded couple in the middle of the waterfront development.

Tilda didn't remember so much activity on the waterfront, but knew the war in Europe was making demands on all the mills for wood products.

"Angie," Tilda said, pointing out the front window of the car, "the Olympic Mountains are standing out clear against the sky today. Do you see George Washington's profile?"

"Of course I do, Mom. That's easy. What I want to see is the front door of the hospital."

Tilda laughed, but, while Charlie concentrated on driving down the steep, curving highway into town, she wrestled with a flood of memories.

Shelton had been their closest town when they lived in the Phoenix Logging Company camps, but it took half a day to get there. Before there were roads out of camp, they rode the speeder to Hoodsport where they kept their car in a rented garage. From there they drove sixteen miles on Highway 101 to Shelton.

In 1936, when they moved to Potlatch, the company town on Hood Canal, things improved. They could get in their car and drive to Shelton in half an hour. Charlie would go off to the hardware store or an auto dealer and she'd take Angie to L & M Department Store and look at dishes or clothes. At noon, they'd meet at the lunch counter in Woolworth's Dime Store. Angie would eat fast, swivel a couple times on the high stool, and slide off to circle through the store. She'd eye games in the toy section and sparkly hairclips and jewelry. They let her buy a ring once, but it turned her finger green. She never asked for jewelry after that.

Charlie slowed at the sign "Shelton General Hospital" on the far edge of the business district.

Tilda remembered well the day Angie was born in this hospital, a happy event in their lives. But there were other memories. Loggers were brought here when they were injured. They brought Charlie's young cousin Johannes here after his logging accident. He died, even though the choker that hit him on the chest had left only a tiny mark.

The hospital could not help Leonard after his accident. Their five-year-old son was taken directly to the funeral home. He was buried in the town cemetery on the top of one of the hills. Tilda felt around in her purse for a handkerchief. This week while they were in Shelton, they would go to their family plot and place flowers on Leonard's and Johannes's graves.

Charlie found a parking place close to the entrance to the hospital. "Bennie beat us here," he said. "I see his truck."

"He didn't have as far to go," Tilda said, shaking off memories of those tragic accidents.

Angie jumped out of the car and ran up the hospital steps. Tilda and Charlie followed close behind. They found Bennie walking back and forth in the waiting room.

"Why the pacing?" Charlie asked. "The baby is already here."

Bennie grinned in return. "Waiting to get my hands on that baby is tough, too. I've only seen her through the glass in the nursery."

"Who's she look like?" Charlie asked.

"Not like you or me, luckily!" Bennie said, still grinning. "Except for blue eyes. She has a deep dimple in one cheek and she's beautiful!"

Tilda had to laugh at that. First-time-father! She figured Charlie, a first-time-grandfather, would agree with him.

"Here we come," Thelma called as a nurse wheeled her and the baby into the waiting room. "I could walk to the car but they won't let me because it's only been ten days! If they'd kept us much longer, Linda could have walked out by herself."

Bennie picked up the snuggly wrapped baby from Thelma's lap. "Heck, I've caught fish bigger than this!" he said, opening the blanket to get a better look. "What do you think, Thelma. Shall we let Linda's Grandma hold her on the way home?"

Tilda took the baby, then, rewrapped her in the blanket, and led the way toward the car. "I wonder if bringing a baby home from the hospital counts as a current event," Angie said, skipping along behind her mother.

Thelma and Bennie's house perched on the side of a fir-covered hill overlooking Shelton. A huge, redwood tree, not often seen in the Northwest, guarded their front door. Bennie helped Thelma up the steps to the door and down the hall to the bedroom. When Thelma protested, Bennie reminded her that the doctor said new mothers need to stay in bed for at least a week after they get home.

Tilda carried the baby to the waiting, lace-trimmed bassinet and left Angie to watch her while she went to the kitchen to see what she could fix for supper. Charlie and Bennie sat down at the dining room table and asked Tilda when the coffee would be ready. Tilda found the coffee pot and cups and in a few minutes was pouring their coffee.

"I guess you're out of sugar lumps," Charlie said in mock seriousness to his son-in-law.

Bennie jumped to his feet and brought out their special, cut-glass sugar bowl. "Want you to know we keep it filled just for your visits."

Charlie placed a sugar lump between his teeth and sucked the hot coffee through it. After several more sips he sighed deeply, set his cup down on the saucer and turned to Bennie. "You're in the Civilian Military Training Corps, is that right?"

"That's right," Bennie said. "CMTC. Put in my annual two weeks of training at Fort Lewis this summer."

Tilda knew what Charlie was leading up to.

"A year ago," Charlie went on, "the Selective Service Act had every man from twenty-one to thirty-five register for the draft. If this country starts drafting men, the first thing they'll need is trained officers—"

"I know what you're thinking," Bennie interrupted. "I've thought about that, too. But the U.S. Army isn't going to draft a married man. Certainly not a married man with a family." He glanced toward the bedroom and smiled widely. "And that's what I am now, you know. A married man with a family!"

14

THANKSGIVING
November 1941

C harlie's lunch bucket clattered when he set it on the kitchen counter.

"Home from work already?" Tilda asked, looking at the clock and wiping her hands on her apron. "I been so busy cooking and baking for tomorrow's Thanksgiving dinner that I lost track of time. Coffee be ready in a minute."

"I smell cookies," Charlie said. He looked at his wife. Tilda had flour on her nose and her cheeks were shiny-pink from rushing around the warm kitchen. He sometimes forgot how pretty she was.

"You do smell cookies," Tilda said. "They're for tomorrow, but you can have one with your coffee."

Charlie liked to eat. Tilda told him that working outside when he logged was why he had such a good appetite. Charlie said it couldn't be that because his appetite was just as good now when he was working inside. Maybe it was because when he was a boy in Finland, he never had enough to eat. He used to tell Telma and now Angie that for supper they often had nothing but "potatoes-and-point." They were so poor his mother would put a tiny piece of meat on a plate in the middle of the table and the family would eat potatoes and point at the meat. The girls knew he'd made that up, but they understood he wanted them to appreciate their food.

Charlie was looking forward to Thanksgiving dinner—the American *smörgåsbord*! Food like turkey and dressing, mashed potatoes and gravy, sweet potatoes, red jello with whipping cream, pumpkin pie, cookies. Then the next day, turkey sandwiches and more pie and cookies. *Lutfisk* dinner on Christmas Eve was still the best, but for a man who likes to eat, Thanksgiving was a fine holiday.

But, he reminded himself, he had more than food to be thankful for. Their life had been good, while the rest of the world had gone crazy. Across one ocean, Germany was on the march, taking over one country after another. Across the other ocean, Japan was moving into China and Indo-China and telling America to stay out of their business. Charlie was thankful that oceans separated him and his family from the fighting.

Charlie sat down by the breakfast-nook window to wait for his coffee. Outside children hopped and skipped down the sidewalk, happy to be out of school for a four-day holiday. A car honked at a boy crossing the street on his bicycle. Another boy, who didn't seem to be in a hurry, kicked his way through the crisp, brown leaves that layered the ground under the maple tree on the corner. Pulsing with the heat and energy of being young, the children carried or dragged their coats behind them in their play, unaware of the chilly November wind.

But a wind in November in Anacortes was nothing like a November wind in Finland. When Charlie ice skated with his brother Vilhelm on the Gulf of Bothnia, the wind blowing across the ice frosted their noses and cheeks so bad they had to rub snow on their faces to thaw them out.

But now, as Charlie thought about Finland, he thought about another wind—not a chilly wind nor a face-freezing wind, but a wind far worse. It was a wind sweeping over Finland, bringing renewed suffering and death. It was the wind of this new war, a war that called back to the battlefield Tilda's nephews, Birger and Edvin, and his nephew Alarik.

Since June, Finland's leaders were committed to taking part in Germany's advance against Russia. Mannerheim hated Nazis, especially the way they treated the Jews, but he saw siding with Germany against Russia as necessary because Russia, in spite of the Peace of Moscow agreement, continued to make demands of Finland.

On July 10, Mannerheim had announced a "holy war" where he would free the people of Karelia. Some thought that this meant he intended to take back more than the area lost in the Winter War, that he planned to create a "Greater Finland" by taking all of Karelia, not just the part that had belonged to Finland. On October 10, Anthony

Eden, the British foreign secretary, warned the Finns that, if they continued to invade Russian territory, England would consider them an open enemy and declare war on them.

America did not as yet threaten to declare war on Finland. Maybe that was because so many Finns lived in America where they were admired or because Finland, in spite of being so poor after World War I, had been the only country to pay its war debt to America. Charlie was very proud of that. But now Mannerheim had made it clear to the world that Finland wanted to take back only the part of Karelia that Russia took from them in the Winter War.

Tilda poured Charlie's coffee and set it in front of him. Then she brought out a plate with two cookies on it. "*Var så god*," she said and kissed him on the forehead.

Charlie picked up his cup and poured a little of the steaming coffee into his saucer. He lifted the saucer, balanced it on the tips of his fingers, blew gently on the coffee to cool it, and then sipped the coffee. "Aah," he sighed.

"I haven't seen you do that in a long time," Tilda said.

"I like to remember old-country custom, even on American holiday."

Tilda smiled at that, poured herself a cup and sat down. "I'm sorry Telma and her family won't be here tomorrow, but they need to stay home when the baby has a bad cold."

"*Moster* and Uncle and Art are coming, aren't they?" Angie asked, running into the kitchen and helping herself to one of her dad's cookies.

"*Ja*, they should be here anytime," Tilda answered. "Art has an appetite like your dad, so I have to do a lot of cooking."

Angie nodded and then announced, "My junior high sold more Defense Savings Stamps and Bonds than either of the grade schools or the high school. Phyllis's dad, Mr. Luvera, is in charge of the sales, and he came to our school and told us."

"That was good," Tilda said.

"He also told us that when we buy stamps or bonds, we are partners with Uncle Sam and we are buying a share in America and defending Democracy."

"Well, if we're doing all that, we'll send a little more money with you next week," Charlie said. "If we can keep the war from crossing the ocean, it's worth the price."

"He told us something else," Angie went on. "Soon there won't be any more tinfoil wrappers for stuff like gum or candy bars. Not even Hershey bars. No lead foil either. And no one will be able to buy typewriter ribbon or film. Mr. Luvera said tinfoil and lead foil are needed for defense products, and us kids need to collect foil that is still in circulation and turn it in."

Charlie poured a little more coffee into his saucer and reached for a sugar lump. The bowl of sugar lumps was always on the kitchen table. "You know, Tilda," he said, "if that's all we have to do to defend America, we really have something to be thankful for on this Thanksgiving."

Charlie was the first to see the Carlsons drive up. Art stepped out of the backseat, golf club in hand.

"No place around here to golf," Charlie called from the back porch.

"I'm just going to practice my swing," Art said. "I haven't had time to golf since school started."

"Well, watch out for Angie. Remember in Potlatch when your club caught her just above the eye?"

"I won't forget that," Art said as Angie ran up and gave him a hug. "Hi, lil' Cuz. Just stand back when I swing. Okay?"

Charlie knew Angie had missed Art since he left for university. The two of them would sit by the radio on Saturday nights and listen to the Hit Parade. Art kept a record of the top ten songs each week in the order of their popularity. On the Saturdays he went out, he had Angie listen and fill in the chart.

Charlie, too, had gotten used to Art living with them the summer he worked at the mill. They especially had a good time when they came home from swing shift. Chee Chee the cat would be the only one up, so, while they ate the coffee bread Tilda had set out for them, they entertained themselves by teasing the cat. One night they tried to poke Chee Chee down the laundry chute. Whenever they got him close to the black hole, he'd spread all four legs straight out. No way would he fit into the opening.

Some nights, Art would take the lid off a can of cat food and set it on the floor, the food still packed in the can. Chee Chee would roll the can around the kitchen floor, trying to get at the food. One night their laughing and the noise of the can spinning across the linoleum and banging against the walls woke Tilda, and she peeked into the kitchen to see what was going on. That ended that game!

"So what do you think of all this defense work?" Charlie asked his brother-in-law, Ida's-Charlie, and Art after supper. They'd settled into comfortable chairs in the front room. The women were in the kitchen doing supper dishes and preparing more food for Thanksgiving Day. "Shipyards in Tacoma are turning out a freighter a month, and they're using them to haul millions of tons of war material to England. Think this country should do that?"

"We help England and we help ourselves," Ida's-Charlie answered.

"We have defense plants springing up all over the place and women leaving their homes and kids to work in factories. That's not healthy for families and not what a woman should be doing."

"But," Art broke in, "Rosie the Riveter is important to our defense force. And, anyway, I think women look swell in pants and flowered bandanas, riveting steel plates onto the sides of huge ships."

"Artur, this is serious," Charlie said.

"Sorry, Uncle. I know it's serious. I knew this whole war situation was serious when I had to register for the draft, but, you know, Roosevelt promised we wouldn't get into this war."

Charlie noticed that Art's dad, sitting in the armchair across the room, looked like he wanted to say something, but changed his mind. They were probably both thinking the same, that young people are so damn sure that everything will turn out all right! Charlie wished he could be as sure.

15

"DAY OF INFAMY"
December 1941

Angie woke up late. She tumbled out of bed and rushed to her closet. Why hadn't Mom called her! Didn't Mom remember she had to be at church early for choir practice? They were working on Christmas music, so it was important! "Mom!" she called. "Where's my white blouse? We're supposed to wear white blouses in choir today."

"I ironed it and hung it in your closet," her mother said as she walked into the room. "You get excited and in a hurry, and you don't see what's in front of your eyes."

Angie turned back to her closet and there it was. Right in front of her eyes.

Mom was right. She did get excited, but so much was going on. Yesterday her and Faith walked to town to see the iron lung on display at the office of Puget Sound Power and Light. The office was jam-packed with people, but she and Faith squeezed to the front of the crowd and watched two nurses demonstrate on volunteers how the tank could help a victim of infantile paralysis breathe.

The nurses helped a volunteer lie down in the huge, metal tank with just her head poking out and a rubber collar around her neck to keep the air in. Then they turned on a pump that changed the air pressure in the tank to raise and lower the woman's chest. This, the nurse explained, makes it possible for a victim of infantile paralysis to breathe, even though the chest is paralyzed.

Then the nurse told everyone that, crippling as polio was, life can go on. She reminded them that President Roosevelt contracted polio when he was thirty-nine years old and never walked again without help. Yet eleven years later, he was elected President of the United States and was now serving a third term.

"You had a big day yesterday," her mother said, interrupting Angie's thoughts, "and you was up late last night so I let you sleep a little bit longer."

"I had to study my part for the Christmas pageant. That's in just two weeks. Paul told us kids—"

"Paul? You mean Reverend Logan? You don't call a minister by his first name."

"All the kids do. He's like one of us."

"I know he's young, but you must show respect!"

Angie did respect him, but he told the kids they didn't have to say "Reverend and Mrs. Logan." They could say "Paul and Margaret." That was the difference between Baptists and Lutherans. The Baptists weren't so particular about things.

"Well, breakfast is ready when you are," her mom said.

For Angie, Sundays were busy. Choir practice at nine, Sunday school at ten, and church at eleven. Then church again at seven in the evening, and after church, BYF Fireside. Now, with Christmas coming and a pageant to put on, she'd be busier than ever. She and about ten other kids.

She and Faith had speaking parts. Bonnie Cross was an angel. Bonnie told Angie that during practices her arms got tired from holding up her wings, but the night of the performance she would keep her arms in the air no matter how tired they got. Some of boys in the pageant didn't go to the Baptist church but took parts because their girlfriends were there. Plus they would be going caroling after the program and then to Faith's house for ice cream and cookies.

"Angie," her mother called from the kitchen, "I thought you was in a hurry. Your mush is getting cold."

Angie scurried to the table. She didn't like mush, but she liked everything else about this day. It was the beginning of the Christmas season. Mom and her would be going Christmas shopping. Her dad would buy a tree and they'd hang lights and ornaments and lots of shiny tinsel. Almost everyone in Anacortes would be stringing colored lights on their houses, and there would be Christmas parties at school. Mom would be secretive and hide stuff in the closet. Angie suddenly felt like singing, "Joy to the World," except her mouth was full of mush. She'd have to wait 'til she got to church to sing out her Christmas joy.

But then it happened. It happened that Sunday, December 7, while they were in church. It happened while their youth choir was singing, "Peace on earth, good will to men." It happened while lighted candles on the windowsills in the sanctuary glowed softly, and while Reverend Logan was at the pulpit telling the congregation to love one another. But it wasn't until after they had sung the last hymn and Paul had given the benediction and people started home, that they heard that the Japanese had bombed Pearl Harbor.

Monday morning, school went on as usual, though everyone had trouble concentrating. It was Faith's week to be stair monitor. She told Angie that a lump filled her throat as she stood at the top of the stairs and watched the usually rambunctious kids move quietly to their first-period classes. Later in the day, Angie and her friends told each other in hushed voices where they were and what they were doing when they first heard that Pearl Harbor had been bombed.

Faith said her family didn't take a newspaper, so she always went to the neighbors after church to read the Sunday funnies. On this Sunday when she heard about the attack, she forgot about the funnies and ran home. Bonnie said she was sitting on the sidewalk with the Owens' kids from next door when she heard Pearl Harbor had been bombed. They all began watching the sky for Japanese planes. Edna said she was walking home after church when Mrs. Causland, her mother's friend who lived on 34th and Commercial, came out on her front porch and told her that the United States was at war. As Edna walked on up the street, she'd wondered what this would mean to her and her family.

Yesterday, Japan had bombed Pearl Harbor and declared war on the United States, and today the United States declared war on Japan. Overnight, anti-aircraft guns had been placed on Whidbey Island beaches, 20 miles from Anacortes, to protect Whidbey Island Naval Air Station. It was expected that Japanese warships would sail across the ocean and down the Straits of Juan de Fuca to attack the naval base. Angie sat with her classmates that morning listening to the President's speech to Congress on the school radio. He spoke very slowly and stumbled a little on the words.

Yesterday, December 7, 1941—a date which will live in infamy—the United States of America was suddenly and deliberately attacked by naval and air forces of the Empire of Japan....

The attack on the Hawaiian Islands has caused severe damage to American naval and military forces. I regret to tell you that very many American lives have been lost. In addition American ships have been reported torpedoed on the high seas between San Francisco and Honolulu....

Hostilities exist. There is no blinking at the fact that our people, our territory and our interests are in grave danger.... I ask that the Congress declare that since the unprovoked and dastardly attack by Japan on Sunday, December 7, a state of war has existed between the United States and the Japanese Empire.

Tuesday morning, Faith was waiting for Angie on the steps of the school before first period class. She was shivering in her light coat and the frosty wind tore at her hair. Angie could tell she'd been crying.

"My brother joined the Marines," she choked out. "He came into the kitchen yesterday and told Mother he had to enlist. Mother said, 'I know.' Then I ran to my room."

Angie thought of Bennie and Art. She thought of the older boys in high school. But mostly, right now, she thought of Faith's brother Bill. He was so handsome with naturally curly hair like Faith's. From what Angie knew, he was a great older brother to Faith and Bobby. His older sister Margery teased him because her friends were always asking about him. Angie had wished a time or two that she was older so he would notice her. Now he was going off to war.

That night at eleven o'clock, someone under government orders threw the big switch in the power station at 15th and Commercial and every street light in town went out. Store owners were told to turn off their lights, and automobiles were ordered off the streets. Policemen and soldiers with blue lights patrolled the neighborhoods to be sure that no light escaped from any house. Angie helped her parents tack blankets over their windows. Japanese planes flying overhead would have no way of knowing that a town lay below. Anacortes, along with the rest of the Puget Sound area and the Pacific Coast, experienced the first night of total blackness.

Wednesday, December 10. Angie heard the newspaper hit the front porch. Before her dad could pick up the paper and shut the door, an icy wind swept into the living room. "'Japanese Forces Invade Philippines,'" he read aloud as he walked back into the kitchen. He swore under his breath as he sat down to read further. Angie moved around behind his chair to read over his shoulder. Her world had been invaded, too, and she struggled to understand.

"Today's December 11," Angie said as she sat down at the kitchen table for her after-school snack. "Dad's fifty-three today, isn't he?" she asked her mom. Her dad wasn't home from work yet, so she could talk freely. "Are we going to have a party for him?"

"*Ja*, it's his birthday, but this is no time for party," her mother said, handing Angie The *Seattle Star* newspaper. "Look at the front page."

"'Germany and Italy Declare war on US; US Declares War on Germany and Italy,'" Angie read aloud.

"It's not fair, Mom!" Angie exclaimed, throwing down the newspaper. "Everything's so different. It's like the blackout isn't just at night. It's all the time!" Angie felt her face getting hot, but she couldn't stop talking. "Me and my friends are supposed to be having fun, but we don't dare laugh around grownups. We hardly talk out loud. We can't have a birthday party—"

"Angie!" her mother interrupted. "Stop that! You can't just think about yourself now. This country is at war and people are going to die. How can we have party at a time like this?"

Angie pushed away from the table and faced her mother. "When we first moved to Anacortes, you and Dad told me to quit moping around, I was only young once and to enjoy it. Now, just when I have friends and am having a good time, the world falls apart. It's not fair, Mom!"

"The world isn't always fair, but we look at what comes and find a way through it. Here's our weekly *Anacortes American*. See what people in Anacortes are doing to help."

Angie hadn't paid much attention to newspapers except to read the funnies and to find current events for her social science class, but, to satisfy her mother, she took the paper and scanned the front page.

The American Legion was asking for books, magazines, and radio sets for the sailors at the base. A community canteen for use by the servicemen and those in the volunteer Civil Defense Corps would be open Friday on the first floor of the Legion Hall. Women were asked to sign up to help run the canteen.

Mrs. Frank Kinsey of Kinsey's Market presented a plan called "Cookies for Rookies," asking the women of the city to bake cookies and cakes for the servicemen. The market, she stated, would be the headquarters of the cookie drive and she would see that the cookies were delivered to the base.

L. E. Stearns, chairman of the Anacortes chapter of American Red Cross, said the Red Cross was launching a War Drive, a campaign for funds for the armed forces and distressed civilians on the home front.

Arthur Donald Blackrud, twenty-three, was listed as the first Anacortes casualty of World War II. He was killed at Pearl Harbor. He attended Anacortes High School before enlisting in the U.S. Navy.

Also on the front page, the Anacortes Sea Hawks beat Coupeville in last Friday's basketball game. On this Friday, the Sea Hawks would face the Snohomish team, which beat Everett, Bellingham, and other big schools. Coach Boulton said that Irvin Ryberg, Anacortes captain and center and star player, will be back in the game after a brief illness.

In the days that followed, Angie continued to read the newspaper. On December 15, she read that the United States appropriated $10 billion for "open warfare." On December 20, the Draft Act required men 18–65 to register; men 20–45 could expect to be drafted into active duty.

On December 21, the First Baptist Church in Anacortes put on their pageant to celebrate the birth of the Prince of Peace. The youth group cancelled their plan to go caroling, however, due to blackout restrictions.

16

CHRISTMAS
December 1941

"Come in," Tilda called. "My hands are in the bread dough, so I can't get the door. Just open it up and step in." It was probably Mrs. Carlson. She sometimes stopped by for mid-morning coffee.

The door opened a crack and Mrs. Charlot peeked in. "Mrs. Lind, I have something to show you," she said.

Tilda was surprised to see Faith's mother. Tilda didn't have much social contact with people outside her circle of Scandinavian friends, and she always felt a little shy around Mrs. Charlot.

"Please come in," Tilda said, washing her hands and wiping them on her apron.

"My, it smells good in here!" Mrs. Charlot said.

"*Ja*, I just finished baking Christmas cookies. We can sample them with a cup of coffee." She hurried to the cupboard and took down two cups and saucers. "I can't believe Christmas is just a week away."

"I can't believe it either," Mrs. Charlot said. "I can only stay a few minutes, but I want you to see what came in the mail today." She took a small box out of her shopping bag and opened it on the table. "Mr. Lind's brother's family in Finland sent me this beautiful silver ladle for Christmas as a thank you for the clothes I gave you for Nadine and Elli. They didn't need to do that, but wasn't it thoughtful? And isn't it lovely?"

Tilda picked up the ladle and turned it in her hand. The light from the window danced off the silver smoothness of its oval-shaped bowl. A fine, filigree pattern of wheat decorated the end of the gently curved handle. The ladle must have been in their family because they could not have bought something as fine as this.

"It's beautiful," Tilda whispered, "and it was right that she give it to you."

"I'll treasure it," Mrs. Charlot said. She sat down at the table. "How are your relatives in Finland doing now?"

Tilda filled the coffee cups and brought them and a plate of *fattigmand* to the table. "You know Finland is at war again."

"Yes, I know, but I haven't heard much about it lately because the radio is filled with reports on our own war. You know that the President proclaimed New Year's Day a National Day of Prayer? We do need to ask for God's help in the days to come."

Tilda agreed and then suddenly remembered. "I'm sorry I didn't ask about your boy. Angie told me he enlisted in the Marines the day after Japan attacked Pearl Harbor. It's a worry, isn't it?"

"Yes, it is. The Christmas season is especially hard without him." She studied her coffee, stirring it even though she hadn't added cream or sugar. A sigh escaped her, but her attention returned to Tilda. "Tell me about your Finland family. I've thought of them often after you told me how difficult life was for them after the Winter War."

Tilda took a deep breath. "In June, just a little more than a year after Finland and Russia signed the Peace of Moscow Treaty, Finland attacked Russia and, with the help of the Germans, took back the Karelian Isthmus that they lost in the Winter War. My two nephews, Birger and Edvin, and Charlie's nephew Alarik were called back into the army to help guard the border. Every time the Russians attack, the Finn boys drive them back. That part of Karelia always belonged to Finland, you know."

The electric clock on the wall hummed softly. Charlie bought this clock for her last Christmas so she wouldn't have to carry the alarm clock from the bedroom when she was getting Angie off to school. She never thought she would have two clocks in one house. It showed how well off they were now. It reminded her how poor things were in Finland, but there was some good news.

She told Mrs. Charlot how 160,000 refugees from the Karelian Isthmus were moving back to their homes. Their houses and barns were gone, and villages and farms were torn up from the bombs, but they were already rebuilding. The important thing to them was they had their land back.

"I'll pray for them," Mrs. Charlot said, "when I pray for Bill and for all of us. I must go now. I have to do some last minute Christmas shopping. I seem to get more behind every year," she said, laughing at herself. "Merry Christmas, Mrs. Lind. I'm glad you and your family moved to Anacortes."

The next day, Charlie picked up a tree at a Christmas tree lot on 5th and Commercial. Angie helped carry the tree into the front room and Charlie placed it in a stand next to the corner windows. Tilda pulled a string of lights out of the Christmas box.

"Why bother stringing lights on the tree and putting it next to the windows when we can't have our blinds open?" Angie fussed. "No one will see the tree."

"We'll see it," Tilda said.

Tilda understood why Angie was upset. Last year people left their living-room curtains open so you could see their lighted trees. On Christmas Eve, Charlie had driven them around Anacortes to see the bright Christmas lights shining from rooftops and front-yard shrubbery. People hung strings of lights around their front doors and left their porch lights on in case company or carolers came by. This year, outside lights were forbidden and everyone was required to close all curtains and blinds.

On Christmas Eve Angie complained that it didn't feel like Christmas this year.

"*Ja*, Angie," Tilda said, "you can't tell it's Christmas when you look outside. But we have Christmas lights inside, and Telma and Bennie and the baby will be here any time to help us celebrate. Christmas is family, you know."

"Then why aren't *Moster* and Uncle and Art coming?"

"I think I told you why. Uncle couldn't get enough time off from the mill in Vancouver to make the long trip. But listen! I think I heard some car doors—."

Angie disappeared out the back door before Tilda could finish her sentence. She followed Angie and Charlie into the backyard where Bennic parked the car. Thelma got out with the baby, hugged her mom and dad and gave Angie a quick kiss. She explained that Linda

needed an immediate change and started for the house with the dia-
per bag over her shoulder.

Charlie stood by the car in the winter darkness shining a flashlight into the back seat. "You need all this for one baby?" he asked
Bennie. "Are you staying for a month?"

Bennie laughed. "There's more in the trunk!" he said as he handed
things out. First came the baby's lace-trimmed bassinet. Next, a box
filled with heavy flannel diapers and another with baby blankets,
powder, and lotions. Then, a small suitcase.

"This is full of baby clothes," Bennie explained.

"Angie, take the suitcase in to Telma," Tilda said. "I'll carry the
diapers, but then I have to get busy with supper and you need to set
the table. We'll eat early so we be ready to sit down around the tree
when Santa comes."

"Aw, Mom," Angie said, taking the suitcase and starting for the
bedroom. "You forget I'm thirteen years old!"

Tilda didn't forget. It was just that time had gone so fast. She
liked to remember past Christmas Eves when they lived in camp and
Telma and Leonard were little. Charlie would tape a straggly white
beard to his chin, put on his red bathrobe, black rubber boots, and a
red stocking cap and then sneak out the back door to knock on the
front door. Telma always got to the door first, but Leonard would be
close behind. Charlie would come in, a bulging gunnysack over his
shoulder, sit down and ask if they had been good. They both said,
"Yes," but Tilda suspected Telma had her fingers crossed.

Then Santa would open his sack and give them maybe two presents and an orange each, and some nuts and candy. That was all
because times were hard. Tilda shook her head as she started for the
kitchen. Now when they could give their children so much, they couldn't
give them what they needed the most—the promise of a safe future.

Bennie strode into the kitchen and gave Tilda a hug. "Thanks for
helping. The car's unloaded, Linda's asleep in her bassinette, and
we're ready for the festivities to begin. So, is it *lutfisk* tonight?"

Tilda always liked her son-in-law's quick ways and cheerful man-
ner, but it was especially welcome this Christmas Eve with spirits
dampened by war.

"You know it's *lutfisk* tonight," Thelma said, walking out of the
bedroom. "Dad always has to have *lutfisk* on Christmas Eve."

"Well, I like the way your dad fixes it," Bennie said. "When he covers his plate with pieces of boiled potatoes, lays chunks of fish on the potatoes, pours lots of cream gravy over the top, and then sprinkles it all with black pepper, it's not bad. Fact is, it's not only not bad, it's darn good."

"Glad to hear that," Charlie said. "Telma never liked it. Tonight Tilda fixed Swedish meatballs for her and Angie."

"It doesn't hurt to spoil them a little on Christmas Eve," Tilda said.

"Well, I might like *lutfisk* more," Thelma said, "if I didn't feel the poor fish was worn out before it reached the table. Dad, I don't think you've ever told Bennie what happens to the fish before you ever eat it."

"Well," Charlie began, "the sea in Finland is covered with ice this time of year, so fishermen try to catch enough whitefish, usually cod, in the summer to see them through the winter. Before refrigeration, they kept the fish from spoiling by salting them and hanging them on wooden racks in the cold air until they were dry as boards. At Christmas time, they softened the fish."

"Angie," Tilda interrupted, "you were with me two weeks ago when I bought this fish at Luvera's Market. Do you remember saying that the fish stacked outside his store looked like firewood?"

Angie nodded.

"Well, anyway," Charlie went on, "we bring one of these fish home and soak it for a week in lye water to soften it. Then we soak and rinse it over and over again in plain water for about three days to get out the lye. Then we can boil the fish for supper."

"And the lye that's not rinsed out turns the spoon and the kettle black!" Thelma added. "And it doesn't smell very good either."

Tilda laughed, "If you keep your nose out of the kettle while it's cooking, you'll be all right. It doesn't smell bad after you dish it up. And that's what I'm going to do right now! Everybody sit down at the table and I bring you your supper. Then we go sit by the tree and open presents."

Thelma and Angie helped with the dishes, but then hurried into the front room to sit by the Christmas tree. "I'll be right there," Tilda called after them. She reached into the high cupboard above the stove for the two-pound Hill's Brothers Coffee cans where she stored cookies. She dusted the curly *fattigmand* with powdered sugar and set them in the middle of a special plate. She placed the creamy-white *spritsar* around the edge. On another plate, the delicate *sand bakkels*. Tilda felt lucky getting those out of their molds and onto the cookie plate without breaking any.

"I'm coming," she called, taking off her apron and joining the others in the front room.

"About time," Thelma teased her mother. "We were ready to open presents without you."

"Now you're the one not ready," Tilda laughed. "I hear the baby."

"Good," Thelma said, jumping to her feet. "She can join us by the tree. I'll change her and be right back."

Tilda was glad for a break in the activity. She had been on the run all week to get ready for their Christmas—shopping, wrapping presents, decorating the house, cooking and baking, helping put the lights on the tree. Tilda remembered her girlhood in Finland....

December nights were twenty hours long! On December 13, families celebrated the Festival of Light. Early in the morning in some households in Sweden and the Swedish-speaking part of Finland, the oldest girl put on her head a crown of lingonberry greens and seven lighted candles. Her brothers and sisters, all dressed in white, followed her as she carried a tray of coffee and special rolls to their sleeping parents.

Tilda and Ida grew up in a home too poor to practice this custom, but they took part in a "festival of lights" Christmas Day. At five or six in the morning, they bundled up in their warmest clothes and, with a lantern or torch, joined others in a long, bright parade of light ending at their church. Horses in the parade wore little bells around their necks and everyone sang carols.

When she and Charlie were married and lived in the logging camp where there was no electricity, they celebrated Christmas Eve with lighted candles on their Christmas tree. How easy it was now! They wound a string of electric lights around their tree and plugged in the cord—

"Angie," Tilda exclaimed, "Chee Chee's in the tree again! Quick! Put him out before he tears it apart."

"Aren't you glad Linda's not crawling?" Thelma asked, coming into the room with the baby and sitting on the floor next to the tree. Linda, awake from her nap, swaddled in a satin-edged blanket, lay in Thelma's lap and stared wide-eyed at the lights on the tree.

"I can hardly wait to see what she does to a Christmas tree next year," Bennie said. "She could do more damage than Chee Chee!"

"Let's take care of one Christmas at a time," Tilda said. "And pray to God that we're all together again next Christmas."

"And that we won't have to close the blinds," Angie added.

PART IV - 1942

17

SHATTERED GLASS
January

Mrs. Garhardt stood in front of the classroom with hands clasped behind her back. She usually smiled as students entered the room, but today her mouth was tight. Teaching Sir Walter Scott's "Lady of the Lake" day after day was affecting her. Angie liked eighth-grade literature, but reading this ballad was affecting her, too. The story, written in the English of the early nineteenth century, was hard to understand. Maybe that was why kids referred to "Lady of the Lake" as "Bag of the Bog" or "Sack of the Swamp."

Angie buttoned and unbuttoned her sweater as she waited for Mrs. Garhardt to start class. She wore her pink cardigan often now. The two girls who had taunted her lost interest in their game when she didn't react. Angie had figured out that winning a popularity contest, even if it had been real, didn't mean anything. Angie felt sad for Laura though. She must have needed friends more than anybody to make up such a contest.

Tomorrow, Saturday afternoon, Angie and Faith and other friends from church were going to another roller-skating party in Burlington. Baptist kids from all over the area would be there. Sometimes boys from Mount Vernon asked girls from Anacortes to skate. Angie hadn't skated very long, just since they moved to Anacortes and had sidewalks, but she hoped a boy would ask her to skate.

"Psst! Angie."

Joyce sat across the aisle from her.

"I'm going to the Baptist skating party with you and Faith tomorrow," Joyce whispered. Class hadn't started, but Mrs. Garhardt expected everyone to sit quietly while they waited for the bell to ring. "Faith said her mother was driving one of the cars and you were riding with them and I could, too."

"Good!" Angie whispered back. "Wait a minute. You go to the Lutheran church!"

"Not any more! When we first moved here, a neighbor invited us to go with them to the Lutheran church. We went because we're Episcopalians and there's no Episcopal church in Anacortes. Yesterday, the Lutheran pastor called Mom and told her that the Masonic Lodge was a secret organization and, if I joined the Masonic Lodge's Rainbow Girls like I'd planned, I'd go to Hell. Mom didn't agree and told him so. Now I can go to the Baptist church with you and to the skating party."

"Class, it's time to begin," Mrs. Garhardt said, getting up from her desk. "But you can leave your books closed and put your homework away. I want to talk to you about something most important."

Angie heard the boy behind her whisper, "I thought the 'Bag of the Bog' was most important." A girl giggled. Someone shushed them. Papers rustled and feet shuffled as the class waited for their teacher to continue.

Mrs. Garhardt was already tall, but she had drawn herself up until her head looked as high as the top of the blackboard. "Children," she said, "it is no longer a matter of if we are bombed, but when we are bombed."

She waited. The room was silent. Angie found herself looking out the window, searching the sky.

"All classes this afternoon will be discussing the seriousness of this war and what we should do if an attack comes when we are in school. I mention the seriousness of the war because some people in our community have yet to realize it. Groups gathered downtown on Commercial Avenue during our first blackout 'to share the excitement,' they said." She paused and took a sip of water from the glass she kept on her desk. "I expect you children to be more mature than that when we begin our air-raid drills."

Mrs. Garhardt went on to explain that when the air-raid warning sounds, the class will walk in an orderly fashion to the nearest exit and continue walking, but at a quickened pace—still orderly—into the trees behind the school. There they will crouch down and fold their arms over their heads for protection against flying debris. Should the enemy be too close for them to reach the protection of the trees, they must slip under their desks and assume the same crouched position.

"Mrs. Garhardt," a student said, waving her hand in the air. "When will we have these drills?"

"We will probably take part in the drills no less than once a week, but we will not know when. We don't know what day of the week the bombs will drop, so we have to be prepared at all times. Just as we don't have blackouts every night but must be prepared to cover our windows immediately when we hear the air-raid siren. Are there any more questions?"

No one stirred. Mrs. Garhardt continued.

"Sometime today the school's fire alarm will sound and you will proceed as I have instructed to the nearest exit and then walk quickly into the woods." She took another sip of water. Angie's mouth was dry, too. The troubles of the lady of the lake were nothing compared to what the days ahead might bring.

Burlington had the biggest and newest skating rink in the area. It was centrally located for groups that came from as far away as Everett and Bellingham. The party started in the early afternoon, so that those who drove a distance could get home before dark.

Angie enjoyed the drive to Burlington. Farms with weathered barns and grazing cattle and horses bordered both sides of the highway. Closer to Burlington, open fields gave way to smaller farms with field crops and nurseries with greenhouses.

"Angie, Joyce, look!" Faith said, pointing out the window. "Mom, look at that greenhouse! Has there been a storm here? A hail storm?"

Mrs. Charlot glanced over at the nursery next to the highway. "I don't remember a hail storm," she said.

"All the windows in the greenhouse are broken!" Faith exclaimed. "Even if we'd had a hail storm, it couldn't break all the windows, could it?"

They drove on in silence, perhaps each trying to make sense of the broken windows. As they neared Burlington, Mrs. Charlot said, "I'm afraid I know what that was about."

Angie leaned forward from the back seat to hear Mrs. Charlot better.

"Four years ago last November, a terrible thing happened in Germany. It was the beginning of many terrible things. The Nazis had been persecuting the Jews, arresting some and demanding that others leave the country. A seventeen-year-old Jewish boy whose parents had been deported struck back by shooting a German officer.

"One of Hitler's leaders, Joseph Goebbels, told supporters of the Nazi party in all parts of the country that on a certain night they were to attack Jewish homes and destroy all synagogues. These men, called the 'Brown Shirts,' were to loot the Jewish-owned shops and shatter all the windows. One-hundred Jews were killed and 30,000 were arrested and placed in concentration camps. This night of riots has been called 'Crystal Night' because of the shattered glass."

Faith stared out the window. "Shattered glass. Like that greenhouse. We know the family that owns that nursery. Two of their kids are in the Burlington BYF! They're Japanese...."

Mrs. Charlot finished Faith's sentence. "and someone is telling them they are no longer welcome in this area. I'm afraid the vandalism we saw is just the beginning."

"Two Japanese American girls go to Whitney Grade School," Faith said. "Kiki and Kimiko Okawa. I don't know them because they are a lot younger, but my friend Phyllis Wagner knows them. She said their parents were born in Japan."

"I didn't know there were Japanese people in Anacortes. Where do they live?" Joyce asked.

"Out Oakes Avenue," Faith said. "Their house is between the house with the flowering cherry trees and Guemes Channel. Phyllis was invited to a birthday party there once and she said the family was real nice. Phyllis told me their mother gave all the kids at the party presents and candy and flowers. Phyllis got a glass candy dish with a horse's head on the lid. It was full of candy!"

"I remember seeing those girls when I was at Whitney," Angie said. "They were always dressed so cute. When they walked down the hall, they looked like little dolls. I'd never seen Japanese people before, so I couldn't help staring. When they saw me looking at them, they smiled at me."

"They'll be okay, won't they?" Faith asked her mother.

Mrs. Charlot didn't answer. She seemed to be concentrating hard on her driving.

Tilda had just begun to wonder when the skating party would be over when Angie walked in. Charlie came home a minute later from the Civil Defense meeting wearing a white hard hat, arm band, and badge. He was carrying a flashlight hooded with blue cellophane.

"When I'm on duty, you better follow my orders!" he barked and pulled a whistle out of his pocket. "I'm now an air-raid warden and you have to treat me with respect!"

Angie looked startled, but Tilda knew he was playing. A person needs to make light of things once in a while in a world so troubled. "So what did you learn at the meeting?" Tilda asked.

"Lots of things. The Army expects Japanese planes to start bombing any day. The mayor signed up volunteers to haul and dump sand next week at forty-seven key places in town. The sand will be used to snuff out incendiary bombs that fall near those places."

Charlie sat down at the table. "Lots of volunteers at the meeting. Bill West, John Carlson, Vic Haglund, Ed Frantz, Axel Anderson, other men from the mill, and some from town I didn't know. Charlie Kilgore volunteered to be plane-spotter. Important job."

"What do you do as air-raid warden?"

"I monitor blackouts. When I hear the air-raid signal, I take this special flashlight and walk through the neighborhood checking houses to be sure no light shows. If I see light, I knock on the door and ask the people to fix it."

"What's the air-raid signal sound like?" Angie asked.

"It's the Morrison Mill whistle. You've heard it. It blows once every day at quitting time, but the signal for an air raid will be different. Three long blasts, six short blasts, and one more long blast."

"What if we're listening to the radio and don't hear it?"

"You'll hear it. They'll repeat it for two straight minutes. Anyway, we should be listening for signals. The Japs could bomb us any time. Submarines are prowling our coast right now. They told us that in the meeting."

Tilda had read it in the newspaper. Nine Japanese submarines were spotted off the Pacific coast in December. Just before Christmas, a General Petroleum tanker, *S.S. Emidio*, out of Seattle was fired on by a Japanese submarine near Crescent City, California. When the crew saw their ship was crippled and drifting, they took to lifeboats. They were later picked up and told their rescuers what happened.

Tilda knew the war in the South Pacific was going bad. In December, Wake Island, an American territory, fell to the Japanese. By January 2, the Japanese had taken Manila and had the U.S. and Philippine armies on the run. With the Japanese military so strong, Tilda could understand why Anacortes and the whole West Coast was on alert.

"So when's supper?" Charlie asked, throwing his coat over a chair. "Time you took care of the warden."

Tilda smiled and turned to the stove to dish up supper. Then, she and Angie joined him at the table. Tilda watched him pile potatoes and meat on his plate and wondered how he would get along if meat was rationed. She'd heard that was coming. As long as they didn't ration coffee, they'd be all right.

"Charlie, you'll be busy during an air raid. What do Angie and I do—after we've covered the windows?"

"If an air raid comes during school," Angie said, "us kids are supposed to run to the woods, or, if there isn't time, hide under our desks."

Charlie set his fork down and looked at Angie. Finally he shook his head and said, "Well, I guess doing something is better than doing nothing."

He was very serious now. "We were told at the Civil Defense meeting that the most important thing is not to panic. If you are home, stay home. Go to an inside room or basement. If you aren't home, find any shelter you can, but don't stay in the street or get into groups with other people. Just don't panic. That's the worst you can do. Stay calm, the army officer told us.

"Something else the officer said. We have to watch for spies. A lot of Japanese live on the West Coast and they can signal planes—let them know where to drop the bombs. Quite a few of them farm right here in Skagit Valley."

"I saw one of their farms when I rode with Faith to the skating party in Burlington," Angie said. "All the windows in their greenhouse were broken. Mrs. Charlot said she knows the family, and Faith said the kids go to BYF skating parties—but they weren't there this time. Heck, Dad, they wouldn't be spies!"

"I don't know," Charlie said. "All I know is what the officer said."

"I read in the *Seattle Star* that all the headstones in the Japanese cemetery near Seattle were broken to pieces," Tilda said. "I can't believe families of those buried there could be spies. They've probably lived in Seattle for generations."

"I don't know about that either. What I do know is that Anacortes is now in Military Zone One. That means no Japanese, even those born in this country, can live here."

Now Angie set down her fork. "But what about the Okawas? They live here and have two girls in school!"

"*Ja*, that came up at the meeting. The Anacortes police chief knows the family and put in a word for them." Charlie related what the police chief had said.

Frank, the father, was foreman at Robinson's Fisheries on Oakes Avenue and Ito, the mother, worked there during the busy season. Frank was in charge of the payroll, too. The Okawa family had never been in trouble with the law.

The day following Pearl Harbor, Frank was fired from his job because the people in the plant said they wouldn't work if he were there. Military soldiers with guns immediately surrounded the Okawa house and Frank was told to keep all the blinds pulled down. The police came and searched the house for contraband like short wave radios, cameras, firearms, hunting equipment, and photographs. The police found nothing incriminating.

The family is not allowed to leave the house between eight in the evening and eight in the morning. They are not allowed to travel more than a five-mile radius without special permission from the police. The girls can continue to attend Whitney Grade School since it is only about a mile from their house.

"The army officer listened to the police chief," Charlie said, "but then the officer told everyone at the meeting that there was nothing he could do about helping the Okawa family. Anyway, he told us, before long all Japanese will be behind barbed wire somewhere away from the coast. 'You can't trust aliens from an enemy country,' the officer said."

Tilda found it difficult to eat her supper. "What about aliens from other enemy countries, like Germany and Italy—and Finland?"

Charlie didn't answer. He knew what she knew, that President Roosevelt was again ordering all aliens to register. Her and Charlie had registered at the courthouse a year ago September, but the President was repeating the order. Probably now, with the country at war, he wanted to be sure he had a complete record of all non-citizens, especially those from countries like Finland that were considered enemies of the United States and its allies. But what would the President do with this information? Would he decide that the Lind family had to be locked up, too?

18

"UNCLE SAM WANTS YOU"
February 1942

"Today's your birthday, Mom. Isn't it?" Angie asked as she sat down at the kitchen table. She wasn't really asking, but wanted her mom to know she remembered. She'd sewn an apron for her in home economics class, and had wrapped and hidden it under her bed.

Angie helped herself to a cookie and sipped her milk. She liked after-school snack time, especially when it was just the two of them. This time of day, Mom would sit down with Angie and ask how school went or how she did on her arithmetic test. When Dad came home from day shift at the mill, he and Mom mostly talked to each other about blackouts and rationing and what-in-the-world was going to happen next.

"Well, isn't today your birthday?" Angie asked again, licking the sugar off the top of her cookie.

"*Ja*, I think it might be," she finally said.

"What do you mean, you 'think'? It is or it isn't."

"That's true," her mom answered, smiling behind her coffee cup.

Angie set down her half-eaten cookie and stared at her mother.

"Well, records in church say I was born February 24," her mom said, serious now, "but emigration papers say February 26. My parents were poor and didn't bother much with keeping records."

"Were they too poor to buy a calendar?" Angie asked.

"Oh, we probably had a calendar, but time of year was more important to them than day of the week. When birch trees leafed out, it was spring and time to plant. When leaves turned yellow, it was fall and time to harvest. When snow fell, it was winter. When ground was hard and dry, it was summer. That was all they needed to know."

Angie wasn't satisfied. "But your mom would know the date you were born! Didn't you ask her?"

"I was six when Mother died. Too young to think about birth dates."

Angie sipped her milk and studied her mom over the top of the glass. "I didn't know your mother died when you were six. You've never told me anything about when you were little."

"You never asked."

Angie thought about that. "How did you get along without a mother?" she asked.

"My older sister Alma took care of our brother Ivar, Ida, and me until Father remarried. Then Alma married and moved to America with her husband and baby. We lost track of her then, but were told she died in 1925. She was forty-one years old."

Angie suddenly realized she knew very little about her mother. If they were poor, how did they buy tickets to America? Her mom must have read her thoughts.

"When Ivar, my brother was old enough, he sailed to America to earn money so he could buy the land we lived on, and the acreage he and Father farmed," her mom explained. "He came back to Finland when he'd saved enough to do this. While he lived in America, he sent money for Ida and me to join him. It was spring of 1912. I was sixteen, three years older than you are now, and Ida, your *moster*, was eighteen.

"The trip over was hard. We were crowded into steerage with hundreds of other immigrants. Steerage is the lowest part of the ship, you know, where the air is bad and a lot of people are seasick."

"Weren't you scared, traveling by yourselves?" Angie asked, her glass of milk, forgotten.

"We were really scared. Father told us when we went ashore to watch out for white slave-traders who kidnap young immigrant girls and sell them to evil men. And for thieves who act like they want to help you with your suitcases and then run off with them. On the train to Portland, we held our suitcases on our laps and were afraid to leave our seats. We'd bought bananas at the railroad station in New York before we got on the train, so we lived on them. For a long time, I never wanted to see another banana!"

"You said you didn't know any English, so what did you do when you got to Portland?"

"Ivar met us and helped us get jobs as maids for $12 a month. Lots of Swedish-speaking girls did this. We were told that when we learned to speak English, we could work in homes with fewer children and better pay, but we didn't think about that. We already felt rich by just being in America."

"Was the work hard?" Angie asked, thinking about how she hated to help her mom clean house.

"*Ja*, but maids had Thursday afternoons off, and we met at an ice cream parlor on 5th and Washington in downtown Portland. We cried together when we thought about families left behind, but we laughed a lot, too, especially when we told about things that happened at work because of language problem."

"Like what?" Angie asked.

"Well, on my first day of work, the lady told me to go to the cellar and bring up the clothes basket. I didn't understand her, so she showed me with her hands what she wanted. So down I went and up I came with the wrong thing. The lady said the word again, louder, like my hearing was bad. After more trips down and up the stairs, the lady showed me again that what she wanted was this long and round. This time I thought I knew and brought up a toilet plunger.

"'No! Clothes basket!' she hollered. Finally, I got it right. The clothes basket was under the steps, so I didn't see it until there was nothing else to bring up. I never forgot the word, 'clothes basket.'"

"Did the lady get mad?"

"I thought so, but I think she just didn't know what to do with me. That night when I was serving dinner, she saw I'd been crying. After the family finished their dinner, she told me to sit down and then she served me my dinner."

Angie took another cookie and slid back in her chair. "What else happened to you?" Angie asked, not wanting the stories to stop.

"Well, once I served food at a wedding. The bride was beautiful in a long, white dress. Everything went fine, I thought, but just as the bride and groom were leaving, she turned around and threw her bouquet at her bridesmaids. Someone had to explain that custom to me!"

"You had lots of problems...."

"*Ja,*" Mom said, "but one thing never troubled us immigrant girls, and that was how to have a good time."

This time Angie slid forward in her chair.

"An organization of Swedish young people called 'Temperance Society,' now 'Runeburg Lodge,' met Saturday nights for basket-socials and Sunday nights at Finnia Hall for dancing. Another Swedish organization called 'Vasa Order' had dances on Thursday nights. Maybe this was because the maids had Thursday afternoons off work and could get ready." Mom smiled and then went on. "It was at one of these dances that I met your *pappa.*"

"Tell me about that!"

"Well, I was there with a date. He introduced me to his logger friend Charlie Lind who was in town for the weekend. Charlie, your dad, kept asking me to dance. The boy I came with didn't like this, and, when your dad asked to take me home, my date got really mad. Of course I told your dad, 'No!' Next morning he called where I worked and asked if I would go out with him on Sunday when I had the day off."

"Did you go?"

"*Ja*, I did. I thought he was very handsome. We took streetcar to the amusement park on Council Crest in the west hills of Portland. We went on merry-go-round and Ferris wheel and other rides, and we ate hot dogs and cotton candy until dark."

"Then what?" Angie asked, leaning into the table, milk and cookie forgotten.

"Then he took me home on the streetcar, and after that he came to Portland from camp every weekend. In 1917, we got married and moved to Ballard in Seattle. Your dad found a job in the cedar mill there. I didn't want him to log any more because it was terrible dangerous work."

"But he did go back to logging and you moved into a logging camp...."

"That's right. He liked logging—being outside, falling big trees and bucking them up. I didn't want to move from Seattle, but I could see he was unhappy, living in the city."

Angie wasn't through asking questions. "Mom, why is Dad's last name 'Lind' and his brother Vilhelm's last name, 'Sjöroos'?"

Her mom seemed pleased that Angie was taking an interest in her parents. "When your dad first came to this country," she explained, "he took his grandfather's name, 'Jobbens,' because he knew 'Sjöroos' would be hard for people in America to pronounce and spell. He wasn't in this country long before he changed 'Jobbens' to 'Johnson' because that was a more familiar name in America."

"So why isn't our last name 'Johnson'?"

"When he worked in the logging camps, he found that a lot of other Swedes had taken the name 'Johnson,' too. So he decided to change his name to 'Lind.' Easy to say and easy to spell. In those days, a person didn't have to go to court to change his name. He just let people know—"

The door flew open and Dad stepped into the kitchen. He threw his hat onto the kitchen counter. "Have you heard the news?" he asked.

Angie could tell by the tone of his voice that it was not good news. She and her mother shook their heads.

"It's been on the radio all day," he said, pulling out his chair and sitting down at the table. "A Jap sub attacked the coast of California! Where the hell were the civilian spotters? Where was the Coast Guard? Don't they know there's a war on?"

"I'll get you coffee," Mama said, and rushed to the stove.

"The President was delivering his Fireside Chat," her dad went on, "so they figure everyone in the Goleta area near Santa Barbara where the first rocket hit was tuned in to the radio and not paying attention to what was happening right under their noses. The funny part is that Roosevelt was talking about what to do in case of a coastal attack."

Angie knew what her dad was talking about but had forgotten to tell her mom. Her social science teacher kept them up to date on the war. He decorated his classroom with patriotic signs like "Buy War Bonds" and "Uncle Sam Wants You."

"Was anyone killed?" Mama asked.

"No one was hit, but everyone felt the jolts and saw the red flashes from the gun muzzles on the submarine. A delivery man from the *Santa Barbara News Press* was at the top of a hill and counted twenty-nine flashes before the sub sailed back out to sea."

"So, what happens now?" Mama asked.

"Oh, no!" Angie exclaimed, noticing the clock and jumping to her feet. "I almost forgot! I'm meeting Faith and other kids from school at four o'clock to collect scrap metal for tanks and guns. We're supposed to look through alleys and empty lots for tin cans or any other pieces of metal."

"How will you carry all that?" Mom asked, getting to her feet, too, like she was going to help.

"Some of the kids are bringing little kids' wagons." Angie grabbed her coat off the chair. "Got to go!" As she ran out the back door, she hollered over her shoulder, "Uncle Sam needs me!"

19

ENEMY ALIENS
April 1942

Charlie sat down on the back porch step, pulled off his work shoes, and banged them together to knock off the sawdust. He turned them over and examined the soles. Clean! Not like when he worked in the woods. This time of year, mud wedged itself around the caulks of his boots until at the end of the day he felt half a foot taller than when he'd left for work in the morning.

Working in the mill out of the weather had its advantages, but he still missed the woods this time of year when alders and maples sprouted green, and dogwoods and rhododendrons were starting to bloom. When pussy willows grew next to the creeks and snow-white trilliums pushed up through the mat of winter leaves, he knew it was spring. When the long-absent sun slipped between the tall fir and hemlock and reached the forest floor, the warm smell of earth and new life pressed in around him. *Ja*, he missed that.

Charlie picked up his lunch bucket and stood to go into the house. He paused with his hand on the doorknob and looked around. Spring in Anacortes was good, too, he had to admit. The lawn was greening up and the maple trees next to the street were leafing out. The soil in the parking strip between the sidewalk and the street looked good for growing potatoes. He breathed deep and inhaled fresh, salt air from Guemes Channel and, just now, something more. Coffee!

"So, Tilda," he said as he walked into the kitchen. "Coffee's ready this time."

"Charlie, you know coffee is always ready when you come home from work."

Charlie started to remind her she'd missed a time or two, but she spoke first. "Well, almost always." She gave her husband a quick smile and then became very serious. "Telma called this morning."

"Telma called? She having another baby?"

Tilda shook her head. Charlie could see she wasn't in a joking mood, that something was wrong. "So what is it?" he asked.

"Bennie got his orders. He has to report to Fort Lewis in three days."

Charlie sat down. "I've been afraid of that, the way the war was going."

"The Army is sending his company to Willows, California, for a week of training and to get malaria shots. Then the Army is shipping them to the South Pacific. Telma and Linda are going to take the train to Willows so they can spend the week together before he leaves." Tilda poured their coffee. "Charlie, Bennie is a married man with a six-month old baby!"

"*Ja*, it don't seem right."

"Telma said because Bennie was in the Civilian Military Training Corps, he'll go as a second lieutenant. I guess that's the only good news."

Charlie put a sugar lump in his mouth and sipped his coffee. Tilda carried the coffee pot back to the stove and then joined him at the table. Neither spoke. The late afternoon sun crept into the little breakfast nook between the slats of the venetian blinds and warmed Charlie's shoulders. It wasn't enough. The thought of Bennie going to war had chilled him through.

Charlie listened to the radio and read the newspaper every day. When he and Tilda went to a movie, "March of Time" newsreels of battles filled the screen. They couldn't get away from it. And the news was always bad. In January, when the Philippine forces withdrew to the Bataan Peninsula, they thought they could hold on there. Yesterday radio news reported that the Japanese had taken over the Bataan Peninsula and thousands of men were injured or killed in the fighting.

"You know, Charlie," Tilda said, breaking into his thoughts, "if Leonard was alive today, he would be twenty-three. He would be in this war. Maybe the accident saved him from something worse."

Charlie studied Tilda, trying to wrap his mind around what she'd said. "Maybe it did," he finally admitted. "But it would have been good to have had him a little longer."

A cloud moved across the sun. "The kitchen is getting cold," Tilda said. "If you bring up some kindling, I'll light a fire in the stove."

Charlie was glad for the diversion. When he got back from the basement with the wood, Tilda had already stuffed newspaper into the trash burner and set a match to it. Charlie sat back down at the table and watched her poke sticks of kindling, one at a time, into the flames.

"You know, Charlie, I'm thinking of our boys in Finland and of Bennie and other boys in this country, and, I don't like to say it, but sending young men to war is like feeding kindling to a fire. God help us all if this war keeps on."

Tilda refilled their coffee cups before she sat down. Charlie looked out the window. "Here comes Angie with an armload of books. Look at that, Tilda. She's dragging her feet like she had troubles of her own."

Angie stepped in the back door, set her books on the kitchen counter, and joined them in the breakfast nook.

"So what's wrong?" Charlie asked. "Teacher give you a spanking today?"

"Aw, Dad. You know better," Angie responded.

Charlie saw that Angie wasn't in a joking mood either. "Well, what happened then?" he asked.

Tilda poured Angie a glass of milk and sat down again. Angie began.

"Phyllis is in Mrs. Pardis's math class and yesterday, when Mrs. Pardis was writing on the blackboard, Mr. Hall, our principal, stuck his head in the door and asked her to come with him to the office. She told her class to start on their homework and she'd be right back."

Angie studied her glass of milk.

"Pretty soon Mr. Hall walked into the room. He told the class that Mrs. Pardis's son had been killed in action." Angie pushed her glass of milk aside. "Phyllis said that after a few more minutes, Mrs. Pardis came back and class went on."

Charlie looked at Tilda. War was hitting close to home—

"And something else!" Angie exclaimed.

Charlie looked at his daughter.

"Our social science teacher showed us the April 6 issue of *Life* magazine. It had a long article with photographs of Japanese volunteers, 1,000 of them, being sent to Manzanar Internment Camp in California. They were to get the camp ready for thousands of Japanese, and a thousand German and Italian aliens. The article said the camp was comfortable and everyone was cheerful about the move! I can't believe Faith's Japanese friends from Mount Vernon, the ones with the greenhouse, were cheerful when they were taken from their home and locked up in a camp, no matter how comfortable the camp was!"

Charlie thought about the Civil Defense meeting where they were told to be alert for spies. "Well, the government has to do that for the safety of the country," he said. "Anyway, living in camps for the rest of the war shouldn't be too bad. Remember, Angie, we spent many years in camps."

"I don't suppose it's the same thing," Tilda said. "We didn't have much in the logging camps, but we were free to come and go."

Charlie knew she was right. And Angie was probably right, too. It wasn't fair to lock up Japanese people who were living peacefully in this country. And it didn't seem right to lock up Italian and German people who weren't citizens, even though they were from countries that were now America's enemies.

But maybe this country had no choice. Maybe when it came to war, the Japanese and Germans and Italians would be loyal to the country of their ancestors and sabotage this country. Still he didn't think so. After all, he and Tilda were aliens from a country considered America's enemy, and they would never consider an act of sabotage.

Suddenly he was tired of the whole thing. He set his coffee cup down and left the table. This was a good time to spade up the parking strip for his potato crop.

20

ANGEL WINGS
June 1942

Angie could hear that her mom was getting impatient.

"I know it's a beautiful Sunday afternoon," Mom went on, "but you have to finish your job before you go to Alexander Beach."

"But, Mom, it's a BYF picnic. You wouldn't want me to miss that. And anyway, I thought we weren't supposed to work on Sundays." Angie knew that was a weak argument.

"We all have to do our bit for the war effort. You know that!"

"But how is squeezing a capsule of yellow dye into a bag of white margarine helping the war effort?"

"There's shortage of butter because government needs it for troops. Anyway, margarine is cheaper and there's nothing wrong with butter substitute when we can make it look like butter. You used to think it was fun to pop the capsule and work in the color."

"I was younger then. Anyhow, my hands get tired squeezing the bag and I can't get the color even."

"Don't worry. Even if it isn't perfect, it will taste fine on your toast."

Angie set the plastic bag down and stretched her fingers. Her mom was sitting across the kitchen table with heavy scissors for cutting sugar. A bowl of sugar lumps was in front of her, the special sugar lumps shaped like small dominoes. She picked up one piece after another and cut it in half. Sugar sprinkles scattered onto the tablecloth each time she clamped down on a piece.

"I think I have your Daddy do this next time," her mother said as she put down the scissors. She brushed the sprinkles to the edge of the table with the edge of her hand and funneled them into a sugar bowl. "My hands get tired, too, Angie, from bearing down on these scissors."

"Are we so short of sugar that Dad can't have a whole lump with his coffee?" Angie asked.

"I'm afraid so." Mom dabbed her neck with her handkerchief. "My, but it's a hot afternoon."

Angie remembered when sugar rationing started. Her mom had to go to the grade school and declare how much sugar she had in the cupboard. From that someone calculated when she could start getting coupons. They had coupons now, but each person's sugar ration was only eight ounces a week, so they had to be careful.

Angie picked up the plastic bag of margarine and started working it again. She knew she should be more understanding. There were worse things than shortages and rationing, and she really was concerned about what was happening. Faith told her that her Japanese friends in Mount Vernon were given only three days to store their stuff, put their greenhouse up for sale, and pack their bags before they were sent to an internment camp. Angie heard some families had only forty-eight hours to pack!

And from what she'd been reading, the internment camps weren't anything like *Life* magazine described. The barracks or sheds the people moved into in April were drafty and cold, and, now with summer here, they were terribly hot. There were no trees to protect the people from the sun, and sand blew in through the cracks in the walls. They slept on army cots. Sometimes more than one family lived in one room with only blankets for dividers. People shared common showers and the bathrooms were outhouses on the edge of the camp.

"How are you getting to the beach?" Mom asked.

"A couple Moms are driving and some of the older kids in BYF are taking their dads' cars."

Angie heard a car drive up and glanced out the window. "They're here, Mom. Marivonne and her mom are picking up Joyce, Faith, and me."

Angie tossed the bag of margarine onto the counter and grabbed her towel and bottle of pop. She had her swimsuit on under her clothes because there was no place to change at the beach. "I'll finish squeezing the margarine when I get back," she called as she ran out the door.

Alexander Beach lay about ten miles out Oakes Avenue from Anacortes. It was one of the few beaches on Fidalgo Island with real sand. Like a silvery sliver of moon, the white beach curved for a mile or two along the salt water's edge. Piles of driftwood bordered the beach at the high-tide line. Angie liked searching through the sun-bleached wood for interesting shapes.

She also liked lying on her towel on the smooth sand just out of reach of the incoming tide. Of course, if a motorboat whizzed by, you could still get wet from its wake. But getting wet was part of the fun! The only drawback was the water temperature. Alexander Beach was situated on Burrows Bay, a wide span of Puget Sound as chilly as the Pacific Ocean.

Arloween, Bonnie, and Doris were sitting on a beached log. "Hi Ar! Hi Bon! Hi Dode! You beat us here," Angie called as she got out of the car. She liked the intimacy of nicknames, like "Murf" for Marivonne. Murf's boyfriend Gordie was called "Meatball."

Some kids were wading along the water's edge. A few were swimming. Angie unfurled her towel and allowed it to float down onto the sand. Marivonne, Joyce, and Faith laid out their towels next to hers. Faith had brought baby oil to spread on her skin for a deeper tan. Angie borrowed some from her and rubbed it on her legs and arms and face. Models in magazines all had deep tans.

"Are your moms telling you not to swim in lakes?" Angie asked.

Joyce and Faith nodded. Faith recapped the baby oil, and stretched out on her towel.

"I decided on my own," Marivonne said.

"I guess I know why," Angie said. "You're Joy Kamps' friend."

"The Kamps were our neighbors," Marivonne said. "Joy is two years older than me, but we used to play dolls together. When Joy got polio, they had to sell their house and move in with her grandparents."

"Why'd they have to do that?" Angie asked.

"Because of the hospital and doctor bills."

"I don't know Joy, except who she is," Angie said, drawing her name in the sand. "I know she's very friendly. I sat by her brother

Jack in sixth-period math. He always hurried out right after class to meet his sister at her locker. He said he needed to help her with her coat and books and maybe walk home with her."

Marivonne was looking out across the bay to Burrows Island, her eyes squinting from the glare of the water. She waved at the waders and Angie did, too.

"Jack told me that sometimes you go to Joy's locker, too, in case he's late," Angie said.

"I'm her friend and like helping her," Marivonne responded.

Angie dug her toes into the loose sand. "How did Joy get polio?"

"They don't know," Marivonne said. "When she was in second grade, she got awfully sick with a high fever. They took her to the orthopedic hospital in Seattle. Her breathing was okay, so she didn't need to be in an iron lung, but the doctors put her in a cast from her head to her toes with just a small opening so she could go to the bathroom. The cast held her left arm across her chest and her right arm pointing straight up with only the tips of her fingers showing. Like this," Marivonne said, demonstrating with her arms. "She lay in the hospital flat on her back like that for almost a year."

"I don't think I could stand that," Angie said.

"Me neither," Marivonne said. "I wanted to go see her, but the hospital wouldn't even let Jack go in. Only her parents. But there were lots of kids in the hospital with polio, so she had company."

Marivonne went on. "After a year they took the cast off from her waist down and moved her to a convalescent center in Seattle. She was there for more months. Jack told me he remembers getting up at 4:00 Sunday mornings, climbing into the back seat of their 1928 Buick sedan and sleeping all the way to Seattle. It took a lot of gas to drive to Seattle, so their dad walked to work during the week. Clear to the pulp mill!"

"Gas wasn't rationed then, was it?" Angie asked.

"No, but gas costs money, and they had so many bills," Marivonne explained as she took a bottle of pop and an opener out of a paper bag. Angie borrowed the opener for her pop.

"Joy studied a lot while she was in the hospital, but she still lost a year of school," Marivonne continued. "When she came back to Nelson, she was in the fourth grade, just one grade ahead of me instead of two. We still have fun together, but she can't do much. Her legs are thin and her arms don't work right."

"I've seen that," Angie said. "What's wrong with her arms?"

"When the doctors took off her upper cast, they had to break both arms to straighten them because they had been in the same positions for so long. She still can't put her own coat on, so Bonnie, Gloria, me, and others in school like to help her. She's always patient and never complains."

Angie decided she wouldn't complain about anything any more. Not about pimples or mousy-colored hair or flat breasts.

"The doctors don't know where Joy contracted the disease," Marivonne said. "Lots of kids swim in the lakes all summer long and don't get polio."

"Swimming pools are supposed to be bad, too, but that's no problem for us," Faith said, smiling at her own joke.

Angie understood. Anacortes had no swimming pools.

"Yesterday's paper said there were two more cases of polio in Skagit County," Joyce said. "It's good we're swimming in the bay. No germs could live in water that cold."

"And I think it's easier to swim in salt water," Faith said. "It buoys you up."

Angie turned over on her back to tan the front of her neck and legs. The afternoon was very hot. She could feel drops of sweat sliding down her sides.

"Time we got wet," Joyce exclaimed and stood up. The others jumped up and ran after her to the water's edge. "Last one in's a rotten egg," she shouted, ran waist-deep into the water, and sat down. The water lapped at her chin. "Whoa!" she cried a second later, jumping up and running for the beach. "That water's too darn cold!"

"It buoyed you up though," Faith said. "Straight up!"

Everyone laughed and then gradually, painfully, each ducked down into the water. "It's not bad once you're in," Faith said.

"It's even better when you're out," Angie said, and sprinted out of the water. Soon the others joined her and stretched back out on their towels.

"I love summer," Faith said.

"I do, too, but I miss seeing friends," Joyce said.

"But we're all here!" Marivonne said with a sweeping gesture. They all laughed.

"I wish we could stay 'til dark," Faith said. "We could float on our backs and move our arms back and forth 'til the phosphorus in the water lights up and sparkles like angel wings."

"I wish we could, too," Angie said. Then she thought of Joy. Of her patience. Her acceptance. Joy didn't need to swim at night in salt water to make angel wings. She was an angel already.

"Hey, you bathing beauties," one of the boys shouted. "Get up and join the games. We're choosing up sides for softball."

Food followed games, and then it was time to go home. The girls pulled their clothes on over their dry swimsuits. They shook the sand off their towels and stuffed them into the paper bags that had held their clothes and carried the bags to the car. Marivonne's mother had returned and waited patiently.

The car was hot from sitting in the sun, but as they drove down Oakes Avenue toward town, they rolled down the windows and breathed in the fresh, cool air from Guemes Channel. Happy chatter filled the car.

"I think of the Okawas when I ride down Oakes Avenue," Faith said. "You can't see their house from the street, but it's behind the house with the cherry trees. Could we stop a minute and see if they're all right?"

Angie had also wondered if the family was okay with so many Japanese being sent to internment camps.

Marivonne's mom pulled over. The girls chatted as they walked up a driveway that led to Okawa's house. When they saw the house, their words trailed off and they stood silent.

"Their grass hasn't been cut," Marivonne whispered. The sun moved behind a cloud contributing to an aura of foreboding.

Angie walked up to the front porch. The others followed. A lawn chair lay upside down on the porch. The window in the door was broken. Pieces of glass were scattered across on the porch. The only sound was the cry of a seagull in the distance. Goose bumps rose on the back of Angie's neck.

"What do you think?" Faith whispered.

No one answered.

"Girls," a voice called from a neighboring yard. "Did you see the 'No Trespassing' sign?"

They saw it then. Tall grass had partly hidden it from view.

"I'm Mrs. Trafton," the woman said. "You could get in trouble ignoring the sign." The woman looked concerned. "Are you friends of the Okawas?"

"Angie and I used to see the girls when we were in Whitney Grade School," Faith said. "Where is everybody?"

"They're gone," Mrs. Trafton answered. "Soldiers took them away two weeks ago. Just before school was out."

"Where'd they take them?" Joyce asked.

"Some place called Tule Lake Internment Camp in northern California." She crossed the yard and stood with the girls. "My husband's father owns Robinson's Fisheries where Frank Okawa worked. Said he was a good worker. Dependable."

Mrs. Trafton walked up on the porch and righted the overturned chair. "They were good neighbors," she said. "Beautiful flower beds. Neatly trimmed lawn." She looked at the yard and shook her head. "One afternoon Mrs. Okawa, and I had tea, right there." She pointed to a spot under a tree. "Ito told me she knew it wouldn't be long before they were taken, and that they considered themselves lucky to have stayed in Anacortes as long as they did."

21
DIMOUT
August/December 1942

"Artur," Tilda exclaimed, "don't slam the refrigerator door!"

"I'm sorry, *Moster*. I keep forgetting."

"Forgetting there's a war on?"

"No. Forgetting that, because of the war, no one can buy new appliances, so we better take care of the ones we've got! I don't know how I could forget that!"

Art poured himself a glass of milk and returned the bottle to the refrigerator. This time he closed the door very carefully and grinned over his shoulder at his aunt. Tilda had to laugh. That mischievous grin had been with him since he was a boy and always made her laugh. She'd miss him when he went back to university in a few weeks.

Art sat down at the kitchen table with his glass of milk and the newspaper. Tilda set out a plate of coffee bread and cookies. Art and Charlie were always hungry when they came home from work in the afternoon. This was the first batch of cookies she'd made since sugar rationing started, so she knew it was a treat. Art grinned his thanks.

"Where's Unc?" he asked.

"He said he was going to stop at a garage after work to see about new tires. The newspaper said there's a quota for August."

Art paged through the paper as he bit into a cookie. "How about this, *Moster*. The paper says the entire salmon pack of the four canneries has been set aside by the War Production Board for military and Lend-Lease purposes. Guess Unc will have to catch his own salmon."

"He likes to fish," Tilda said, "so we'll get along." She poured herself a cup of coffee and joined her nephew. She watched as he turned the newspaper inside out and laid it on the table in front of him. He moved his glass of milk onto the newspaper.

"Here's something else," Art said. "The Civil Defense Board's dimout rules. It says they go into effect the twentieth of this month."

"Are dimout rules different than blackout rules?" Tilda asked.

"Looks like it," Art said as he read on. "Dimout rules are in effect every day for the duration of the war, it says. No bright signs. No neon signs. No porch light or outside light brighter than 50 watts, and it must be shielded so light doesn't shine up. No lights visible to the sea." He took another bite of cookie. "For you, that would be Guemes Channel," he noted and then read on.

"Shades must always be drawn at night. Venetian blinds are okay if tightly closed. No light should be left on in the house in case a blackout occurs while you're gone. It explains that the dimout is to protect certain areas like Anacortes that are likely bombing targets. Army men will be inspecting the area to be sure everyone is complying."

"We'll follow the rules," Tilda said, "but sometimes I wish I could do more to help."

"Well, here's something for you!" Art said, pointing to an article on the next page of the *American*. "The Red Cross is setting up a Production Department in a room in the community building downtown. With the help of some sailors, they've moved in big cutting and packing tables." Art set his empty glass aside. "It doesn't say what they'll be cutting—oh, here it is. The tables are for seamstresses. They also want knitters—that's you, *Moster*—and anyone else who can help provide clothes for needy civilians and families of American soldiers."

Tilda thought about that. It was a good idea, but her broken English made her uncomfortable around people she didn't know. Anyway, she and other women in her sewing club and her friends in Ladies Aid at the church were knitting wool hats and stockings for the needy in Finland.

Arthur must have read her mind. "What do you hear from our relatives in the old country?" he asked, setting the newspaper aside.

"I haven't heard from my sister-in-law Ester since first of summer. I know she's busy keeping the farm going. It's harvest time now, so I still won't hear for a while. She has Ture, but his handicaps keep him from doing very much. Neighbors help each other because their young men are gone, too. Old men in the village and children do what they can for each other."

"What about Birger and Edvin?" Art said. "Are they still in the army?"

Art often asked Tilda about his cousins. In1931, when the Depression threw so many in America out of work, Art's dad decided they should move back to Finland and live on his family farm. Art's grandfather was a respected town councilman and known as the best mechanic in the community. Art's dad could work for him. Art was ten then. They stayed only four months, times being worse in Finland than in America.

But during that summer Art got to know his cousins. Birger was fourteen, Edvin, thirteen, and Ture, eleven. The boys ran together in the fields, fished in the streams, and swam in the lakes and the sea. Art was full of stories of the good times he'd had with his cousins.

"*Ja*, when I last heard from Ester, Birger and Edvin were still at the front," Tilda said in answer to Art's question. "Even though the Finnish army, with the help of Germany, took Karelian Isthmus back from the Russians, they have to fight to hold it." Tilda sipped her coffee. "In Birger's last letter to his mother, he wrote about one of his close calls. He and Edvin were fighting near each other in the Tienhaara area. Birger rode a bicycle to see his brother. Half an hour after he got back to his regiment, a Russian offensive started right where he'd been. Birger said a lot of Russian eyes must have watched him peddle through the front lines."

Art shook his head. "And Bennie? Does Thelma know where he is?"

"All she knows is that he's somewhere in the South Pacific. Bennie wrote that the Army had been in such a hurry to ship them overseas they didn't give them malaria shots. Now many in his battalion have malaria, but so far he's been lucky. We know from the news the Army invaded Solomon Islands and there's hand-to-hand fighting." Tilda sighed. "We pray that Bennie isn't there, but we don't know."

"Say, *Moster*, speaking of whereabouts, where's the little squirt?"

Tilda laughed, but then scolded. "Angie wouldn't want to hear you say that. She feels quite grown-up these days. You know she's going into ninth grade this fall? She turned fourteen August 4."

"I know," Art said. "I ate some of her birthday cake. But I still think of her as a little kid. So, where is she?"

"She went with Phyllis and some other friends to collect newspapers for a paper drive. Did you know that the government is blaming the shortage of paper on the shortage of manpower in the woods—so many loggers have been drafted. Charlie says if the bureaucrats in Washington would cut back on paper work, there'd be no shortage."

Art laughed. "Sounds like Unc. How is he handling the butter and sugar shortage?"

"He fusses about it, but now there's a bigger worry. There's talk of rationing coffee and gasoline!"

"Charlie, don't throw out yesterday's coffee!" Tilda exclaimed.

It was no longer talk. It had happened. November 28, coffee rationing began. December 1, nationwide gas rationing went into effect. No wonder Tilda felt cross.

"I wasn't going to throw it out!" Charlie retorted. "I know better than that. I was just looking in the pot to see if there was any left."

Tilda shouldn't snap at Charlie, but the rationing was getting to her. One pound of coffee every five weeks! That was less than a cup a day for each of them! She'd been rebrewing the grounds for their afternoon coffee. It didn't taste so good, but it was better than nothing. To think there was lots of coffee in South America, but there was no ships to bring it to the United States. The ships were all being used for war purposes.

"We're out of milk," she said as she slipped into her winter coat and tied a wool scarf on her head. "I'm going to run to the store."

A few weeks ago, "run to the store" meant Charlie driving to the store. Well, they all had to do their best to conserve gas. It was their patriotic duty. Tilda closed the door behind her and leaned into the wind.

Winter had settled over the town like a dark shroud. The mid-afternoon sun was low on the horizon and offered no heat. She didn't like walking the six blocks each way to Luvera's Market, but Charlie said their gas coupons should be saved for Saturday grocery shopping and driving to work and church. And she had to agree.

Life had changed for her and Charlie, as well as others. No more Sunday drives, something she'd always enjoyed. Like last year, there would be no outside Christmas lights, and now they weren't supposed to send Christmas cards because of the paper shortage. To buy a new tube of toothpaste, they had to turn in an empty tube. And making sure their sugar, butter, coffee, and gas coupons lasted until the next ones were issued was a headache.

Dimout rules were inconvenient, too, but she knew they were necessary. In June, a Japanese submarine shelled Fort Stevens in Oregon. On September 9, a Japanese submarine carried a small plane called a *Zero* across the ocean. The plane dropped two incendiary bombs on the woods along the Oregon coast. Their purpose was to start a firestorm that would sweep down the coast. Luckily, a fire didn't start. They tried again on September 29, and again the forest didn't ignite.

Tilda turned up her coat collar against the icy wind, hung her pocketbook on her arm, and stuffed both hands into her pockets. She shivered and stepped up her pace. Then she thought of the young men fighting on two continents, living in jungles or desert heat or Arctic cold. Suddenly she was ashamed to be complaining, even to herself. She had much to be thankful for. So far, her son-in-law in the South Pacific and her nephews in Finland had survived their battles. And then she thought of the family she'd just read about, the Sullivans of Iowa.

When the five Sullivan boys heard that a friend had died at Pearl Harbor, they immediately enlisted in the Navy and insisted that they be allowed to stay together on their tour of duty. On November 12, their sea force met up against a Japanese force. Their ship, the *Juneau*, survived the sea battle and was limping toward its base when a torpedo from a Japanese submarine hit the part of the ship where ammunition was stored. There was a huge explosion. Only ten men from the ship survived.

The parents couldn't understand why letters from their sons had suddenly stopped coming. For security reasons, according to the newspaper, the Navy had not immediately reported the loss of the ship. Finally the parents' worst nightmare was realized. They were notified that four of their sons had died in the explosion and the fifth, some days later in the shark-infested water.

Five sons! Gone! She and Charlie had lost one son, and the pain had been almost more than they could bear. Twenty years had gone by since the terrible accident took their boy, but Tilda's heart still ached at times 'til she didn't know what to do. And this mother and father had lost five boys!

God in heaven, help that mother and dad. God help us all.

PART V - 1943

22

SLUMBER PARTY
February

Angie had Mr. Ellis for social science in eighth grade and now again in ninth grade. They studied different stuff, but one thing remained the same. The students were expected to bring current events to class on Fridays.

Mr. Ellis stood in front of the class with his hands clasped behind his back as he waited for everyone to settle down. It was Friday, and Angie had her news article on the desk in front of her. The headline read "Rationing Procedures Confuse Housewives." Angie knew that without reading it in the newspaper. She'd seen her mom puzzle over the ration books every time she went to the store.

The news article went on to say the OPA, Office of Price Administration, was making every attempt to simplify procedures and warning people not to hoard or buy goods on the Black Market. Buying counterfeit ration stamps or paying outrageous prices for scarce items was playing into the hands of organized crime. Stocking up on scarce items like flashlight batteries or anything made of metal, like can openers, bobby pins, even paper clips, was unpatriotic.

Angie wished she could give her report first to get it over with, but she had to wait her turn. They were to summarize briefly what they'd read in the newspaper, or they could read the article aloud, but standing up in front of the class always made her nervous. She pulled a clean sheet of paper out of her notebook and prepared to take notes. Mr. Ellis was strict about that. Angie looked at her pencil. Too late to sharpen it now. She licked the point like she'd seen her mother do when the lead was dull, and then she sat up and listened to her classmates give their reports.

"Bombing raids over Germany by U.S. Air Force have begun. In the Pacific area of the war, the U.S. Marines recaptured Guadalcanal, but at an enormous loss of life. The U.S. was also victorious in the Battle of Bismarck Sea."

"Ten permanent internment camps have been set up in isolated sections of six western states and Arkansas to house 110,000 Japanese and Japanese Americans. Nearly two-thirds of the internees are American citizens. The federal government is attempting to enlist men in the camps who pass a loyalty test to serve in the Army. They would be stationed in Europe."

"Women in overwhelming numbers are reporting for work in shipyards across the country, this creating a desperate need for housing and child-care. Residents are asked to rent rooms to these workers who are vital to the defense program."

"February 7 nationwide shoe rationing went into effect as the leather is needed for combat boots. Each person will be issued no more than three pairs a year. Tennis shoes will not be available because of the rubber shortage."

"The Anacortes Seahawks' basketball team took first place in the county," one of the junior-high basketball players reported.

"Rah for the Seahawks!" a boy in the back of the room called out. Someone else whistled and the class cheered. Mr. Ellis smiled briefly and then called the class back to order.

"We're all proud of our team," he said, "but we need to move along with our reports."

Someone groaned, but the student next in order stood up and read her news item. "Although the government encourages people to build bomb shelters, a shortage of building material has hampered this program."

"Bacon grease and fat yield glycerin for high explosives. One can turn in bacon grease for ration points. Silk stockings are no longer available in the stores as silk is used for parachutes. Wool yardage cannot be purchased, it being used for uniforms. Sugar is rationed because the cane is needed to make molasses to make industrial alcohol necessary for explosives. Housewives despair because flour is now being rationed."

"The best selling book in 1942 was the *Red Cross First Aid Manual*. The Department of Defense encourages people to take first aid training."

"Anacortes High School, along with other high schools across the nation, is offering a Commando Class to prepare boys for basic training."

"Children are asked to bring nickels and dimes to school to buy defense stamps. They can also take part in the war effort by collecting scrap iron, rubber products like overshoes, and tin cans, which they are expected to flatten and take to a collection depot. They can also collect milkweed pods to be used for the fluffy insides of life jackets."

"Popular music like 'Praise the Lord and Pass the Ammunition' and 'Coming in on a Wing and a Prayer,' reflects a military theme. Comic strip characters like Joe Palooka and Daddy Warbucks in

Little Orphan Annie now wear military uniforms and take part in war adventures."

"All public transportation is jammed with military personnel moving from one camp to another and with wives traveling with babies to be near their husbands. People are urged to rent out rooms to families of servicemen."

"Scrap metal and paper drives are important. Iron from one old shovel makes four hand grenades. Scrap paper is used for packaging the armaments being sent overseas. Plastics, a new product, is replacing metal and paper."

Finally it was Angie's turn. She put her pencil down, stretched her fingers, and picked up her news article. Her knees trembled as she stood beside her desk and summarized the information. A boy asked a question about the black market. She didn't know the answer, but Mr. Ellis did. Then she sat down. Giving her report turned out to be easier than taking notes.

Mr. Ellis must have realized their fingers were tired from writing, or maybe he had become bored with all the reporting. He announced the class would spend the rest of the period reading from their textbooks. They could finish their oral reports on Monday.

Saturday evening, Faith and Joyce arrived at Angie's house right on time. Seven o'clock. Their mothers had already driven off when Angie answered the door.

"My mom said I could come to your slumber party if I wasn't late for Sunday school in the morning," Faith said as she handed Angie her coat. "I told her I knew you and Joyce would be going to Sunday school, too, so not to worry."

"When I told my mom I wanted to have a 'slumber party,'" Angie said, "she asked what kind of party was that? She'd never heard of 'slumber party.'"

The girls giggled.

"They probably didn't have slumber parties in the old country when she was a girl," Angie went on. "I explained that even though

I hadn't been to one, I knew all about them from other girls. It was when you ate cookies and drank pop and then went to bed and talked all night."

"Mostly about boys," Faith added.

The girls giggled again. Angie took Joyce's coat and headscarf.

"Joyce!" both girls said at the same time. "What have you done?"

Joyce smiled and fluffed the back of her hair with her hand, like beautiful women do in the movies.

"You've bleached your bangs!" Faith exclaimed.

No one giggled.

"They came out whiter than I planned," Joyce said, "but I thought it would be fun to look different."

"Do you think Paul—Reverend Logan—will let you sing in choir tomorrow? In front of all the congregation?" Angie asked.

"I don't know. I didn't think of that."

"What did your mom say?" Faith asked.

"She just shook her head, and then she said she didn't want me staying awake and talking all night because that makes me crabby the next day."

"Wish Edna could have come," Angie said, "but she has to be at her church early tomorrow morning for confirmation class. We'll be three musketeers tonight instead of four musketeers."

The girls giggled. Angie led them into the kitchen where the table was set for the three of them, but, instead of cookies on a plate in the middle of the table, there were apple slices. Angie's mom stood by the kitchen counter welcoming them.

"I'm sorry about no cookies," she said. "Angie wants me to fix Swedish hotcakes for breakfast, and that will use up the last of our sugar 'til the next stamp is good." Faith slid behind the table and sat down. Joyce and Angie followed. "Later, I make you root-beer floats," Mom said.

Much later the girls in their pajamas were in Angie's bedroom with the door closed. "Elmer's Tune" blared out from her dad's radio. They had found a good station with the latest hits and had danced for more than an hour. They were used to dancing with girls, like at noon dances and after-school sock-hops, because mostly freshmen boys didn't care much about dancing.

Finally, Faith dropped down on the bed. "I'm ready to rest," she said.

"I'm not," Joyce said. "Can you turn up the volume?"

"I better not or Dad will make us turn it off and go to bed," Angie said. "In fact, I better turn it down."

She and Joyce flopped onto the bed on either side of Faith.

"We all three have to sleep in this bed," Angie said, a little anxious.

"That's okay," Faith said. She sat up. "I have a secret." She turned her face slowly from one girl to the other. "Notice anything different about me?"

Angie and Joyce sat up and studied Faith's face.

"You're sweating."

"You're wearing lipstick."

"You're both right, but you haven't guessed it yet."

Angie and Joyce peered into her face again and then gave up.

"I cut off the tips of my eyelashes," Faith said and fluttered her eyelids.

"No!" Angie said, and both girls leaned into Faith's face.

"Jeepers, I think you did," Joyce exclaimed. "But why?"

"I read in a fashion magazine that if you cut off the tips of your eyelashes, they'll grow longer."

"You already had long lashes," Joyce said. "I'm the one who should do that."

"Or me," Angie said, "but I don't think I will. Anyway, I have a secret, too."

"What?" both girls exclaimed.

"I stuff my bra!"

The girls stared at her, incredulous. Joyce whispered, "What with?"

"My bobby socks."

No one spoke for a minute. They just looked at each other. White bangs, clipped eyelashes, stuffed bra. It was too much. They started to laugh.

"Think we should share these beauty secrets in current events next Friday?" Faith asked.

Joyce and Angie screamed with delight and threw themselves backwards on the bed. Faith dropped to the floor. She laughed and laughed, finally gripping her sides.

Angie's mom knocked on the bedroom door. "Time to be quiet now and go to sleep. Sunday school tomorrow."

The girls held their hands over their mouths and crawled under the covers. The bed shook from giggles. Someone hiccupped igniting more giggles, but gradually the giggles subsided, and the room became quiet, and the bed, still.

Angie broke the silence. "Faith," she whispered, "have you ever kissed a boy?"

"Not yet," Faith said, "but I'll bet Joyce has." Faith reached under the covers and tickled Joyce's ribs.

No answer.

Both Angie and Faith raised up on their elbows to look at Joyce. They knew she had a boyfriend. "Come on. Tell us," Faith said. "Do you and your boyfriend kiss?"

"Of course," Joyce said, ducking under the covers. Angie and Faith sat straight up and pulled the blanket off Joyce's face.

"Where do you put your nose when you kiss?" Angie asked.

"That's no problem," Joyce said, her eyes moving back and forth between the girls. "You don't kiss straight on like when you kiss your parents. The boy tips his head one way and the girl tips her head the other way. So lips touch without smashing noses."

"What if you both tip your heads the same way?" Angie asked. "Do you crash heads?"

No answer. Just a round of muffled giggles.

"Is it fun to kiss a boy?" Faith asked.

Joyce nodded vigorously and ducked back under the covers.

"What about French kissing?" Faith whispered.

Joyce flipped the covers back. "You know about French kissing?"

"What is French kissing?" Angie asked.

"That's when a boy puts his tongue in your mouth when he kisses you," Faith answered.

"Yuck!" Angie said.

"My sister Margie says not to let a boy do that," Faith went on. "You could get pregnant!"

"That's not how you get pregnant!" Joyce exclaimed.

"Margie says it's the first step," Faith said. "When the boy French kisses a girl, he gets excited and touches her in personal places, and then she gets excited and that leads to going all-the-way, and that's how you get pregnant."

Angie lay back down on her pillow. Her mind whirled.

"A girl dropped out of high school last year," Joyce said. "Kids say she was pregnant."

"Girls!" Mom's voice behind the door. "Girls, stop talking now or I won't be able to wake you in the morning. And I still hear the radio!"

"Whoops," Angie said and jumped out of bed. She turned off the radio and slipped back into bed between her two friends. "Good night," she whispered.

"Good Night," Faith and Joyce said in unison.

"Can we talk some more about this tomorrow?" Angie whispered.

23

PRESS CLUB
March 1943

The Columbia Junior High Press Club announced to the school that the March issue of their bi-weekly *Columbian Journal* newspaper would be the last issue of the school year. Faith as editor-in-chief and Angie as circulation manager weren't too disappointed because publishing and distributing the newspaper was a lot of work.

But the newspaper served an important role in the life of the school. Sometimes it published important announcements. Sometimes, calls to action. The March issue did both:

> Due to war conditions, it is believed that the annual freshman picnic will not be held this year. Under the present circumstances, gas will not be provided to transport students to their usual gathering place at Similk, and food rationing does not provide for school picnics.

> What are you doing for the war effort? Buying stamps every week? Well, that's a good investment, but there are other things you can do to help. This summer, instead of doing morning exercises to the 'Reduce with Music' program, you should be doing your exercising in a berry patch or potato field. The farmers are crying for help. Besides this, there is a need for air-raid messengers, practice victims, first-aiders, etc. in the Defenses Mobilization Program. Our allies are all working to win a war, which will mean freedom for us, so the least we can do is to give all possible support on the Home Front. Kathleen Meagher, Associate Editor

24

EASTER SUNDAY
March 1943

Angie had set her alarm for five o'clock and told her mom not to get up, but she did anyway. Her mom wanted to be sure Angie was dressed warm enough. It would be cold and windy on Cap Sante so early in the morning. There, even in the summer, you needed a sweater.

Mama said she should eat something, but Angie reminded her that Faith's mom was fixing breakfast for the BYF group after the sunrise service.

Angie heard the Charlot's car horn. She ran out and crawled into the back seat with Faith and Margie. Mr. Charlot drove down Eighth Street, turned left on Commercial and right on Fourth. He stopped to pick up Arloween, and then continued on up the steep, curvy road to the parking area near the crest of Cap Sante. The girls jumped out of the car the minute it stopped and ran the rest of the way to the top. The sun was not yet up, but it was light enough to pick out the BYF kids standing in a group among the adults. Joyce, Marivonne, Bonnie, and Doris motioned them to hurry.

From the crest of Cap Sante—the high, rocky peninsula jutting out from Anacortes—Angie could see the whole town, Fidalgo Bay, and the San Juan Islands. Now as she looked out over the bay, the gray sky was turning pink, and a brilliant sliver of light was edging over the horizon. Faith whispered, "Any minute now," and one of the adults said, "Ssh!" Reverend Logan asked that they all bow their heads and thank God for the beginning of a beautiful day. Then he started his sermon.

Angie listened to Reverend Logan's words about the resurrection. She liked hearing that there was life after death. It meant that someday she would meet her brother Leonard and that their whole family would be together forever.

But her mind wandered a little, too. Angie had been told that some years it rained during the Easter sunrise service. Maybe God knew that this year people needed to see something beautiful when the world had become so ugly. Four Anacortes boys had died since the war began. Arthur Blackrud was the first reported death at Pearl Harbor. Then, James Gray. Harding Smith, and Corporal Dick White were killed in action and Dick Haddon was listed as a prisoner of war. Angie didn't know them, but a lot of people in Anacortes did. Paul—Reverend Logan—had two brothers in the service and one of them had been killed.

Almost everyone had someone to worry about. People didn't know where their loved ones were because letters were censored. Bennie had written in one letter that he enjoyed playing with the little native children, but that could have been anywhere in the South Pacific. Angie wondered if he would watch the sunrise from some island this Easter morning and think about home.

The sun was up and starting to move across the sky. Angie looked at the crowd. Dwinal Smith, their youth advisor, was there. Gladys, his wife, would be helping Mrs. Charlot with breakfast. Angie knew most of the adults from the Baptist church. Some people came from other churches, as everyone was welcome.

Two sailors and their wives stood at the edge of the crowd. Both the Kilgores and the Charlots, along with others in Anacortes, rented bedrooms in their homes to navy wives so they could live near their husbands stationed at the naval air station. Angie didn't see any single sailors, probably because it was so early, and it was a long drive from the base. Several would be at the eleven o'clock church service, she knew. Often families invited sailors home to dinner after church, even when it wasn't Easter.

The sermon was long. Margaret—Mrs. Logan—had found a rock to sit on. Angie wanted to do the same, but decided against it.

She thought again about the young sailors who came to church. Most of them looked about the age of the older kids at school. A boy could enlist at seventeen, and some did. Some waited to be drafted at eighteen. Sometimes sailors asked older high-school girls to go roller-skating or to the movies with them. Sometimes Angie wished she were older.

After the closing prayer, Angie and the others hurried to the car. Faith's mother and Gladys would have breakfast ready by now.

Pancakes and eggs. Toast, juice, milk. Coffee for the adults. Mrs. Charlot apologized for not fixing ham or bacon, but they didn't have enough meat coupons for a crowd. She and Mr. Charlot didn't drink much coffee, so they had enough stamps to offer that with the breakfast.

Angie counted twenty kids in the group. Eight sat at the dining-room table and the rest, at card tables in the living room, which was the same room. Angie asked Faith if they'd moved the sofa into another room to make space for tables. Faith said the American Legion Auxiliary was fixing up a room for servicemen at Legion Hall and needed furniture, so her mom gave them their sofa.

After breakfast, a committee of older BYF kids did the dishes. Angie sat on the front steps with other girls. Mr. Charlot and Dwinal— Mr. Smith—sat in the porch swing. Angie's parents never allowed her to call adults by their first names, but sometimes she forgot. Even her mom and her lady friends addressed each other by their last names. Mrs. Carlson, Mrs. Eriks, Mrs. Haglund. Her dad and his friends called each other by their first names. Hard to figure out.

"It's a beautiful day," they heard Mr. Charlot say.

"It is," Dwinal agreed, "and Cap Sante's a great place to be at sunrise."

Arloween giggled. The girls turned to look at her. "What's funny?" Angie asked.

"It's a perfect place at sunset, too," Arloween whispered.

"And perfect when the moon comes up!" Marivonne added, just loud enough for the girls to hear. Now all the girls giggled, except Angie.

"What do you mean?" Angie whispered. She figured this was not information they shared with adults.

"Don't you know?" Joyce said, shaking her head. Her back was to the men in the swing.

Angie again felt like the dumb one in the group.

"It's where kids go to neck," Arloween said. "From where I live, I see carloads of kids drive up to Cap Sante all the time."

Angie glanced at the men in the swing. They weren't listening.

"These are boys and girls that go steady?" Angie asked.

"Some do," Arloween said. "Some just like to neck."

Angie put her hands over her mouth and giggled with the rest of the girls. She didn't know what else to do. She was glad when Faith and Margie came out on the porch and interrupted their conversation.

Margie had dressed for church. She wore a filmy, blue dress that fell above the knees, and a navy blue hat and navy pumps to match. Margie really knew how to dress!

"What do you think?" Margie asked, spinning on her heels.

"Your dress is beautiful," Joyce said.

"Notice anything else?" Margie turned around again.

"Your hair is fixed different." "Your shoes are new." "Your dress is extra short." The girls kept guessing.

"You're wearing silk stockings!" Joyce exclaimed, pointing at Margie's legs. "I thought you couldn't buy them because silk is needed for parachutes."

"You can't," Margie said. "Look again."

"You've painted your legs!" Arloween exclaimed.

"That's right," Margie said. "These are stockings from a bottle. The color lasts three days if I don't take a bath."

"And I drew the seam up the back with her eyebrow pencil," Faith said, holding up the pencil.

Mrs. Charlot came out of the house. She was wiping her hands on a dish towel. "It's time for everyone to go home and get ready for church," she said. "We need to go to the regular eleven o'clock Easter service even though Reverend Logan already gave us much to think about."

It was only about six blocks from Faith's house to Angie's house. Angie wished the walk were a little longer as she had lots to think about besides Rev. Logan's Easter sermon.

25

LETTER FROM MOLPE
April 1943

Charlie picked up the mail at the front door and leafed through it. Telephone bill. Light bill. A pamphlet from Civil Defense. A letter from Molpe! This was the first time he'd heard from his brother in a long time. Vilhelm was like Charlie—lazy about writing. This reminded Charlie. It had been a while since he wrote to his mother. She'd be looking for a letter from him.

Charlie hadn't always been slow to write. In 1906, when he first came to America, he missed his mother and brother very much. But gradually, over the years, he wrote less often—every three months and then every six months, mainly to send money because they had it so poor in Finland. Tilda would get after him for not writing. Once Tilda put the tablet and pen on the kitchen table and told him to sit down and write to his mother. Then to soften it a little, she set a cup of coffee on the table next to the pen.

It wasn't that he didn't think of his mother often. He did! But when it came to writing, he was either tired from work or doing things with family and friends or maybe going fishing. But he always wrote to his mother at Christmas and sent her money. And then he'd try to write and send money once more during the year.

His father died in 1900 when Charlie was twelve. He remembered that after his father died, his mother really struggled to keep food on the table and warm clothes on her boys. Vilhelm was only three, so Charlie did all the work in the hay field and cut and hauled firewood from the nearby forest. Mother gardened and canned, mended and patched. Even their shoes were patched. Nobody had anything in those days, so it was all right.

In 1917, he planned to go home for a visit, but his mother wrote not to come then because he would be taken into the Army to fight the Germans. Another time he made plans to visit Finland, but he lost his job and decided he'd better wait until things got a little better for him. The last time he planned the trip was in 1930. He wanted his mother to meet Tilda and his two daughters. They had passport pictures taken and went to the bank in Seattle to draw out money for tickets.

The doors of the bank were locked. The bank had gone broke, and, like other people at the beginning of the Depression, they'd lost their savings and had to start all over again.

But he and Tilda hadn't given up. They had a little savings again, and they could travel as soon as the war was over. Charlie wondered if his mother would know him after almost forty years. He hoped he would know her. Her hair would be white, but he figured her smile would be the same. People's smiles didn't change. It wasn't too late to plan a trip to Finland to see his mother.

"Tilda," he called, "letter from Vilhelm! Come in the kitchen and sit down and we read it."

Charlie read the letter twice and then handed it to Tilda.

Another cold winter racked Finland. Wood supply was short, so the house was cold most of the time. Food was poor. No meat. Even flour to make bread was scarce. Times were hard, especially for the old. Mother wanted to hold out to see him and meet Tilda and the girls, Vilhelm wrote, but she couldn't make it. She died March 25 of pneumonia. Their mother was buried next to their father in the graveyard by the Lutheran church in Molpe.

It was too late after all.

26

CRISES
May 1943

Angie walked in the back door and threw her schoolbooks on the kitchen counter. "I'm home," she called. No answer. "Hey, Mom, I'm home."

The house was cold, but that was not unusual. Everyone was told to keep thermostats no higher than 65°. When Angie complained, her mom told her to put on a sweater. Whenever anyone complained about shortages, the answer was always, "Don't you know there's a war on?"

She guessed she knew! They'd just heard from Art. He said he's going to join the Navy. She was already writing a letter to Bennie every week, and now she'd have to write letters to Art, too. It was a citizen's patriotic duty to write to servicemen. She didn't mind, except it was hard to think of something to write. Nothing much exciting happened. School, church, and sometimes a movie or roller skating with friends at the rink above City Hall. Where the heck was Mom?

Angie had picked up her books and started to her room when she noticed the note on the kitchen table.

> *Dear Angie,*
>   *Daddy took me to doctor this morning for bad stomach ache. Doctor said I must go to hospital for tests. Daddy will sit with me, but be home for supper. You're big girl now and can help around the house 'til I get home.   Mama*

Angie studied the note. She shivered, but not from the cold. She was scared. Mama often had really bad headaches—migraine headaches—but she'd never gone to the hospital.

The hospital was only two blocks away. Still in her coat, she darted out the door and raced down 9th Street.

Anacortes General Hospital, a white, one-story building, was surrounded by neatly trimmed shrubbery and lawns. As she approached the front entrance, she slowed to a walk. This wasn't just a building. This place dealt with life and death. People didn't go to the hospital unless they were very sick. Her mom must be very sick. She caught her breath, ran up the walk, and opened the front door.

The hall inside the hospital was white like the outside. Angie looked around and saw above a counter a sign that said "Nurse's Station." A woman dressed in white called her over and stated firmly that visiting hours for the afternoon were over. If she wanted to see someone, she could come back in the evening between seven and eight.

Angie was breathing hard and trying not to cry.

"Who did you want to see?" the nurse asked, gently this time.

"My mom, Tilda Lind."

The nurse opened a notebook on her desk. "Mrs. Lind went into surgery at two o'clock this afternoon. Mr. Lind is in the waiting room." The nurse patted Angie on the shoulder. "I'll take you there," she said. Angie could read sympathy in her eyes.

The waiting room was a short distance down the hall. Her dad was the only one in the room and stood up when he saw her. Angie ran to him and threw her arms around his waist. Now she could cry.

"It's all right," her dad said, patting her on the shoulder as the nurse had done. "The doctor was just here. Mama came through the operation fine and I can see her in a few minutes."

"Will she be okay?" Angie asked. "What was wrong with her?"

"You know, Mama doesn't complain much, but she had stomach trouble for quite a while. This morning it was so bad she let me take her to doctor. He said it looked like gall-bladder problem, so this afternoon he operated and took out her gall bladder."

Angie remembered sometimes her mom held her stomach and looked uncomfortable. Angie wished she'd paid attention and helped more. Once she overheard Thelma telling their mother that she spoiled Angie, always doing everything for her. Even ironing her socks! It was time Angie learned how to iron and how to cook and help a little around the house. When she was Angie's age—

Then Mom had interrupted and told Thelma she had to help when they lived in camp because life was hard. They had to keep a fire going in the wood stove to heat water for cooking and baths and to wash clothes. They washed clothes on a washboard and wrung them out by hand. They heated flat irons on the stove and ironed as best they could on a folded sheet on the kitchen table. They grew their own vegetables and canned—

Then Thelma interrupted. "I know all that," she'd said, "but here it's like the world revolves around Angie!"

"Well, if I remember right," Mama said with a smile in her voice, "you enjoyed spoiling her when she was little. I was surprised she learned to walk when you carried her everywhere."

"That doesn't count!" Thelma exclaimed.

Then Mom sounded cross. "Well, maybe I should expect more of her, but housework is easy now with electric stove and washing machine and iron and, besides, I have time. I like doing things for Angie. I like seeing her coming and going with friends and enjoying every day. Besides, she has grown up a lot this last year and become very responsible—"

Then Angie had interrupted. She'd decided she'd heard enough and walked into the kitchen. She remembered asking when dinner would be ready and Thelma giving their mom some kind of look. Angie thought she'd better offer to set the table and when she did, Mom smiled and gave Thelma a look. Adults seemed to have their own language!

The waiting room in the hospital was like a living room. Comfortable chairs, pictures on the walls, a table covered with magazines.

"Can I wait with you, Dad, and see Mom?"

"You can wait here with me, but I don't know if they let you in her room. Anyway, she'll be groggy from the ether. I just go in for a minute and then you can ride home with me."

Angie picked up a magazine and paged through it without really seeing it.

"But, Dad, can Mom get along without a gall bladder?"

"Doctor says if she watches what she eats, she'll get along fine. She'll have to stay a week or more in hospital and then in bed a while at home, but I told her not to worry because Angie can keep house and shop and cook for us."

The first day Mom was in the hospital, Anna Carlson provided supper for Angie and her dad. Mr. Carlson and Edwin brought the food in from the car while Mrs. Carlson set the table. Swedish meatballs, boiled potatoes, string beans, and salad. Best of all, apple pie for dessert. The second day, Mrs. Haglund cooked supper, and she and Mr. Haglund and Edna brought it over. Angie started to take Edna to her room to show her something and then remembered she was in charge. She let Edna help her set the table.

The third day, Mrs. Eriks cooked supper. Then Mrs. Frantz, and then Mrs. Ness. When Mom came home, Angie had to admit that all she'd done for supper all week was set the table. Her dad said he'd never had so many Sunday dinners in one week. Mom was glad to hear that, but she told her friends that Angie and Charlie would take care of things now she was home.

Then she wanted to talk to Angie.

Mom was sitting up in bed in her pink bed jacket. Her face was pale, but that was probably because she hadn't put on any rouge since she got home. Not knowing what else to do for her mother, Angie fluffed up her pillows. She'd seen that in movies when the leading lady was sick.

"I'm going to get better," Mama told Angie, "but doctor says I have to stay in bed another week. I know you can get along mornings with dry mush for breakfast."

"Mom, you mean 'cereal.'"

"*Ja*, cereal. Cornflakes." She went on. "Last week you and Daddy packed your lunches for school and work. That was good. When it comes to fixing supper, you and Daddy can work together. He batched before we were married, so he knows a little about cooking. But now comes the hard part."

"What's that?" Angie asked. She thought her mother had covered it all.

"The hard part is shopping for groceries. Bring me the ration books from the drawer in the kitchen, and I go over them with you."

Angie was back in a minute with the books. Her mother motioned her to sit on the edge of the bed.

"I want you to understand this rationing business, so you can help when I can't do the shopping," Mama said. "We start with the red book.

"These stamps are for meat, fish, butter, and cheese," her mom explained. "When you get to the meat counter, you see signs that give prices of meat per pound and how many stamps or points per pound. A pound of hamburger or pork chops costs forty-three cents and eight points. We each get only 64 red points a month, so you have to plan ahead. You already know about Meatless Tuesdays and Fridays. Those are the days we have soup."

Angie nodded. This wasn't going to be so hard.

"But soup comes in cans, and anything that comes in cans is rationed, too. This is what the blue stamps are for. We each get 48 blue stamps a month for canned food."

"Why is canned food rationed?" Angie asked.

"Because the cans are made of tin, and tin is needed by the Army for canteens and for some armaments, they tell us."

Angie became restless. How much more was there to learn?

"You have to watch the dates on the stamps. They are usually good for a month, and then you get new ones. Sometimes the new stamps are worth more or less points, depending on food supply, so you have to watch that." Mama picked up the sugar-ration book. "The Office of Price Administration gave us sugar coupons for a year, but each stamp is good for only a week. Each sugar stamp is dated, too—only good during certain weeks. It's the same with the coffee stamps."

There was more to shopping than Angie thought.

"I planned to pick up sugar and coffee next time I went to the store, but I'm laid up. I want you to walk to Luvera's Market this afternoon and buy sugar and coffee, as much as they'll give you for the stamps that are good. My purse is in the kitchen cupboard. Take the $5 bill so you have enough money." Then Mama sighed and slid down in the bed.

Angie tucked the covers around her mother's shoulders. She picked up the ration books and tiptoed to the kitchen. She put the red and blue books back in the drawer and set the sugar and coffee coupon books on the counter. The afternoon was warm, so she didn't need a coat. She folded the $5 bill into the sugar book and worked the two books into her small purse next to a note pad, her comb, a handkerchief, and last Sunday's church bulletin. As she started out the back door, her mother called, "Hang on tight to ration books. We can't eat without them."

Angie walked the half block on K Avenue to 8th Street and turned the corner toward town. The big, brick Christian Science church stood tall on the corner of 8th and K, right across the alley behind their house. Angie often looked at it out the kitchen window and wondered what that church was about. The name puzzled her. Christians in the Baptist church believed God created the world in seven days, but her science teacher said it took a lot longer. So how could "Christian" and "science" be part of the same name? She'd ask Reverend Logan about that next Sunday. He knew a lot.

Two more blocks and she was in front of the city library. Someone named Carnegie built it, she supposed, as his name was carved above the front door. Almost every Saturday, she and Phyllis walked to the library to pick up books for the week. Angie usually checked out two, but Phyllis checked out ten or twelve until one day the librarian said she couldn't do that any more, that she couldn't possibly read that many books in a week. Phyllis was upset. She did read that many and now she'd have to go to the library every other day.

Angie had spent several evenings in the library this spring. She was researching and writing a report on plastics for her science class. Plastics was a new product with a great future, she learned, and it was taking the place of metal and rubber products that were scarce because of the war.

Angie crossed catty-corner from the library to Causland Park, which covered a whole city block. The park was built as a memorial to World War I soldiers. The early developers of the park planted unusual trees and bushes, and created an amphitheater out of the side of a small rise on one side of the park. The tiers of seats faced a raised stage built of colorful rock from the area. Four pillars of the same rock arranged in a mosaic design supported the roof. Daffodils and tulips were in full bloom around the base of the open stage.

In the summer, when bands or other musical groups performed on the stage, people could wander around or sit and listen as long as they wanted. Once last summer, Angie and a couple of friends happened by during a wedding. They hid in the bushes and watched, and then ran when the bride and groom turned to greet the guests.

No one was around today, so Angie hopped down the seating tiers and darted onto the stage, spinning and whirling as a ballerina might, and then dashed out the other side and started down 7th Street. Trees along the street were sprouting tiny, soft-green leaves. One tree was covered with pink blossoms, like the trees next to where Okawas used to live.

Okawas had been gone a year now. Angie wondered if she'd ever see the little girls again. Faith said Mrs. Trafton had heard from Ito, their mother, a few months after they left. Mrs. Okawa wrote that the train ride to Tule Lake was frightening. All curtains in the rail cars had to be closed night and day, and a soldier stood between each car with a gun.

Tule Lake Internment Camp had been set up in a dried-out lakebed so dust storms were terrible. The walls and floors of their barracks had wide cracks between the boards. Whirlwinds ripped tarpaper off the barrack walls. Even with the windows closed, everything was covered with gritty sand. School was held in one of the barracks. Kiki and Kimiko said they didn't like their teacher and there weren't enough books. Mrs. Okawa hoped that things would get better.

Angie swung her purse in circles as she continued her walk to Luvera's Market. She thought about her mom telling Thelma that Angie was quite grown up now and very responsible. Proof of her mom's trust was in her purse. A $5 bill and ration books for coffee and sugar!

She also had the last fifty cents from last year's strawberry-picking money in her purse. She and Edna had picked together, but Edna made more money. They'd start down a row at the same time and, when Angie looked up, Edna would be half a row ahead of her. Still, Angie had made a little spending money.

She walked and skipped the last two blocks to Commercial Avenue.

Angie paused on the corner at Luvera's Market. The Diamond Five-and-Ten-Cent Store was two blocks away on her left. The dime store was her favorite place to shop.... It wasn't much out of the way.... She had those two quarters in her purse.... Her mom was taking a nap so Angie was sure she wouldn't notice if it took a little extra time to shop.

As Angie walked toward the dime store, she noticed the sign on the side of the building.

Use it up.
Wear it out.
Make it do
Or do without.

The same posters were all over town. They reminded people to conserve because of war shortages. The first time her mom saw the poster, she'd said there was nothing new in that. Her and Dad had grown up with those rules.

Angie continued on to the dime store.

A lot of people were shopping, probably because it was Saturday. Angie worked her way through a cluster of older kids to the cosmetic counter. The lipsticks were displayed in colorful rows next to the nail polish. Most of her friends were wearing lipstick now, so she wanted to, too. Angie chose Tangee because it was least expensive. She picked out a light pink shade and wondered if she had enough money to buy polish to match.

The lady at the cash register watched while Angie opened her purse and felt around for her coins. Too much stuff packed into one little bag! She took out her handkerchief and felt around until she found one quarter, but she couldn't find the other. Finally she emptied her purse on the counter.

"Here's the other quarter!" she told the patient clerk, and handed her the two quarters. The lady gave Angie the lipstick and her fifteen cents change. Angie dropped the coins and her lipstick into her purse. She picked up her handkerchief and comb, the ration books, note pad, and church bulletin and hurried back to the cosmetic counter. She studied the bright bottles of fingernail polish. All shades of pink and red. She set her things down, got out her lipstick, and began sorting through the bottles until she found a pink polish that matched the color of the lipstick.

"How much is the fingernail polish?" she called to the lady at the cash register. She was busy with customers but finally answered, "Twenty cents."

Angie set the bottle back into the display and her lipstick back into her purse. Probably Dad would give her five cents for being so responsible since Mom had been sick, and she could come back and buy the fingernail polish.

Angie looked at the clock on the wall. She'd taken too long! Her mom would be awake and worried. She grabbed her purse and ran from the store.

Mr. Luvera was everyone's friend. He called Angie by name when she walked into his store. "How's Mrs. Lind doing?" he asked.

"She's home from the hospital and doing just fine," Angie answered. "She sent me for coffee and sugar."

"She trusts you with the ration books?" he asked, smiling widely. The ceiling light reflected off the top of his smooth, tan head. He took a lot of good-natured teasing for being almost bald at such a young age, but he never minded.

"Yes, she trusts me," Angie answered, returning his smile.

As Mr. Luvera turned to go to the shelves at the back of the store, Angie snapped open her purse. A prickly heat unrelated to the warm day crawled up her back. Her throat tightened. Perspiration broke out on her neck. Her knees lost their strength and she leaned against the upright freezer next to the meat counter. She looked in her purse again. It was empty except for the lipstick and a dime and a nickel.

"Are you all right?" Mr. Luvera asked. His kind face was next to hers. "Here's a chair...."

Angie didn't sit down. She ran from the market, down the street toward the dime store. She prayed as she ran. *Oh, God, don't let me lose our ration books. I promise anything if I can find them. I'll help more at home. I'll teach Bible school this summer....*

She was at the dime store. She darted down the aisle to the lipsticks and nail polish. Nothing! She turned the display upside down, searching frantically. The clerk came out from behind her cash register and shouted at her. Then she looked at Angie.

"Oh, you're the girl who left the ration books," she said. "I put the books and your other things in the drawer under the cash register. Let me get them for you before you make a bigger mess here."

Angie wished she had Mr. Luvera's chair now. She was almost too weak to follow the lady to the front of the store.

"You know," the lady said as she handed Angie the books, "ration books are worth more than money these days. You're lucky the person that found them was honest and turned them in."

When Angie had the ration books in her hands and saw the $5 bill was still in the sugar book, she ran back to the grocery store. Two scary things in a row! Mama sick and lost ration books. At least when she wrote to Bennie this week, she'd have something to write about!

27

THIRTY-DAY LEAVE
Summer 1943

Faith was at the door. Quick raps, harder the second time. An emergency, Tilda thought, as she ran to open the door. Faith must have heard Tilda's heels click across the linoleum because she opened the door before Tilda got there.

"What's wrong?" Tilda exclaimed.

"Nothing's wrong," Faith answered, feet dancing in place. "We just got a telegram from Bill and he's coming home on leave!"

Angie came running from her room. "Bill's coming home?"

"He's on his way right now," Faith exclaimed and hugged Angie. "He said in the telegram he's being sent back to the states. He's been sick, but we shouldn't worry. He's fine—just needs to rest. He'll be here sometime next week!"

Tilda was happy for the Charlot family. Bill had been gone since the war started and, like all families, they'd worried about him every day.

Charlie had just heard from his brother Vilhelm in Finland. He and Hulda worried, too. Their boy Alarik had come through the Winter War without injury, but, after a short leave at home, he had to return to duty. Their nineteen-year-old son Mauritz was in the military now too, and their seventeen-year-old boy Manne was anxious to sign up. Tilda's sister-in-law Ester, too, had written with a heavy heart. Birger and Edvin had lived at home for a year following the Winter War, but had been called back into the service.

"Faith," Tilda said, "tell your mama we are happy your brother is coming home."

Angie, Joyce, and Edna were through picking strawberries now and had summer jobs at Lefeber Bulb Farm on Skagit Flats between Mount Vernon and Anacortes. Six o'clock every morning, an open truck from the farm picked up girls and boys in Anacortes and took them to the fields.

Each spring when the tulips were through blooming, the farmer plowed them under. As the plow turned over the soil, the bulbs came up on top, ready to be harvested. The pickers crawled or scooted along on their seats in the furrow the plow had left, and gathered the exposed bulbs into baskets. Angie didn't mind crawling in the ditch because the ground was usually cool and damp.

Picking bulbs was easier than picking strawberries, Angie told her mother, because you didn't have to bend over, but the rows looked terribly long at the beginning of the day. Still she earned more money picking bulbs than strawberries, and she liked riding in the back of the truck with other kids.

Tilda had heard that the boys told dirty jokes to tease the girls, but Angie never mentioned that. Angie did tell her the kids this week were excited about Faith's brother coming home on leave. To the boys, a Marine fighting in the South Pacific was a hero. To the girls, Bill was a heartthrob. To Angie, he was both.

Tilda glanced out the breakfast-nook window and saw Faith walking toward the back porch. It had been exactly a week since Faith ran to tell them Bill was on his way home. Tilda hurried to open the door.

"Is Angie here?" Faith asked, standing back from the door.

"*Ja*, she is," Tilda said. Angie had come up beside her.

"Bill got home today," Faith said.

Faith was so serious, Tilda noticed. No dancing feet. "Is your brother all right?" she asked uneasily.

"I think so, or at least he will be," Faith answered.

"Well, let's not stand here. Come in. We sit down." Tilda led the way to the kitchen table.

"What's wrong with him?" Angie asked.

"He's awful thin and very nervous. He just rests. Mother plans to cook his favorite dishes to cheer him up and help him gain weight."

Tilda and Angie sat quietly, waiting for Faith to go on.

"He was in the Solomon Island campaign. Guadalcanal. Fighting was heavy, he said, but he was lucky. His only wound was shrapnel in his leg. There was no anesthetic, but the medic removed the shrapnel anyway. Bobby wanted to see the shrapnel, but Bill said he didn't keep it. All he could show him was where it had been."

Tilda stood up and went to the refrigerator. She poured a glass of milk for each of the girls and put a couple cookies on a plate.

"While on Guadalcanal," Faith continued, "he heard that a friend from Anacortes was stationed nearby. Bill got permission to go see him. When he got there, he was told his friend had been killed the night before by one of their own sentries. The sentry had commanded him to halt and identify himself, and he hadn't done so. They think he didn't hear the command."

"Who was his friend?" Tilda asked.

"Dick White. He graduated from high school with Bill."

Tilda remembered reading in the paper Corporal Dick White had been killed in action.

Faith seemed to want to keep talking. "Before Bill left Guadalcanal, he came down with malaria. When his unit moved to New Zealand, he was in and out of the hospital eighteen times. He'd be discharged from the hospital and the malaria would come back again. That's why he was sent back to the states."

The summer days were unusually hot. Tilda sometimes wished that she could be like the young girls and run around in shorts. She saw a few women her age wearing shorts, but it didn't look right to her. It helped to put on a different clean, crisp, cotton housedress each day, even when it added to the ironing. Then she'd remember their tiny camp houses on clear-cut land with no protection from the sun, and she'd be ashamed for complaining. Now they lived in a well-insulated house and, if it got too hot, they could go to the cool basement.

Tilda was sorry for Angie, though, crawling along in a dirt field with no protection from the sun. She'd be brown as a berry by the end of summer! Angie said that was the part of the job she liked. She wore shorts and halter to get her shoulders, arms and legs tan. She tied her hair up in a bandana to keep the dust out, she told her mother, but Tilda knew it was to expose all of her face to the sun.

And she and her friends had a good time working together. Once, though, Tilda had to scold Angie. Just before noon, Angie found five tiny, pink, newborn field mice huddled together in their nest among the bulbs. Angie put nest and all into her basket.

When they reached the shade tree at the edge of the field where they ate lunch, Angie saw her chance. Joyce had set down her lunch bucket and was off talking to someone. Angie took wax paper from her own sandwich, wrapped up the baby mice, and slipped them into Joyce's lunch bucket. Then she waited. Finally Joyce sat down next to her and opened her lunch. She unwrapped what she thought was her sandwich. The baby mice wiggled and Joyce screamed and threw them in the air. Angie giggled as she finished telling the story.

Tilda told Angie she didn't think it was funny.

"Everyone else did," Angie protested.

"What about Joyce? Did she think it was funny?"

"Well, not right away," Angie admitted. "But later in the truck on the way home, she laughed about it."

"You know when you pull a trick on someone, you can expect something in return!" Tilda said.

Angie stopped smiling. "I didn't know that," she said.

Bill was getting his strength back, Mrs. Charlot told Tilda. He didn't have a lot to do except rest, his high-school friends being in the service. But he was still very nervous. And he was uncomfortable when treated like a hometown hero, Mrs. Charlot said. He didn't consider himself a hero, but, when the mayor and city council invited him to speak at one of their meetings, he did so. Later, when he was asked to ride on a float in a parade, he accepted only because the parade was promoting war bonds.

One of Bill's friends, Pat Buchanan, was home on leave while Bill was home. He was in the Army Air Corps and had been wounded in action. He walked with a cane, but, Faith said, he was a real dreamboat. And nice, too. He would always include Faith in the conversation when he was visiting with Bill. He could get a medical discharge if he wanted it, but he said he'd stay in the service because the war wasn't won yet. Faith promised to write to him and he said he would like that—and did she have a picture of herself to give him? Angie told her mom that Faith had a real crush on him and she thought he liked her, too.

Tilda asked Angie when Bill would have to return to duty. She thought Angie would know because she was spending a lot of time at the Charlot house. She'd come home from the bulb fields, clean up, and run to Faith's.

Angie said Bill's leave was thirty days. He planned to spend time with the family and once in a while date girls from his high-school class.

Angie told her mother she wished she'd been in Bill's high-school class.

PART VI - 1944

28

THE PLAYROOM
January

Angie sat at the kitchen table, her chin in her hands, her elbows resting on her open notebook. She stared out the window. Icicles hung from the eaves; a dusting of snow covered the ground. Frost in lacy patterns edged the outside of the windowpane. Angie thought of turning up the thermostat, but knew better. She'd put on a sweater.

It was Sunday, January 2. They'd been to church and finished their dinner, and Mom and Dad had gone to Carlsons for afternoon coffee. Angie was invited, too, but Mrs. Beard had given her English students an assignment to do over Christmas vacation and she had put it off until the last minute.

Mrs. Beard asked her students to think back over the past six months and list interesting or important events in the lives of their families and friends. They were to keep their notes as a source of ideas for future writing assignments. Angie was glad to be alone now because this required real concentration.

She walked to the sink and drank a glass of water. She checked to see that there was food in Chee Chee's dish, combed her hair in front of the bathroom mirror, and wrote "Johnny" in ink on the palm of her hand. She sat back down at the table, picked up her pencil, and stared at the blank piece of notebook paper. First, she'd think about family happenings.

In June, Art entered the Navy V-12 program at the university as a Seaman 3rd class. This meant he couldn't work at the mill during the summer, but he could visit on weekends.

This he did, and each time he came he brought a different date with him. Angie was visiting Thelma the weekend he brought Alice home. Her mom said he seemed to especially like this one. He'd met her on a blind date. She had dark brown, naturally curly hair, wide brown eyes, and a big smile. She had completed a year at Reed College in Portland and was leaving in September for Baltimore to enter the School of Nursing at the University of Maryland. But Art would still be at the University of Washington in Seattle, so probably nothing would come of it. Angie made a note about her cousin Art and his girlfriends.

Thelma had found a job working in the business office of L & M Department Store in Shelton. Bennie's mother took care of Linda. Thelma said working made the time go faster while Bennie was gone, and it helped keep her mind off the possibility that Bennie might not come home.

Her dad's brother Vilhelm Sjöroos in Finland wrote that seventeen-year-old Manne, their youngest son, had joined the army and was assigned to a machinegun company. Now all three of Angie's cousins on her dad's side were in the war, as well as her two cousins on her mom's side. Angie made a note of that.

She didn't know any other family news, so she'd think about her friends.

In early August, Faith's brother Bill returned to his marine outfit in the South Pacific. Everyone was glad he got his strength back, but was sorry to see him leave. Angie asked Faith if it would be all right if she wrote to him—just to be patriotic!

Angie, Joyce, and Edna made enough money picking bulbs during the summer to buy their school clothes. Joyce and two other girls took a bus to Seattle to shop. Angie wanted to go too, but her mom said Penney's in Anacortes had everything she needed for school.

Mom was right when she said if you play a trick on someone, expect a trick in return. On one of the last days at the bulb farm, Angie opened her lunch bucket to find her thermos of milk missing and a bottle of beer in its place. She tried to hide the beer under her napkin, but Joyce made sure everyone saw it. The kids poked each other and smiled. Several laughed out loud. Angie knew what they were thinking. Girls who spent as much time in church as she did should not be drinking beer. Angie wrote in her notebook, "Joyce gets even."

Entering high school as a sophomore had been a big event in Angie's life. Different classes and new teachers. Biology was the hardest. Students had to memorize a long list of chemical elements and their symbols. Angie liked Miss Carter, but she was a very strict teacher. Angie knew her from church where she taught the adult Sunday school class. This was one time Angie was glad she wasn't an adult!

There was a lot going on in high school besides classes. Girls Athletic Club, Home Ec. Club, Pep Club, Honor Society, Choir— Angie joined them all and so did most of her friends. Everyone liked Choir, partly because everyone's favorite English teacher, Mrs. Beard, was also the choir leader. The choir had sung for several city clubs during the Christmas season and performed at the Baptist church the night an important evangelist was guest speaker.

Angie went to the refrigerator and poured herself a glass of milk. She drank it while standing at the sink. She was remembering what she'd like to forget.

It was shortly before Thanksgiving when Angie suggested to Reverend Logan that he invite the high-school choir to sing the evening the evangelist was to speak at the Baptist church. Mrs. Beard accepted the invitation on behalf of the choir and told the choir they could thank Angie Lind for initiating the invitation.

The newspapers reported the evangelist's presence in the city. They wrote that during the past summer, people in Seattle, Everett, and Bellingham had crowded into tents to hear this evangelist. Anacortes was very fortunate, the papers said, to have such a renowned preacher lead a worship service in one of their local churches.

As expected, the church was packed. Folding chairs were placed down the center aisle and around the edges of the sanctuary for extra seating, and still people had to stand. The raised platform at the front of the sanctuary was filled to overflowing with members of the large high school choir. Angie, as part of the choir, could hardly contain her excitement as they marched into church wearing their performance robes. This was a big event, for both the high school and the church.

Several years in a row, the choir under Mrs. Beard's direction had won superior ratings in district competitions. They sang without accompaniment and had been told their music was like that of angels. They lived up to their reputation on this evening as they sang two sacred numbers flawlessly. The congregation sat in rapt attention. The evangelist complimented the choir and then turned to the congregation.

His tone was soft at first, his words gentle. Then he began to build, much as the choir had in one of their numbers. But his words became harsh. "We are all sinners and deserve God's punishment," he said. "Hell is as real as the hand before your face and, without salvation, you will burn forever!" Soon the evangelist was shouting and perspiring and pounding the pulpit. "Come to Jesus now," he said. "Give up your evil ways. Walk down the aisle as a public confession of your faith and be born again. I'll meet you there and we'll kneel together and pray for the salvation of your sinful souls."

Gradually, one person after another walked to the front of the church and the evangelist laid his hands on each head and prayed for each one of them. Mrs. Beard directed the choir in one more number, but Angie had trouble keeping her eyes on her directing. People in the congregation were still coming forward to kneel in front of the preacher. Angie wasn't sure if she felt exhilarated by the power of the sermon or ashamed to be a part of the sinful human race the preacher described. One thing she knew. It was an unforgettable evening and she looked forward to talking about it with her friends in choir class.

When Angie walked into the choir room the next morning, no one looked at her. The students were unusually quiet. Mrs. Beard was very serious. Angie hurried to her seat.

As soon as the bell rang to start class, Mrs. Beard turned to her and thanked her for inviting the choir to sing at her church. Mrs. Beard looked at the whole choir then and went on to say that it was not up to us to judge how some people worshiped, but to accept differences. She smiled at Angie then, but all the choir members were studying their music books. Angie had rushed out of the room when class ended.

Angie's face burned as she remembered that morning. Was she "some" people? She would not include this event in her list of ideas for compositions.

She set her empty glass in the sink and returned to the table. She checked the palm of her hand. Her hands were sweaty from thinking about that morning in choir, and the ink was smeared. She rewrote "Johnny" on her palm and picked up her notebook. She carried it into the living room and sat down on the couch.

Sometimes Angie wished she had a little brother or sister to liven things up. When her mom and dad went visiting on Sunday afternoons, the house was always too quiet. Not that her parents were noisy, but she'd hear the back door slam when her dad went in and out of the house. And her mom always hummed or sang softly to herself as she worked in the kitchen.

Angie turned onto her knees and rested her arms on the back of the sofa. She peered out between the slats of the venetian blinds. The duplex across the street where they lived when they moved to Anacortes four years ago looked the same. Not that she expected it to look different. Houses don't change. People change. She felt herself changing.

Angie still thought about Faith's brother Bill, but some of the high-school boys had become interesting to her, too. Don, Hap, and Ishmael had recently moved to Anacortes from different states and were coming to BYF. They were fun, but the brown haired, dark-eyed boy named Johnny had caught her attention. To Angie, his slightly bucked teeth and chipped front tooth didn't take away from his good looks. Arloween, who knew him as a neighbor as well as a classmate, whispered to her one day that Johnny had noticed Angie, too.

Johnny was in high-school band and his father was the band teacher. Before the school year started, Angie had decided to sign up for band class. The band needed clarinet players, she was told, so she'd learn to play the clarinet. Her mom was glad she was showing an interest in music again!

The clarinet was harder to play than the piano. When you struck a key on the piano, you could count on a certain sound. With the clarinet, you had to fuss with a reed and blow just right to hit the right note, even with your fingers on the right keys. The band teacher told Angie he expected her to practice hard every day if she wanted to join the high-school band second semester.

Mrs. Green, Angie's home economics teacher, also expected a lot of her students. The girls in her classes not only had to learn to cook and sew but also had to do a major project outside the classroom. They could wait until second semester and plant a victory garden and can the vegetables, or pick berries and make jam. If they wanted to begin their project right away, they could do something like sew curtains or recover a chair or decorate a room. They could have adult help as long as they reported on their own part in the project.

Last September when Angie told her parents about the assignment, her mom had said they'd been wondering what best to do with the unused part of the basement. If Angie wanted to, she could decorate it and make it into a playroom where she could bring friends. Her dad said he'd help fix up the room. He'd been looking for a project now that he'd harvested his potatoes.

Angie had immediately begun drawing plans for the room. She'd made other plans, too. When the room was finished, she'd have a party and invite both girls and boys—and Johnny would be one of the boys.

Angie sat back down on the couch. The house was too quiet. She wondered when her folks would get home. She checked the palm of her hand again. The ink was holding.

Angie and her parents started the playroom project in October. One part of the basement had cement walls on three sides. Angie asked her dad if he could build a fourth wall. He did this, leaving an opening for a doorway. Then he nailed plywood across the ceiling joists. Together Angie and her dad painted the walls, the ceiling and the cement floor. With her mom's Eldredge Rotary Sewing Machine, Angie sewed curtains for the two high windows and to cover the open doorway.

When Art came from the University one weekend for a visit and saw what they were doing, he had an idea. The next weekend he brought woven-wicker car seats from a wrecked car and helped Angie's dad built supports for them. They set the two seats in a corner at right angles to each other and built a table to go in the space between them.

Angie's plan called for a serving counter in another corner of the room. Her dad brought home more plywood and built a bar with shelves underneath for glasses. Her mom fussed a little about the sawdust flying around right next to where she washed clothes, but she didn't mind too much. She liked the way the new room was developing. When it was time to paint the corner car seats and table and the bar, she offered to help, but Angie wanted to do this herself.

The project took until Christmas to finish, but, when Mrs. Green visited to evaluate the work, she was very pleased. Angie had reported carefully what her dad and mom and Art had done, and what she had done. Mrs. Green said they each deserved an A+ for the project.

Angie decided the best day for the party would be the Friday before Christmas vacation. She'd invite certain boys and girls as she ran into them at school. "Friday night," she told each one. "Seven-thirty." They could bring records if they wanted because she had a phonograph. They could dance or just sit around and listen to the music. Because more boys went to noon dances in the gym now that they were sophomores, Angie thought they would probably want to dance.

The hard part she left for last. It was Thursday morning before she'd found the courage to invite Johnny.

Angie approached him after band class as he was putting his music away.

"I'm going to have a party at my house tomorrow night," she told him. "Seven-thirty. We're going to listen to records. Maybe dance."

Johnny went on putting his sheet music into his band folder. He nodded without looking at her, placed his saxophone in its case, and carried it into the next room where some of the students stored their instruments. Then he left. Angie snapped shut her clarinet case and carried it down the hall to her locker. Her face was hot from the encounter, and her heart raced, but she had found the courage to invite Johnny!

That afternoon Angie hurried home from school to get the new room ready for the party. Her dad had bought a sofa at the second-hand store and set it against one of the concrete walls. It had a few spots on it, so Angie covered it with one of her mom's hand-knit Afghans. Then she carried a small table from her room and placed her phonograph and records on it. She already had "Jersey Bounce," "Elmer's Tune," and "In the Mood," and Joyce was bringing "Sentimental Journey."

Friday after school Angie went with her mom to buy ice cream and root beer. She could imagine herself standing behind the bar making root beer floats, just like they did at the Polar Bear. Popcorn wasn't rationed, so they bought a big bag of popcorn to pop. Finally, Angie had her dad help her hang strips of crepe paper from the ceiling light fixture to the corners of the room.

That evening Angie had been too excited to eat supper. Instead, she spent the time in front of the bathroom mirror arranging her hair in the popular Ida Lupino style. She parted her hair on one side and swept it down and across her forehead and fastened it in place with a bobby pin. She put on a skirt and blouse she usually saved for church and she was ready. Edna's family had gone out of town for Christmas vacation, but no one else had said they couldn't come.

Joyce and Faith arrived right at 7:30. Angie hurried them downstairs, eager to show them the new room. Then she ran upstairs to check the clock. "It's quarter to eight!" she exclaimed as she ran back into the recreation room. "Where is everybody?"

"It's fashionable to be late," Joyce said. Joyce read a lot of women's magazines, so she knew about those things. But, in spite of Joyce's reassurance, Faith and Angie took turns standing on a chair next to the high window to watch for headlights. Parents should be dropping off their kids any time now.

"Maybe they don't know where you live," Faith said.

"It's eight o'clock," Mom called down the stairs. "What time did you tell your friends to come?"

"Seven-thirty, Mom! You know that!"

"They be here soon," her mom said.

Sometimes Angie couldn't stand the way her mom was always so calm, even in a possible crisis.

"Let's play some records," Joyce said. "The music will help pass the time."

Angie put on "Elmer's Tune" and then "Jersey Bounce." She went to the bar to rearrange the glasses and napkins. At nine o'clock she put "In the Mood" on the phonograph and rearranged the glasses again. At ten o'clock, Joyce's dad and Faith's mother honked their car horns and the girls left. Angie sat alone on the sofa in her new playroom.

"Maybe the boys and girls thought the party was tomorrow night," her mom said, peeking into the playroom. "It's easy to get mixed up on the days."

Angie didn't answer.

"You know the flu is going around—"

"Never mind, Mom. It's okay," Angie had said before dashing up the stairs to her room.

Chee Chee jumped up on the sofa beside Angie, startling her, bringing her back to the present—a slow afternoon, a too-quiet afternoon. So quiet she could hear the seagulls on the beach calling to each other. They sounded lonesome, too. She should have gone to Carlsons with her parents. She and Edwin could have played Flinch or Chinese checkers.

Angie invited her kitty onto her lap. Chee Chee curled up and began kneading Angie's stomach with his paws. Angie stroked Chee Chee's back and he purred his thanks. Angie looked at her open notebook on the couch beside her. The page was nearly blank. What had she been doing all afternoon? She dumped Chee Chee off her lap and began writing furiously. She'd nearly finished her assignment when she heard the basement garage door open.

Mom asked if she'd finished her homework and Angie asked what Edwin and Roy did all afternoon. Mama noticed how cold the house was and asked Dad if they could turn up the thermostat a little. He reminded her that oil was rationed and to put on an extra sweater, and didn't she know there was a war on?

29

"DANNY BOY"
January 1944

"**M**om, I'm meeting Joyce downtown," Angie announced when she walked in the door from school. "We're going to the Polar Bear. Could I have a dime for a milkshake?"

"I'll get my pocketbook," her mom answered. She was back in a minute with the dime. "I'm glad you've been wearing your heavy coat. Ever since school started again, it's been terrible cold and windy. You don't want to get sick!"

Angie put the dime in her purse, retied her wool scarf under her chin, and left. Mom was right about the weather. Her mom was right about a lot of things, but Angie wished she didn't worry so much. She worried about how Thelma was getting along—alone with the baby, and about Angie catching cold, and about how Angie felt when no one came to her party. It was good to get out of the house.

Angie took a shortcut to 8th Street across the backyard of the Christian Science church. Her mind spun like dry leaves caught in a wind. She looked forward to talking to Joyce. Maybe Joyce had figured out what happened the night of the party. Joyce was six months older than Angie and even had a boyfriend.

When Angie moved to Anacortes in the middle of sixth grade, she'd thought her world would end. She missed her friends in Potlatch. At the end of the next year, she was told she had been voted the second-most-popular girl in the seventh grade only to discover the contest was a fake. She'd had embarrassing moments since then, too, but she'd also learned there were bigger problems in the world. Still, the party was a crushing disappointment.

As Angie walked by the library, she heard someone call from the top of the stairs. Phyllis was waving at her. She watched her friend skip down the steps with an armload of books.

"Hey, I haven't had a chance to talk to you since your party," Phyllis said. "I wanted to tell you I'm sorry I couldn't be there. We had company and Mom needed me to help with dinner. I'll bet you had a good time."

For a minute Angie thought Phyllis was teasing, but then she knew better. Phyllis was too kind to tease.

"Is that why you didn't come?" Angie asked.

"That's why. I would have called, but you said just come if I could. You probably didn't even miss me with all the kids you invited."

"It's okay," Angie said. "I figured you had a reason."

The girls exchanged good-byes and each went her own way. Angie hurried now. She didn't want to keep Joyce waiting.

When Angie entered the Polar Bear, she saw that Joyce was sitting with Bonnie and Doris, two of her friends who hadn't come to her party.

"Can you believe the new skirt length?" Joyce was saying as Angie walked up to the table. "Skirts are really short because the Army needs the material for uniforms. And now dresses, jackets, coats—everything has broad shoulders with huge shoulder pads. The military look! We'll look like generals, or football players!"

"Maybe the boys will think we're football players," Bonnie said, "and tackle us!"

They giggled. Angie had to laugh, too. The girls greeted Angie and pulled a chair out for her.

"Angie, how was your party?" Doris asked. "Did you play Sinatra records?" She sucked noisily at the last of her milkshake. "Sure wish I could've been there."

"Remember when Frank Sinatra was mobbed at the Paramount Theater in New York?" Bonnie said. "When he sang, 30,000 girls screamed and some even climbed right onto the stage."

"I guess I'd scream, too, if I saw him in person," Doris said.

"I want to scream when I hear his records," Joyce said. She turned to Angie and spoke quietly. "I didn't tell them what happened to your party."

"You mean what didn't happen," Angie responded under her breath. She scooted her chair up to the table. The tabletop was sticky.

"My parents were going out, so I didn't have any way to get there," Doris explained.

"I didn't have any way to get there either," Bonnie said. "I'll be glad when I'm old enough to drive." She finished the last of her milkshake, scrunched up her lipstick-tipped straw, and dropped it into the glass ashtray.

"Sorry we have to go just when you get here," Bonnie said to Angie. "We're supposed to meet my mom at the drug store about now. Bye!"

Angie and Joyce watched the girls pay their bills and waved to them as they went out the door.

"We didn't think about it that night, but there was a lot going on besides your party," Joyce said, following up on their conversation with their friends. "A lot of people went out of town for Christmas, and there was a family Christmas party at Eagles' Hall and a new movie at the Empire starring Paulette Goddard."

The waitress came over and picked up the used napkins and straws, and wiped off the table. She asked what they wanted to order. Joyce said a strawberry shake. Angie ordered a chocolate shake, but her mind was elsewhere. She was thinking about what Phyllis and Joyce and the others had said. She suddenly realized that her invitations weren't clear, and that she'd chosen a bad night. It was that simple. Kids not coming had nothing to do with her—

"We should go see the movie before it leaves town," Joyce said, seemingly unaware of the impact her words had had on Angie. "Paulette Goddard marries an Air-Force captain played by Meredith Burgess. He's so handsome in his uniform. War stories are so romantic!"

"I'd like to go," Angie said, happy to be looking ahead. "I'll ask my mom."

"I'll loan you the fifteen cents for admission, if you want," Joyce said.

"Thanks. I'll let you know."

"Are you girls talking about movies?" Mr. Hauglund asked, breaking into their conversation. Angie hadn't noticed him walk up to their table. All the kids knew him even though he wasn't always in his ice cream parlor.

"We are," Joyce said. "There's a good one on at the Empire."

"There's no such thing as a good movie," Mr. Hauglund said. "Movies are the work of the Devil. They show people drinking and smoking and dancing. And passionate kissing! You know that, don't you?"

Angie knew what the movies were about, but she didn't know that it was bad. She didn't like to see people drink and smoke, but she didn't realize dancing and kissing were the work of the Devil. She did know that Mr. Hauglund and his family went to the Pentecostal church, or Holy Roller Church, as the kids called it.

Joyce told her that once she and her friend Dorothy tried to sneak up to the window of the church to see if people really did roll on the floor. Joyce's dad had suspected the girls weren't going to the store as they said and followed them. When the girls neared the side of the church where there was a low window, Mr. Kilgore stopped them and took them home. He was more upset about Joyce's lying than what they intended to do, Joyce had told her.

Mr. Hauglund cleared his throat. "I didn't come to your table to talk about the evils of movies, though somebody needs to," he said. "I came to show you the headlines in today's paper. Have you read this?" He pointed to an article on the front page of the January 6 *Anacortes American*.

Both girls gasped.

Mr. Hauglund read it aloud. "Brother of Reverend Logan Dies."

Joyce grabbed the paper out of his hands to read the rest of the article. Angie read over her shoulder.

> Rev. Paul Logan of the Baptist Church in Anacortes has received word that his brother, Second Lieut. Daniel S. Logan, 23, of Raymond, Washington, was one of the ten army flyers killed in the crash of a bomber near Muroc Army Base in California early this week. This is the second brother of the Anacortes minister who has been killed in the service of his country.

The waitress brought the two milkshakes and set them on the table. She placed a napkin and a straw next to each glass, wiped her hands on her apron and left. Mr. Hauglund took back the newspaper and walked away shaking his head. Angie wondered if he shook his head because of the sad news or because they were going to a movie.

They didn't drink their milkshakes. They paid their bills and left for home.

Reverend Logan wasn't in the pulpit on Sunday. He had left for California to take charge of his brother's body and accompany it to Raymond, Washington, where burial services would take place. The substitute minister announced there would be no evening service or BYF meeting. Reverend Logan would return to Anacortes in time to preach next Sunday's sermon.

Angie talked to Faith and Joyce after church and they agreed the BYF kids should get together Sunday evening as usual, even if it wasn't a planned meeting. Angie told them they could come to her house. They invited Marivonne, Marie, and Arloween, Bonnie and Doris, and any other BYF girls who wanted to come.

This time Angie didn't need to watch out the high windows in her playroom to see if anyone was coming. The girls were all there at seven o'clock as planned. Even though it wasn't a regular BYF meeting, Angie got out her Bible and everyone took a turn reading a favorite verse. Then, instead of singing, they listened to the radio and talked about school and boys and church and Paul's brother.

Angie's mom brought down popcorn and a pitcher of lemonade. Angie stood behind the bar and popped the corn and poured lemonade into the empty cheese glasses that her mom let her keep at the bar. Some of the girls sat on the couch and some, cross-legged on the floor, their lemonade glasses next to them. Then they all heard it. The radio was playing "Danny Boy."

Faith started crying first. Then one by one the others began to cry. Angie tried to hold back because she was watching the next batch of popcorn to be sure it didn't burn. Finally she gave in and cried along with the others.

The reality had struck home. War was not about running around with friends collecting scrap metal. Or parties for the class that collected the most paper in a paper drive. It wasn't about romance—beautiful girls falling in love with handsome men in uniforms. It was about being afraid for someone you love, about being lonesome, and about death.

30

NIGHT SCHOOL
January 1944

Tilda stood at the kitchen sink scrubbing potatoes for dinner. It was good that Charlie dug up the last of his parking-strip crop before the cold weather set in. Now the ground was frozen solid. She glanced out the window—

"Oh my! Here they are!" she exclaimed aloud, startling Chee Chee as he slept by the heat register in the breakfast nook. Tilda dried her hands on the dishtowel and ran to the refrigerator. Chee Chee followed her, trying to rub against her legs.

"I promised them hot chocolate when they got home from ice-skating!" she told Chee Chee as she reached for the milk.

She heard the garage door in the basement raise up, car doors open and shut, and the garage door slam down. She heard Angie run up the basement stairs, taking steps two at a time from the sound of it. You'd think she'd be tired after ice-skating all afternoon.

The door from the basement steps flew open. "Mom, we're home!"

"I can see that. Where's your daddy?"

"He's putting away our skates. Boy, did we have fun! I didn't know Dad could skate like that! He's really good! Us kids took hold of hands and Dad pulled the whole string of us across the lake. Then he swung us around like a whip and we went sailing off in all directions—"

"Slow down and catch your breath," Tilda said. "Were you warm enough out there on the ice?"

"I was plenty warm. I didn't even wear my jacket."

"Too warm," Charlie said as he came into the kitchen. "I'm afraid the ice won't be good tomorrow. Too bad this January isn't like last year. Remember, the temperature was ten degrees for most of a week, and then went down to six degrees and then four. That's when I should have gotten out my ice skates."

"*Ja*, that was an awful cold spell," Tilda said. "School closed down for three days." She poured milk into a kettle and carried it to the stove.

"I liked it!" Angie said. "We had six inches of snow. We skied and sledded down the steep street near Phyllis's house."

"*Ja*," Tilda said, "and you tied your sleds to the back bumper of Ishmael's car and rode around the neighborhood. I put a stop to that!"

"But it was fun while it lasted," Angie said, grinning at her mother. "Where's our hot chocolate?"

"It's coming," Tilda said, stirring the powdered cocoa into the warming milk. She added half a teaspoon of sugar. They'd gotten used to using less sugar in their food and drink. "Well, who else was skating?" she asked.

"Joyce, Marie, Marivonne, Arloween. Ethel and Olive from Lake Campbell. Sally Isaacson. Boy, you should see Sally skate! She flies across the ice like she had wings."

"Don't forget the boys," Charlie said.

"Oh, yeah," Angie said, dropping her voice.

Tilda looked at her. Angie had come into the kitchen with pink cheeks and red nose from the cold, but now her whole face was red. "Well?" Tilda said.

"Well, Gordon Christenson and Mark Gilkey."

"And?" Charlie prompted.

"And Johnny Waldorf. When's our hot chocolate ready?"

Tilda smiled to herself. "You can sit down. I bring the cups to the table."

"I didn't have as good a time yesterday as you did," Tilda told Charlie the next morning as they finished their breakfast. She held up the *Anacortes American*. "I spent the afternoon studying the Ration Calendar on the front page. It's supposed to make shopping easy for the average housewife!"

Charlie reached across the breakfast table, took the paper from her, and looked it over.

Processed Foods: Green stamps D-E-F valid now thru Jan. 20. Green stamps G-H-J valid Jan. 1 thru Feb. 20. Meats,

> Fats, Rationed Dairy Products: Brown stamps R-S valid now thru Jan. 29. Brown stamp T valid Jan. 9 thru Jan. 29. Shoes: stamp 18 War Ration Book 1 valid indefinitely, stamp 1 War Ration Book 3 "airplane sheet" valid indefinitely. Sugar: Stamp 29 Book 4 valid through January 15.

"*Ja*," Charlie said, "that takes some careful study. But did you read the rest of the calendar? The part I have to figure out?"

> Gasoline: No. 9 coupons, A Book, valid Nov. 22 thru Jan. 21. B and C books may be renewed within, but not before, 15 days from date on book cover. T coupons expire Dec. 31. New serial strip T coupons valid Jan. 1. Tire Inspections: A-car deadline March 30. B every 4 months; T every 6 months or 5,000 miles of driving.

> Fuel Oil: Period 1 coupon, class 4, 5 and 6, valid to Jan 3. Period 2 coupons valid Nov. 30 thru Feb. 7. Maximum consumption to Dec. 27 of total annual yearly rations should not exceed 32% west of Cascade Mountains, 37% east.

"Tilda, it says that next month the OPA is putting out ration tokens along with coupons. You'll get blue tokens in change for blue stamps, red for red stamps. You spend the tokens like coupons—"

Tilda wasn't listening. "Charlie, if this calendar is easy for the average person, then I'm not average. And, if I'm not average, how can I pass my citizenship test?"

Charlie looked like he was going to say something, but instead shook his head and walked to the window.

The kitchen was quiet. Tilda heard seagulls down by the water. Sometime during the night, a fog had moved in from Guemes Channel. It blurred everything but the nearest tree. She knew Charlie wouldn't be able to see much across the yard, but she knew he wasn't looking there anyway. He was looking toward their home half a world away. Lately, he'd become very quiet every time she brought up going to school to become an American citizen.

Tilda carried their mush bowls and coffee cups to the sink, washed and dried them, and put them in the cupboard. A week ago she'd been working at the sink like this when Charlie told her he'd decided not to take citizenship class. She couldn't believe what she was hearing. Even in the logging camp, they'd talked about becoming citizens some day when they lived where they could get classes.

She'd reminded him that they were registered "enemy aliens," citizens of a country that was fighting along side the Germans and that some Germans in this country who didn't have citizenship papers had been interned. She'd asked how long he thought they would escape the same treatment. He'd grumbled and walked out of the room. They didn't speak to each other the rest of the day. That afternoon Tilda had gone ahead on her own and registered for the class.

She'd met with the Naturalization Class the following Saturday evening at eight o'clock in Carpenter's Hall on Commercial. In May Charlie would drive her to the Superior Court of Skagit County in Mount Vernon and if she passed the test, she'd be sworn in as an American citizen.

Their first assignment was to memorize the Preamble to the Constitution. Tilda found that easy. As a girl in Finland, she'd had no trouble memorizing long passages in the Bible for her confirmation class. She had done well in school, too, and hated to see it end with eighth grade. She liked history. Finland's history made her sad though, to learn how her country had struggled under the rule of Sweden first and then Russia.

The teacher of the Naturalization Class told them they would be reading some American history, but mostly they'd be studying the Constitution and Bill of Rights. The form of the U.S. government with its branches—executive, legislative, and judicial—and the responsibilities of each sounded like a lot to learn. But her teacher in Finland had said she was an above-average student, so she shouldn't be nervous about the work required of her in this class.

But, if she was above average, why was she having so much trouble with the Ration Calendar? She went to the kitchen drawer, found paper and pencil, gathered up her ration books and returned to the table. She'd make a list of groceries they needed for the week, and then check to see if she had enough stamps with the right date. She'd figure this out if it took all morning!

Charlie turned from the window and saw his wife back at the table, head bent over ration books and papers. The ceiling light picked up some gray in her hair. What was that song they used to sing? "Silver Threads Among the Gold"? Tilda's hair was brown, but the idea was the same. It was all right to show a little gray. Tilda was forty-seven now. He himself had a lot of gray hair, but he was eight years older than his wife. Anyway, the barber cut his hair so short it was hard to tell what color it was.

He wanted to sit down now and tell her he was sorry he couldn't take the naturalization class with her. He wanted to make her understand something he himself hardly understood. To become an American citizen, a person had to renounce allegiance and loyalty to the country of his birth. Even thinking about doing that when Finland was having so many troubles made him feel disloyal.

In the winter of 1941, Finland had succeeded, with the help of the German army and German supplies, in taking back the Karelian Isthmus, the territory Russia took from Finland in 1940. But Finland didn't feel allied to Germany, Charlie was sure of that. Finland didn't approve of Germany's invading other countries or of their treatment of the Jews. Finland had made concessions to the Germans only because they were fighting a common enemy. The Finnish army advanced only until they regained the Karelian Isthmus.

Ice-skating with Angie and the other young people brought back memories of his own boyhood and skating on the Bothnia Sea. There he could race across miles of unbroken ice, through frosted air that snapped at his nose and cheeks until his whole face was numb. Sometimes in fun he would race up to a friend, turn his skates for a quick stop, and cover his friend with a blizzard of ice shavings. Other times he and the other boys would race each other to the snow-crusted islands that dotted Finland's coastline. They'd boast that one day they'd race across the sea to Sweden and spend the night in some unsuspecting farmer's hay barn before skating home the next day.

A sigh escaped him as he sat back down at the kitchen table.

He watched Tilda write the list of groceries they needed. She wrote evenly with letters rounded where they should be. And, besides that, she was smart. And she was determined. When she made up her mind to do something, she did it. She'd pass the citizenship test, he was sure.

31

"HELP WANTED"
March 1944

"Thank you, Mrs. Lind," Faith said, wiping the melted butter off her chin with her napkin. "This was the best breakfast ever!"

Angie's friends liked to spend the night at her house because they loved her mom's Swedish hotcakes.

"I'm glad you like them," Mom said. "But, you know, in Finland people don't eat these for breakfast. They eat them for supper. They fold the hotcake over fruit, like berries, and put whipped cream on top. When I was a girl, we were very poor, but we picked wild berries in the woods next to our house. With cream skimmed off the milk from our cow, we had a great supper."

"Berries and whipping cream sound good," Faith said, "but I like the way you did it today. Sprinkling sugar on the hot cake, rolling it up, and dipping it into melted butter! Yum!"

"I don't fix Swedish hotcakes very much now, with both sugar and butter rationed. But I like to make them when Angie has such nice company." Tilda smiled at Faith.

Angie, embarrassed, ducked her head, but Faith went on talking to her mom. Angie started paying attention.

"How long you been working at Safeway?" Mom asked.

"Since I turned sixteen in November," Faith answered. "With all the men employees and some of the women gone to the service, the store was desperate. I work as produce manager and sometimes as cashier. It's really fun and I like earning money. I'm saving up to buy a bicycle."

"I didn't know you didn't have a bike," Angie said. "You went on the Girls' Athletic Club's twenty-five-mile bike ride to Oak Harbor—"

"I borrowed a bike. Wasn't that trip fun? Except I remember your dill pickle leaked in the paper bag that held your lunch. Your nickel for a treat fell through the wet bottom. We looked for it, but it must have dropped through somewhere along the way."

Angie groaned. "I tried not to cry, but I was so hot and tired! We rode ten miles without stopping before we got to the country store. Everyone bought pop or ice cream, except me!"

"I hope I gave you a lick of my ice cream cone. I don't remember."

"I don't remember either. All I remember is drinking water and acting like that was all I wanted."

"Anyway," Faith said, "we met the GAC challenge and rode fifty miles in one day!" She looked at the clock. "I better go. Mom always has things for me to do Saturday mornings, and I work at Safeway this afternoon." She carried her plate and glass to the sink. "Thank you, again."

"Mom, I want a job!" Angie said as soon as the door closed behind Faith.

"You got jobs," her mother said. "You set the table every night at supper, and you dry the dishes and dust the furniture when I ask you to."

"Mom, I mean a real job. I want to earn money and, besides, it's my patriotic duty! In history class, Mr. Smith said there aren't enough people to fill the vacancies left by men and women joining the service. He said child-labor laws have been changed so you can work in manufacturing plants when you're sixteen."

"You're only fifteen," Tilda said.

"Mr. Smith said almost three million teen-agers now work in fields and defense plants—"

"We don't have defense plants in Anacortes, but you've picked strawberries and worked in the bulb fields. You're doing what you can."

"That's summer work. I want to work now—after school and weekends. Most places don't care how old you are as long as you can do the job. Mom, you know Edwin's been working in the print shop at *The Daily Mercury* since he was fourteen!"

"I know, but when do you do your homework when you work after school?"

"Edwin gets his homework done!"

Mom shook her head.

Angie wasn't going to give up. "Joyce saw a sign that said 'Ushers Needed' in the box office window at the Empire Theatre. And Edna said Mr. Hauglund put a 'Help Wanted' sign on the counter in his ice-cream store and she's going to apply."

"Well, Edna should get the job, with the same last name."

"Aw, Mom. It's not the same name. Edna's name doesn't have a 'u' in it, and they're not even pronounced the same."

Her mom hadn't said 'no' about the job. Angie was winning! After all, her mother knew she'd had jobs before.

The first summer they lived in Anacortes, Angie rode her bike down 12th Street almost half way to Alexander Beach delivering newspapers. The next year she worked mopping floors after school at the hospital. Dinner came with the job, so she told her dad she was saving him money, so it would be fair if he paid her fifty cents each day she didn't eat at home. Her dad had laughed at first, but then agreed to the idea, but thought twenty-five cents was enough for the meals she didn't eat. Angie remembered he'd winked at Mama. Sometimes parents were strange.

Anyway, the job didn't last long because the hospital found a woman to do the work. But finding people to fill jobs was even harder now than three years ago. Mr. Smith said a cosmetic factory lost so many employees they had to stop manufacturing artificial eyelashes. Movie stars and models were now making eyelashes out of their own hair! He said he read that in the newspaper!

"If I was eighteen, I'd join the WACs," Angie said as she carried her plate to the kitchen sink. "Mr. Smith said that women by the thousands are doing their bit for their country by going into the service. They take the place of men in offices so the men can go off and fight."

Angie sat back down in the breakfast nook. She rested her elbows on the table, her chin on her hands. "I can't join the WACs because I'm not old enough," she said, "but I can fill the place of someone who's joined the WACs. 'Help Wanted' signs are everywhere. It's my patriotic duty to get a job!"

Angie's first night as usher at the Empire Theatre went very well. She got to wear a badge that said, "USHER," and carry a large flashlight—almost as big as the one her dad carried on Civil Defense duty. The manager showed her how to shine the flashlight on the floor just ahead of the customers as she led them down the aisle of the dark theater. When she came to a row with empty seats, she was to direct the person or persons to their seats by shining the flashlight on the floor of that row. When she was not seating people, she was to stand in the lobby at the head of the aisle and keep the heavy drape closed so no light would enter the theater where the movie was being shown.

It didn't take long for Angie to decide this was a very boring job. Once she seated everyone and the movie started, there was nothing to do. She couldn't draw the curtain aside to peek at the movie because this would allow light into the theater. Her dad didn't like leaving his comfortable chair in the living room at ten o'clock at night to come get her, and he couldn't come at all when he was working swing shift at the mill. Her mom worried about her walking home in the dark, even though it was only eight blocks. The pay was poor and she couldn't see she was relieving anyone for active duty. She gave notice and quit.

Mr. Hauglund had hired Edna to work at his soda fountain, but he still needed one more girl. Angie applied and got the job. She learned how to make sodas and milkshakes and banana splits. She learned she was to pay for her own food or drink and not sneak tastes of ice cream out of the open cartons in the freezer chest. She learned about workers' unions. A stern-looking man in a suit and necktie came into the shop and asked for the owner. Angie called Mr. Hauglund from the back room, and from then on she and Edna weren't expected to mop floors at closing time.

Angie also learned from Mr. Hauglund that many of the things she liked to do were sinful and, if she did them, she'd burn in Hell. Angie began to look forward to summer at the bulb farm where there weren't so many rules and lectures. Perhaps fieldwork would, after all, be her contribution to the war effort.

And volunteering. There was no end of opportunities to volunteer.

In January, the high-school Girls' Club worked on the Infantile Paralysis Drive. Angie and others addressed and mailed hundreds of letters to townspeople, asking them to drop dimes in the envelopes for the March of Dimes. Some of her friends helped their mothers work at tables in the Post Office where people could donate dimes. A line of dimes a foot long, seventeen dimes, cost $1.70. Eagles Auxiliary bought three feet of dimes, but Elks Lodge bought the most. Six feet of dimes! Angie and Edna thought of their friend Joy Kamps and bought a foot of dimes each with money they'd earned at the ice cream parlor.

Then there were the scrap metal drives with special collections for aluminum. Paper drives, rubber drives, and fat and grease drives. More and more glycerin was needed for high explosives. Mom kept a coffee can under the sink where she poured fat and grease from cooking. When it was full, they took it to the local butcher. Kids of all ages collected anything that was needed by the armed services.

Book publishers began putting out small, soft-cover books they called paperbacks because they used less paper and were cheaper to produce and ship to soldiers overseas. Angie and her friends had gone door-to-door asking for used magazines and paperbacks for USO Centers in Anacortes and Oak Harbor.

Angie was part of a committee of high-school kids who helped with the Fourth Annual War-Loan Drive by distributing information to the two elementary schools, the junior high, and the high school. During the January drive, students in the four schools bought a total of $1,823.80 in war bonds and stamps. Whitney Grade bought $519.60 worth, beating Nelson Grade by $300.00. The junior high beat all the schools by buying $881.05.

Angie was disappointed that the senior high bought only $212.60 worth, but next year the committee would work harder to get donations from classmates. Next year? Were they assuming that the war would still be going on next year? Had war become a way of life?

Angie lost interest in "Help Wanted" signs. Volunteer work felt more important and she met kids other than those in her own grade, like Frances Maricich. Frances was a year younger than Angie. She was the oldest daughter in a big family and had to work a lot at home, but she found time to help collect stuff for the war effort. Her parents were immigrants, too, only from Croatia. Angie's family was part of a community of Scandinavians who were in the plywood business; Frances's family was part of a close-knit fishing community made up mostly of Slavonians. Frances even belonged to a Yugoslavian youth club.

Something else that Angie and Frances had in common was Miss Green's home economic's project. Frances had painted her bedroom and the bathroom with Kemtone, and all the woodwork in both rooms with enamel. Then she sewed curtains for the windows and skirts for her dressing table and chair. Like Angie, she got an "A+" for her project—

"Angie," Mom called from the front room, "would you come here, please?"

Oh, oh! Angie thought, getting up from the breakfast table. I was supposed to dust the furniture this morning.

"I'm studying the Constitution," her mother said, "and I need help. The textbook has study questions and answers. Could you see if I know the answers?"

Her mom hadn't checked the furniture! Better than that, she wanted help in getting her citizenship papers. This was important. Like volunteer work. The kind of work Angie liked best.

32

THE TEST
May 1944

Tilda took first one dress out of the closet, then another. The first one was too flowery. The second one, too bright. A third was navy blue, a good color for a formal ceremony, but it was too plain.

"Charlie," she called, "I don't have the right dress to wear to the naturalization hearing!"

"How do you know what's the right dress?" Charlie asked, walking into the bedroom. "Have you been to lots of these hearings?"

Tilda looked at him to see if he was joking. She saw crinkles at the corners of his eyes and his mouth twitched. She knew him so well. He was proud of her and showed it best by teasing her.

"I think I go shopping," she said.

Angie went with her. "Over here, Mom," she said. "Here where it says 'Better Apparel.'"

Tilda shopped often in Penney's for nightclothes and underclothes—slips and bloomers, stockings when she could get them—but she'd never shopped in "Better Apparel."

"Are you about a size eight?" a pretty young woman asked.

"I think so," Tilda answered. It had been so long since she'd bought a good dress, she wasn't sure.

The girl pulled one dress after another off the rack.

"Too flowery."

"Too bright."

"Too plain."

Tilda saw one she liked and looked at the price. "Too expensive!"

"Mom, you're never going to find anything!" Angie exclaimed.

Tilda thanked the young lady and turned to leave, but, as she started for the door, the sign "Accessories" caught her eye. "You can look around, Angie. I'll be ready to go in a minute."

It took Tilda five minutes, but she found what she wanted and gave the clerk behind the counter a $5 bill. The clerk made out a sales slip and put it and the $5 bill into the small can hanging from a wire above her head, snapped the receptacle shut, and pulled the cord. Tilda watched the metal can zip up the wire that connected to a desk in the balcony. In a few moments the girl on the balcony made change and sent the can sliding back down the wire. The clerk gave Tilda the sales slip, four $1 bills, and some coins in change.

"Let's go, Angie. I'm through shopping."

Tilda leaned across the top of her bureau and examined her face in the mirror. She'd hardly slept and knew she'd find dark shadows under her eyes. Her stomach was in knots. She was lucky she didn't wake up with one of her migraine headaches. Today was the day Charlie would be driving her to Mount Vernon for her naturalization test.

Three weeks ago when classes ended, the teacher had instructed them to fill out a Petition for Naturalization and send the form to the Immigration and Naturalization Service in Mount Vernon. The teacher reminded his ten students that in order to petition, they must have lived in the United States for five years and be of good moral character. A person must not be a drunkard or have committed adultery or be a bigamist, or make his living by gambling or been in jail more than 180 days for any reason or be a convicted murderer. The teacher smiled then and said he thought everyone in class could, with a clear conscience, fill out the petition.

Tilda took her round box of face powder out of the top bureau drawer and dusted her face with the pink powder puff. She put on a little extra rouge and a touch of lipstick because she could see she was pale. She removed her curlers and brushed her hair back carefully, combing the front curls around her finger and bobby-pinning them in place. She sat down on the bed and pulled on her stockings. The young girls painted their legs, but her mended cotton stockings would have to do. She had just slipped her navy blue dress over her head and zipped it up the back when Angie walked into the bedroom.

"Mom, you look great! You bought a new dress after all."

"The only part of the dress that's new is the white collar, but thank you anyway. I bought this lace-piece the day we shopped at Penney's. It's made to fasten at the neckline to decorate the front of a dress. I'm glad you think it looks good."

"Are you still getting ready?" Charlie hollered from the kitchen. "Do you want to be late?"

"I'm late enough, getting my citizenship papers," Tilda called back. "Angie, get your coat. Let's go."

The imposing front of the courthouse spoke of the dignity of the law. Four tall pillars supported the roof of the entry. Across the façade above the pillars, carved into the granite, were the words, "Skagit Covnty Covrt Hovse." Tilda wondered about the spelling.

Four wide, granite steps, a landing, then four more steps led to the dark-stained, oversized, double doors. Tilda was glad Charlie was there to open the heavy door for her and Angie. Dark walnut paneling in the entrance added to the solemnity of the occasion. The open stairway to the second floor was the same dark wood. When they reached the top of the stairs, another set of double doors to their left opened onto a chamber where the ceremony would take place. Tilda took a seat on the bench at the front of the room next to her classmates. Charlie and Angie sat behind them. The spectator benches were nearly full.

Tilda had never been in a courtroom, but it was like she imagined. The judge's seat and desk in the front of the room was slightly raised. Next to his desk was the witness chair, and on the adjoining wall, behind a low barrier, the twelve chairs of the jury box. Tilda wondered why they called it a "box," but it didn't matter what they called it. She was glad she hadn't broken the law and had to face a jury today. Facing the official examiners was bad enough.

Suddenly the judge, gowned in black, walked into the room. Everyone stood until he sat down. An official announced that Judge W. L. Brickey from Bellingham would preside over the Naturalization

Hearing. Howard Caton, also from Bellingham, would be the examining officer.

Tilda recognized the names. These were the same two officials who'd questioned the group applying for papers in January. Twenty-seven people from Skagit County had gotten their citizenship papers that day, but six would have to come before the judge a second time, according to the newspaper.

Seventeen people from the county were applying for citizenship today, with eight of them from Anacortes. Tilda was sitting next to Tillie Frantz. In class, Tillie had always found something to tee-hee about. She hadn't worried as much as Tilda about passing the test, but today she looked as nervous as everyone else.

The last time Tilda had felt this nervous was when she and Ida were immigrant girls standing in line in the huge, domed building on Ellis Island with hundreds of other immigrants. Everyone hoped their papers were in order, and that they could pass a physical examination. If they didn't pass these tests, they would be sent back to the country they came from.

Suddenly the immigration officer had pulled Tilda out of the line and taken her and Ida, who'd insisted on coming along, to a small room with only a high window for light. The officer explained to them why they were being isolated, but the girls didn't understand English. All they knew was that they had failed some part of the immigration test.

After what seemed like hours, a doctor came into the room, examined Tilda's face up close with a bright light, nodded, and left, closing the door behind him. Finally a young woman came in and spoke to them in Swedish. The officer thought Tilda might have smallpox, the woman explained, but the doctor recognized it was just a bad case of acne, and they were admitted to this country.

Now, thirty-two years later, she was again being tested—but for another kind of admission. One just as important!

"Mrs. Lind," Mr. Caton, the examining officer, said. "We will begin the questioning with you." His voice was stern.

Tilda stood up. Her teacher had said she was expected to do this when addressed by the court. She clutched her handkerchief.

"Mrs. Lind, in your own words, what does the First Amendment to the Constitution require of Congress?"

"The First Amendment requires Congress to guarantee freedom of religion, freedom of speech, and freedom of the press," Tilda answered. Her voice came out surprisingly strong. "It guarantees a citizen's right to assemble peacefully and to petition the government for help if they have a serious complaint."

"Thank you," Mr. Caton said. "You memorized that very well," he added with a little smile. Tilda sat down and patted her neck with her knotted-up handkerchief.

The examining officer, continuing down the row of applicants, asked each person a question about the history of the United States or about the Constitution. Then he started down the row again. Tilda and her classmates were all able to answer their questions. No one stumbled. Finally as a group, the class was asked if they intended to reside permanently in the United States, if they would renounce loyalty to any other country and pledge loyalty to the United States, and if they would uphold the laws of the land. Then Mr. Caton addressed each of them individually. Tilda knees felt weak when it was her turn to stand.

> On this tenth day of May in the year of our Lord, nineteen hundred and forty-four, and of our Independence the one hundred and sixty-eighth, you, Vendla Matilda Lind, are now a naturalized citizen of the United States.

Mr. Caton then spoke to the group. "Arthur Eliason, Clerk of the Superior Court, has filled out your Certificate of Naturalization according to the information you gave him in your petition. Now Deputy Clerk Samuel Wilhite will sign your certificates and give them to you."

Then Mr. Caton smiled broadly. "I've been asked to announce that the Kiwanis Club of Mount Vernon and the high-school civics class are honoring you at a reception at the Mount Vernon high-school cafeteria May 17 at 8 p.m. They hope you will all attend."

During the hand-shaking and congratulating, Tilda dabbed at her eyes. She told Charlie her eyes were watering because of the flowers

in the front of the room. Her allergy, you know. Charlie said they'd
have dinner at Amsberry's Café when they got back to Anacortes.

Tilda noted Charlie was quiet on the drive back. "You're thinking about the letter from your brother that came yesterday, aren't
you?" Tilda asked.

Charlie nodded. Vilhelm wrote that Finland wanted to separate
themselves from Germany, as Germany seemed to be losing the war.
This would be hard to do because there were so many German troops
in Finland, especially Lapland. Also, since Finland had regained and
reoccupied the Karelian Isthmus to its 1939 borders, it was ready to
get out of the war entirely.

Finland decided that the only way to keep its freedom and independence was to petition the Soviet Union for peace. They presented
the Russians with a carefully written policy of "good neighborliness." Vilhelm said that in March, Paasikivi, former Finnish Minister to Moscow, was called out of retirement to start negotiations with
Russia that would allow Finland to withdraw from the war.

But negotiations went badly. Moscow's terms in response to
Finland's petition for peace were that Finland expel or intern all
those in the German army by April and that they pay a war indemnity
of $600 million. Finland's new government under Prime Minister
Linkomies said these terms were unacceptable. Vilhelm wrote he
didn't know what was going to happen next.

Then Vilhelm told about his seventeen-year-old boy Manne. He
was wounded during military practice when the water-cooling sleeve
on a machine gun exploded. The skin on his face and eyelids was
shredded and hanging, covered with blood. Manne was sent home
where doctors treated his eyes. They were afraid for his eyesight,
but, in spite of the seriousness of the wound, his eyesight was spared.
He would be scarred, however, for the rest of his life. When his face
was healed, the army sent him back to active duty.

Vilhelm had gotten a letter from Manne a few weeks after he
returned to duty. Manne said that while on a military train, he ran
into his brother Mauritz. They were happy to see each other, but,
while they were talking, bombs started to fall. Many soldiers were
killed, but they were lucky. When the train reached its destination,

the boys parted for their separate assignments. Vilhelm hadn't heard from them since, nor had he heard from his eldest son Alarik. He didn't know where he was fighting.

The letter ended saying Hulda and the girls were well and he hoped the same for Charlie and his family.

"Tilda, can you understand why I'm not ready to give up my Finnish citizenship—to turn my back on my own country?"

"I understand," Tilda said. She guessed she really did understand. "Maybe things will improve for Finland. Maybe next year you'll be ready to become an American citizen." She patted his knee. "And then we can go to Amsberry's Café for a second celebration. I always like to eat out, you know."

33

CABBAGES AND CAULIFLOWER
August 1944

"Mom, do you know what the kids at the bulb farm are saying?" Angie asked as she came in the back door. Fine, brown dust coated her hair and dirt streaked her nose and cheeks.

"No, how would I know that?" Tilda asked, picking three potatoes out of a bag and dropping them into the sink. She smiled at her daughter, though it was hard to see her behind all the dirt. Another summer of crawling along the ditch in the heat picking tulip bulbs! It would be nice if she had a different job.

"I'll tell you what they're saying! They're saying, 'The Russians are rushin'; the Finnish are finished.' That's not true, is it?"

Tilda hesitated. She prayed it wasn't true, but the news looked bad. Russia wouldn't accept Finland's "Policy of Neighborliness" unless Finland met certain demands. The Finnish government considered the demands unreasonable. In June, Russia began another offensive along the Karelian front.

Mannerheim, in charge of the Finnish army, told President Ryti that his troops would not be able to hold out against the Red army. On June 25, Hitler's Foreign Minister Ribbentrop went to Helsinki and told Ryti that, if Finland would not agree to a separate peace with Russia, Germany would continue its military aid and supply the starving Finns with grain and other food staples. President Ryti signed the agreement with Germany.

"It's true that the Russians invaded again," Tilda told Angie, "but it's not true that the Finnish are finished. They don't give in if they can help it."

Angie started for the bathroom to clean up, but then stopped. "Art's in the navy now, isn't he?" she asked.

"*Ja*, you remember, he's at Annapolis Naval Academy in Maryland. He'll be ready for active duty before long." Tilda knew what Angie's next question would be, so she answered it before Angie could ask. "And Bennie is still in the South Pacific. Telma gets letters from him, and so do you, so we know he's all right."

"All Bennie writes about lately is the heat and insects and army food and how he wishes this war was over. And he asks if we've seen Linda lately and what she's doing now."

"He can't write about other things. Telma said he's one of the censors and has to be responsible."

Angie disappeared into the bathroom. Tilda began peeling potatoes for supper. *Ja*, she reflected, Bennie wanted to know about Linda. She was only six months old when he left and she'd be three in September. Bennie didn't hear her first words or see her learn to walk, and now she was talking a blue streak and running everywhere. She could count to ten and sing, "Jesus Loves Me." Bennie was missing it all.

Tilda thought of all the young mothers whose husbands were away because of the war. Most of these women had gone to work, many in defense plants and factories where they sometimes worked seven days a week. The government started day-care centers for the children, but how could that take the place of parents? No dads and only part-time moms! Telma was lucky Bennie's mother lived nearby so she didn't have to leave Linda all day in some kind of center. Tilda knew Telma was lonely, but, with gas rationing, they couldn't drive to Shelton often enough to help.

Another problem. Tilda had read that because of the war there was a rise in divorces. Families were unsettled. Husbands were gone too long and wives were lonely. Young sailors and soldiers were separated from their families and lonely, too, looking for companionship.

Ja, and then there was a rise in marriages. Young men and women about to be separated by the war hurried to find a preacher. Viola, a thirteen-year-old friend of Angie's, eloped with a sailor. Laura Elliot, another friend of Angie's, the one who gave her the pink sweater, married a sailor from the Whidbey Island base. Maybe those two girls knew what they were doing and their marriages would work, but it seemed to Tilda they were awful young.

Young girls were growing up too fast. Many teenage girls were out looking for a good time. Tilda could see it when she went to town. Right in Anacortes on Commercial Avenue, young girls, some younger than Angie, were walking the street wearing bright red lipstick, high heels, and extra-short skirts. They were hoping to meet a sailor, and usually did.

Tilda thought of the young boys in high school. They, too, were being forced to grow up fast. Most of the boys who graduated from Anacortes High School in May joined the service, and the rest said they planned to do the same by the end of summer.

The war had turned the whole world upside down. Germany had taken over France. On June 6, D Day, the Allies came to France's aid by attacking the Germans at Normandy. Planes dropped paratroopers in the night, and American and English warships unloaded men onto the shore. At Omaha Beach, the German army was ready for them.

Thousands of American boys were shot or drowned in the rough ocean that day before reaching the shore. Tilda read that the water ran red with blood. Many who made it to land were shot as they ran up the beach. Thousands of fathers, sons, and husbands died that day. Those who lived to cross the beach drove the Germans back, but the fighting went on in the cities and countryside.

In the South Pacific, American boys were also landing on beaches. They were fighting to take back islands captured by the Japanese. Tilda read that Marines who made it ashore through gunfire on the beaches of Guam and Saipan, had to go on and fight the enemy hand-to-hand in the jungles. According to the newspaper, this battle wasn't over either.

At the first of the year, Tilda had begun cutting articles out of the *American* about those in the service, even if she didn't know them. It was her way of honoring them for the sacrifices they were making. One article said that an Anacortes woman, Mrs. W. L. Barber, had three sons and a daughter in the service. The daughter was a SPUR in the Coast Guard. Nels Nystrom's third son Cecil joined his two brothers in the army. Mrs. Mae Campano had four army sons—one stationed in England, two prisoners of war in Japan, and the fourth son, just drafted. Tilda wondered if these parents dared to read the newspaper. It seemed that every week the *American* reported the capture, missing in action, or death of another local boy.

At the first of the year, Delbert Harris, 19, was killed in a plane crash in Florida, and Silas Adams was reported missing in action in Europe. Both were Anacortes boys. A twenty-five-year-old Marine, Walter Sullivan of Friday Harbor, was killed in the Gilbert Islands.

In February a headline read, "Whidbey Flyers' Plane Lost." The bomber was missing in the North Pacific and pilot, co-pilot, and large crew were lost and presumed dead. This spring, two young men, also from the Whidbey Island Naval Air Station, were killed in a plane crash in Puget Sound. In another accident, Floyd Woody, an Anacortes boy, and two others were killed in the crash of a navy bomber at the base.

Tilda leafed through a different set of articles she'd clipped together. On January 20, "Sergeant Jim Turner Makes Heroic Rescue." The young man rescued a pilot who crashed in the sea at New Hebrides. In the same issue of the *American*, "Local Man Survives Sinking." Kenneth Powers of the U.S. Navy had been reported missing. He was on the destroyer *Perkins,* which was rammed and sunk. Tilda knew she'd probably missed some articles in the newspaper about war deaths and near deaths, but she'd tried—

Charlie swung open the back door! "I been weeding and watering the potato plants," he said, sitting down on the nearest chair. "We have a good crop again this year. If the government rations potatoes, it won't be a problem for us."

Tilda put the clippings down and smiled at her husband. He looked a little like Angie did when she came home from the bulb farm. Sweat lines and dirt on his nose up to his hairline.

"I think next year I plant part of the parking strip in vegetables," he said, removing his shoes. "We'll have a regular Victory Garden. Did you know that twenty-million people in this country have planted victory gardens? See, Tilda, I read the newspapers, too," he said, nodding at Tilda's collection of articles on the table."

"Okay," Angie said. She'd put on clean clothes and poured herself a glass of milk. "We'll plant a Victory Garden. Just don't plant cabbage or cauliflower. No victory is worth that!"

Charlie laughed, but Tilda shook her head. She had been so embedded in war news that Angie's comment seemed wrong. Had war become so common that she could joke about it? Tilda started to say something but caught herself. Charlie and Angie had no way of knowing how gloomy her thoughts had been during the past hour. How worried she was about what was happening to their world.

"Mom, can you guess what I want for my sixteenth birthday?"

"No, Angie. I couldn't guess."

"My driver's license! Mr. Lefeber, my boss at the bulb farm, said as soon as I get my driver's license, he wants me to drive the Anacortes kids to and from work in their farm truck. Won't that be great! Twenty or more kids riding in the open truck, and me at the wheel cruising down the highway. He asked if I had a place to park the truck at night. I said sure. In our backyard. So, it's all set. You know I take my driver's test tomorrow."

Oh no, Tilda thought. Now that's something more to worry about!

Tilda hoarded enough sugar from their monthly ration to bake Angie a chocolate cake for her birthday. She whipped cream for frosting and didn't add any sugar. She was looking in the cupboard for candles when Angie burst in the back door.

"I passed the driver's test!" Angie shouted. "The man who tested me said my dad was a good teacher."

"Well, I guess you were a good learner," Tilda said. "Your dad tried to learn me to drive when we lived in Potlatch, but the car just hopped and jumped every time I let out the clutch. Finally he gave up on me."

"Maybe he should try again. Heck, I learned to double-clutch the farm truck."

"When did you do that?"

"Last week. Mr. Lefeber had me drive around on the farm so I'd be familiar with the truck and ready to drive the kids. That is, when I get back from church camp."

Tilda shook her head. She wasn't happy about Angie driving the kids on the busy highway. Angie had explained that Mr. Lefeber was desperate, that he couldn't spare another person to do this driving. Most of the men and women who worked for him in the summer had either joined the service or left for a better job at the air base. The men who didn't leave were needed for heavy jobs on the farm. The woman who stayed to work didn't know how to drive.

"Where's your dad?" Tilda asked. "Did you leave him at the Motor Vehicles office?"

Angie laughed. "No, he had me park the car in the backyard. He's getting ready to wash it. I think Dad wants it to look good when I drive it."

"Daddy always takes good care of the car, whether you're driving it or not!"

Tilda felt cross. Maybe she was just upset about Angie driving the farm truck.

"I have to finish packing for Seabeck," Angie said. She started for her room, but then stopped. "Baptist church camp will be fun, but I hate being gone a whole week when I could be driving—picking up friends and zipping around Anacortes."

"Angie, there'll be no zipping around. Did you forget about gas rationing? You'll drive only when you have to."

"Well, then I'm glad I have to drive the truck for Mr. Lefeber!"

Tilda shook her head again. She found herself doing that a lot lately.

The week went fast. Before Tilda knew it, Angie was home from Seabeck.

"So how was church camp?" Charlie asked when they sat down for supper.

"It was really swell! We ate lots of food and met new kids from all around the state and talked all night with our roommates. Lois Persons was my roommate. She lives in Everett and is going to come visit me sometime."

"That'll be nice," Tilda said. "What else did you do in camp?"

"We studied the Bible and sang songs around a campfire and prayed and talked about what we want to be when we grow up."

"And what did you say?" Charlie asked. "That you want to be a truck driver?"

"No! I said I want to be a Baptist missionary."

Tilda set down her fork.

Charlie said, "I guess you'll go to Finland to save the Lutherans."

"No, Dad!" Angie said, "but maybe I should. Lutherans do a lot of things wrong. When they baptize someone, they just sprinkle a little water on the head. Baptist preachers don't just sprinkle. They dunk the whole person clear under the water. That way they're sure their sins are washed away.

"And you know what else? Mr. Hauglund was right about sin. It's everywhere. I'm not going to go to movies anymore or dance or wear lipstick."

Tilda looked at Charlie. He was concentrating hard on stirring the gravy into his mashed potatoes.

"So where do you plan to go as a missionary?" Charlie asked.

"Africa," Angie declared. "I'm going to darkest Africa to convert the heathen."

Charlie quit stirring his mashed potatoes and looked up at Angie. "Africans baptize people, too, you know. They baptize missionaries in big, black kettles of boiling water."

"Charlie! That's silly talk!" Tilda scolded, and then turned to Angie. "Maybe you shouldn't make up your mind just yet—"

"Oh, I've made up my mind!" Angie interrupted. "It's the mission field for me!"

Monday morning at 6 a.m., a farm truck drove up on the back lawn. Angie left her unfinished bowl of cornflakes, grabbed her lunch bucket, and ran for the truck. The driver moved over and Angie stepped onto the running board and climbed into the driver's seat. The gears growled as Angie shifted into reverse and backed into the alley. They ground again as she prepared to move ahead. Then the truck hopped once, belched out a cloud of blue exhaust, and took off down the alley to K Avenue. Tilda watched from the kitchen window as the truck made a tight turn onto Ninth Street toward town. The kids would be waiting at corners along Commercial Avenue.

"Don't think she quite got the hang of double clutching," Charlie said as he came into the house.

"Looks like she had trouble seeing out the windshield," Tilda said.

"The driver said the front seat was broken down, so they piled pillows on the seat so Angie could see."

"She looks so small in that big truck."

"She'll do fine."

"Maybe so, but I'll be glad to see the end of summer and the start of a new school year," Tilda said.

34

ROLLER COASTER
September 1944

School began fall semester two days after Labor Day. Angie searched the packed halls for a glimpse of Johnny but didn't see him. She hadn't seen him all summer. She wondered if he'd remember who she was. She'd soon find out. Band class was next. Angie wove her way through the maze of students and hurried toward the band room.

Edwin was already there with his slide trombone on his lap. Joyce came in with her clarinet and sat down beside Angie. She licked the reed and fixed it in place. Angie did the same with her clarinet reed. The seats in the room were filling up. Angie checked the brass section. Johnny wasn't there yet.

Angie was glad school had started. It was good to see friends. And good to be through driving the truck! She hadn't had any problems, but she felt the pressure of the responsibility. Work itself had been easier. She and Joyce were promoted to the sorting table. They worked out of the sun in an open-sided shed where any breeze could reach them. They stood by a moving belt and watched for bulbs of certain quality and size to put into boxes. For this they were paid fifty cents an hour, much more than they made in the field doing piecework. Still she was glad the season was over.

"Hey, Joyce," Edwin said, tapping Joyce on the shoulder. "Understand you're called 'Hot Lips!' now. Where'd you get that name?"

Joyce's face turned red. "You know where that came from. It's because I play the clarinet!" When Edwin and other kids laughed, Joyce laughed, too. It was good to be back with friends.

Over the sounds of students warming up their instruments and turning around in squeaky chairs to talk with friends, Mr. Lunsford, the new band teacher, introduced himself. No one heard him. Then he tapped his baton on his music stand and asked for their full attention.

"Class," he said, "the band has been asked to prepare music for a memorial assembly three weeks from now, so we have no time to waste. The assembly will honor an Anacortes boy killed in action this past summer."

This time the chair scraping, drum tapping, and talking stopped.

"We'll practice 'The Star Spangled Banner,' which you probably already know," Mr. Lunsford said. "We'll learn two new patriotic numbers for the assembly." He took a drink of water from a glass on his desk before continuing. "One of our 1943 graduates was killed June 6, during the D Day invasion of Normandy. I understand he was a very well-liked young man and a popular cheerleader. You knew him as 'Bucko.' He will be remembered."

Angie didn't know Bucko, but Faith's sister Margie was part of the same cheerleading team, so Angie knew who he was.

Mr. Lunsford went on. "We are told that Bucko crossed Omaha Beach safely, but then went back to aid a wounded buddy and was shot before he could get his friend to safety."

No one spoke. Mr. Lunsford went to his desk and picked up a stack of music and began handing it out. Angie noticed that Johnny had slipped in the side door and taken his seat in time to hear Mr. Lunsford's announcement. Johnny would have known Bucko because the guys all knew each other. She guessed she wouldn't try to catch Johnny's eye today.

Faith was waiting outside the band room door for her and Joyce. They hurried toward the library for study hall.

"We're practicing for the memorial assembly," Angie told Faith. "Did you know Bucko?"

"Everyone knew Bucko! Margie was very upset when she heard the news. Seems like the war has everyone on a roller coaster. Bad news, good news, bad news, good news. . ."

"That was certainly bad news. What's the good news?" Angie asked.

"You know. Two weeks ago, Margie announced to the family that she and Joel Prenselaar were engaged. We're happy because we like Joel. They're getting married on September 10."

"I didn't even know she was going with anyone," Angie said. "I've seen him in church and knew he sometimes went to your house for dinner—"

"Two weeks is a short engagement," Joyce said.

"That's because of the war. He's scheduled to ship out two days after the wedding."

The girls reached the library and found an empty table near the window where they could sit together. They'd have to whisper now. Mrs. Webb was very strict. She thought study hall was for study. Angie preferred to visit with her friends while at school and do homework at home. Besides, if she finished her assignments at school, her mom would ask her why she didn't have any homework. Life was complicated.

"Bucko was bad news," Angie said. "Margie was good news. Next, more bad news? I mean besides the war going on and on."

Faith doodled on the cover of her notebook. "Did you see the Russian ship that docked here a few days ago?" she asked.

Joyce and Angie nodded.

"Some sailors came into Safeway when I was working in the produce department. They bought fruit and some vegetables like carrots that they could eat right then. One of the sailors spoke a little English and asked me where he could find a shoe store. He had three children at home and, because of the war, it was impossible to buy shoes. He said his wife got along all right wearing the same pair, but the children outgrew their shoes, and, without shoes, they couldn't go to school. He told me he'd saved a little money and, now that he was in America, he would buy them each a pair." Faith said his face lit up when he said that.

"I told him he could buy children's shoes at Penney's and gave him directions, but then I remembered to tell him that shoes were rationed. He couldn't buy shoes without a shoe coupon."

Mrs. Webb walked over to their table. Like most librarians, she had sharp ears and heard them whispering. Angie opened one of her books and Joyce did the same. Faith opened her notebook and took out some paper. "That was 'bad news,'" she wrote across the top of a sheet of paper. She passed it to Angie and Angie passed it along to Joyce.

When Mrs. Webb returned to her desk, Faith leaned across the table and whispered, "But there's good news!"

Angie and Joyce pushed their books aside.

"I told him to come back to the produce section the next day. I thought maybe I could bring him some of Bobby's outgrown shoes or something. When I told Mom, she went to the kitchen drawer and tore three ration stamps, her year's shoe allotment, out of her ration book and said that if the young man came back, to give him the stamps."

"Did he come back?" Joyce asked.

"He did. I gave him the stamps and he thanked me and said to thank my mother. Then he ran out of the store down the street to Penney's."

"Good-news story!" Joyce said aloud.

Mrs. Webb held a finger to her lips and scowled.

"One problem," Angie said. "If this war has us on a roller coaster, and we've had bad news, good news, bad news, good news...." She hesitated, not sure if she should go on. But she did. "Then bad news is next!"

35

EVEN SEAGULLS CRY
October 1944

D ays were getting shorter in October. Dusk and the gloom of a heavy fog closed in around Angie as she left the high school and started down K Avenue. She didn't really like walking home alone, but Faith wasn't at the Red Cross meeting and the rest of the kids all lived in other directions. She turned up the collar on her wool coat and fastened the top button. She shifted her notebook and history book to her right arm so she could warm her left hand in her pocket. She hoped the foggy, moisture-laden air wouldn't creep into her notebook and crinkle the pages of her nearly completed history project.

Rain would be better than this, she thought. Rain comes straight down and you can protect yourself with an umbrella. Fog circles around you and sneaks up your sleeves and down your collar—and between pages of a book. But it's okay. When you live in a town with water all around, you can expect a little fog.

She'd told her mom she might be late. She was helping her friends in the Junior Red Cross Club finish their project for servicemen overseas, and the work took longer than they expected. All summer the kids in the club had been cutting cartoons and puzzles out of magazines and newspapers. When school started, they made scrapbooks out of butcher paper and bound the pages together with yarn. Today she helped paste in the clippings. Before they left school, they placed textbooks on top of each scrapbook so the pages would dry flat. All that took time. Now she worried that her parents were worried about her.

Angie quickened her step. Her house was only fifteen blocks from the high school, but it seemed farther in the fog. The familiar walk had become unfamiliar. The strange, phantom figures of light poles and street signs ducked in and out of the fog on either side of her. Headlights of cars shone out of the mist with watery, unblinking eyes. In the distance she heard seagulls calling to each other, like ships lost in the fog.

Angie shuddered. The cold, the distortion of headlights, the spectral posts on street corners, all made her uneasy. Or was it something else? A premonition? Was something wrong at home? She hugged her books to her chest with both arms and ran the last three blocks.

"Mom, I'm home," she called as she entered the kitchen and dropped her books on the counter.

"I was starting to worry," her mom said. "You're so late. The table is set and I've had to keep our supper warm in the oven."

"I'm sorry," Angie said, "but we wanted to finish the scrapbooks...."

Her mom wasn't listening. Her dad was sitting at the kitchen table. He hadn't turned to greet her or to scold her for being late. He sat with his back to her, his head down. Once before, when they first moved to Anacortes, he had sat like that when she came from school. Then it was the fear that the mill wouldn't make it, that they would lose their investment and future security.

"Mom, what's wrong?" Angie asked.

"Daddy got a letter today from his brother Vilhelm."

Angie stared at her dad's back. He always stood or sat straight and tall, like he was in charge, like he could handle anything. He made Angie feel safe when he walked into a room. Even if he had reason to scold her, she never minded too much because she knew he was right and that he loved her and Mom. Angie saw his head drop further and his shoulders sag. Was this the bad news that was next on the "roller coaster"?

"Mom," she whispered. "Is Daddy crying?"

Tilda pulled Angie to her and watched with her. The sound of distant seagulls intruded briefly on the quiet moment.

"I don't know if Daddy's crying," Mama whispered, "but if he is, it's okay. You know, Angie, even seagulls cry."

The Tacoma News Tribune, along with other major newspapers, covered the war in the South Pacific and in Europe and regularly updated its readership on the continuing war between Russia and Finland, but Charlie got more specific news about Finland from the Swedish newspaper *Ledstjärnan*, the *Evening Star*.

Finland's President Ryti resigned August 1 and, with his resignation, the agreement to accept Germany's help against Russia also expired. On August 4, Marshall Mannerheim was elected President and ordered peace negotiations with Russia. Finland broke off diplomatic relations with Germany on September 4. The next day, Russia and Finland agreed to an armistice. On September 18, the agreement was signed between the two countries. One of Finland's concessions for peace was to give up the Karelian Isthmus by withdrawing all its troops to the lines established by Russia in 1940 at the end of the Winter War. For a second time, the residents of Karelia would become refugees.

Dad handed the letter to Mom and she translated it for Angie.

The refugees arrived in Molpe on a Sunday morning, Vilhelm wrote. Nearly two-hundred weary people, mostly women and children, climbed out of trucks and wagons. As was the custom, young girls rode in the wagons with the cows, but now led them on tethers into the village. Others guided the horses. Still others herded the sheep and pigs. When the homeless people saw that villagers had gathered to meet them, they rushed forward.

The refugees spoke excitedly to us, Vilhelm said, but when they found we couldn't understand Finnish, their excitement faded. One of the refugee women dropped to the ground and cried in despair. It's like you remember, Charlie, Vilhelm wrote, only a very few people in our part of Finland speak Finnish. But then Vilhelm's neighbor, Helge Mannfors, the sightless man who learned Finnish at the blind school, stepped forward and offered to help us communicate.

The refugee who cried told Helge the Finnish government had promised the evacuees they would still live in Finland. The people didn't know there were Swedish-speaking people in their country, so they thought they had been taken to Sweden. They were relieved to hear they were still in their native land.

The refugees huddled in silent groups in front of our village people. Children of the refugees peeked around their mothers' skirts and stared at us. Then an old man leaning on a crutch limped forward and told of their journey, which Helge again translated into Swedish.

They and their livestock were packed into rail cars and rode the train for several days. When they reached Vasa, they were loaded into trucks for the three-hour drive to Molpe. Their personal belongings and household utensils were coming by coast-steamer from Vasa to the harbor in Molpe, and, from there, their goods would be brought to them by horse and carriage. In the meantime, they had only the clothes on their backs and a bit of food left in their knapsacks.

During the Winter War, most Karelians had left their homes voluntarily because they didn't want to live under Russian rule. Then, they had at least a few days to get ready. When Finland reclaimed the isthmus in the winter of 1941, the refugees returned to their land and rebuilt their homes and barns, and replanted their fields. But this time when Russia took over the Karelian Isthmus, the refugee woman told them, they were given two hours to pack. Now they were again homeless with little hope of returning to their land.

"We are only a small part of the number of people expelled from Karelia," the old man continued. "We have heard that this time ten per cent of the Finnish population, 422,000 people, are displaced, most of them for the second time."

In the evening, Vilhelm said, the community folk took the refugees to the village hall where they could warm themselves in front of the fireplaces. The teacher in the village had a list of who was coming, so a committee checked off their names as they entered the hall and assigned as many as possible to hosts. Another committee served the refugees a meal of potatoes and herring in white sauce. Then those who had been assigned hosts went home with them. One of the villagers covered the floor of the hall with long-straw where the remaining refugees could sleep the first night.

What do we do now? Vilhelm asked Charlie at the end of his letter. Molpe, a small village of 765 people! And then he answered his own question. You know what we do. We make room. We bring them under our roofs or offer them places to sleep in our barns or *lillstugon* or *framstugon* if we have no beds in our house to spare. We add water to the soup and bake extra loaves of bread when we have flour. We cry with the women who have lost their men and we comfort the fatherless children. Then we cry again when we tell them of the husbands and fathers we have lost from this village. And together we curse war and a world that can be so cruel.

Mom refolded the letter and slid it back into its envelope. Dad turned from the table and saw Mom and her standing in the middle of the kitchen, the two of them watching him.

"Don't stand there like you was frozen," Dad said. "I guess we're not having any dinner tonight," he added, wanting to shake the gloom with the teasing game he played.

Mom turned to the oven, grabbed two hot pads and carried the beef and potato platter and the vegetable bowl to the table. Angie dropped her coat on the floor and turned to the refrigerator for milk to fill their glasses. In a minute they joined him at the table. Neither Tilda nor Angie spoke.

"Cat got your tongues?" Dad asked, trying to break the heavy silence.

"It's good Vilhelm wasn't taken into the army," Mom finally said. "He was needed in the village."

"*Ja*, Vilhelm was too old—forty-two when the Winter War started. But he did important work. From his seal hunting, he helped supply both the army and the village with seal meat, seal skin for shoes, and seal oil for water-proofing the shoes—"

"Are there seagulls in Finland?" Angie interrupted.

Her dad looked at her across the supper table. "*Ja*, there are seagulls in Finland," he said.

"Do they cry a lot?"

He looked puzzled at Angie's question. Her mom answered it. "*Ja*, Angie, I think they must cry an awful lot."

36

JUNIOR MIXER
November 1944

"**H**ey, Mom, guess what!" Angie shouted as she came in the back door. She threw her schoolbooks onto the kitchen counter and raced to her room to change out of her school clothes.

"How can I 'guess what' to you when you run away?"

No answer. Tilda shook her head. She was glad Angie was having a good time at school, but sometimes it was hard to keep up with her.

Tilda looked at the November page of the calendar tacked to the wall next to the telephone. Tomorrow Angie had to go to school early for an Honor Society meeting. She had a Girls' Athletic Club meeting after school on Thursday, and then Girls Club, Home Ec. Club, Pep Club, Drill Team, choir rehearsal, band practice, and song-leader practice. All this in one month! It was a wonder she got any schoolwork done!

Angie came out of her room and hurried to the refrigerator.

"So what am I supposed to guess?" Tilda asked.

Angie poured herself a glass of milk and rummaged in the bread drawer for something to eat. With her back still to her mother, she said, "Johnny asked me to the Junior Mixer after the football game Friday."

The first time Tilda heard "mixer" was when Angie was a freshman. Tilda had asked Angie what they were mixing and all Angie had said was, "Oh, Mom!" But Tilda figured it out. It was when boys and girls mixed together, like at a party, usually dancing.

"Are you having a date?" Tilda asked. Telma had moved from camp to Shelton when she was thirteen to go to high school, so Tilda had no experience with young people's doings.

"It's a double date. We're going with Murf and Meatball. He has his dad's car, so we'll probably go to the Polar Bear for ice cream after the dance."

"So you're going to a dance," Tilda said, remembering Angie's decision to give up movies, lipstick, and dancing.

Angie sat down at the table to eat a slice of coffee bread with her milk. "Well, I look at it this way. When I'm a missionary in Africa, there won't be movie theaters or dance halls, or any reason to wear lipstick. So I figure I might as well do those things now while I can."

Tilda nodded. She remembered when Angie wanted to be a lion tamer in a circus when she grew up. And for a while her ambition was to own a string of XXX Root Beer stands along the highway between Anacortes and Seattle. She often talked about being a news-paper reporter. Most recently, Angie tried to talk Joyce into going into business with her selling hotdogs and soda pop to tourists at the Deception Pass Bridge. Tilda was glad Angie had settled on becom-ing a missionary some day, but, for now it was important to have a good time with her high-school friends.

Tilda tossed and turned. She switched on the bed lamp and checked the clock again. Quarter-past one in the morning! "Charlie, wake up. It's after one o'clock and Angie isn't home yet!"

Charlie snorted in his sleep and rolled over, his back to Tilda.

Had Angie come home and she not heard her? Tilda jumped out of bed, ran to her room, and switched on the light. The bed was empty!

"Charlie!" Tilda exclaimed, shaking him by the shoulder. "Wake up! Something's happened to Angie!"

"What's happened?" he exclaimed, sitting straight up in the bed.

"A car accident! She's been in an accident!"

"Gawd, no! Where? When? Is she all right?"

"I don't know, but why else would she be so late? We don't know anything about this Johnny or if the driver has experience. They're only sixteen years old, Charlie. Kids can be so reckless—"

"Slow down," Charlie said, sitting on the side of the bed and feeling around with his feet for his slippers. "You don't know there's been an accident!"

"But what else? I'm so worried. Angie said her and the other girl were meeting the boys at the dance after the football game," Tilda went on. "The dance ends at ten, Angie told me. Charlie, look at the clock!"

Charlie found his bathrobe and sat back down on the bed. He ran his fingers through his hair. "Call the other parents. Maybe they know something."

"I don't know their last names! All I know is 'Murf' and 'Meatball.'"

Charlie mouthed, "Murf and Meatball?"

Oh, how could I be so careless! Angie's first date and I don't know anything—"

"You don't know anything about the kids she's with?"

"I know that Angie and this Murf and another girl are song leaders at the football games and Johnny and Meatball play football. That doesn't tell me if they're good drivers or what kind of homes they come from."

"Then, we just wait."

"*Ja,*" Tilda said. "Worry and wait." She sat down on the bed, all thought of sleep gone. Then she heard the back door open and tiptoeing steps across the kitchen and into the hall. She met Angie there.

"Angie, do you know what time it is?"

"I'm sorry, Mom," Angie said, her voice small. "I didn't have my watch and time got away from me."

"The dance was over three hours ago. Where have you been?"

"We went for ice cream and then we just drove around."

"Drove around?" Charlie exclaimed from the bedroom. "With gas rationing? Are your friends in the black market?"

"No, Dad!"

"All right. Then where did you go after ice cream? It's after one o'clock!" Tilda persisted.

"It was such a beautiful night. The stars were out and the moon was full so we—we drove to Cap Sante. To see the moon reflected on the water...."

Angie had dropped her head and her voice, so Tilda barely heard her over the ticking of the clock in the bedroom. Charlie grumped and crawled back into bed. When Telma was young and did something to upset them, Charlie was quick with the strop, Tilda remembered. She knew Angie was too old for that, but Charlie needed to pay attention. Or maybe he was getting too old. Or maybe he figured there was bigger things to worry about. Whatever the reason, it looked like he was leaving Angie up to her.

Tilda switched on the hall light so she could see her daughter better. Angie's lipstick was smeared and her hair, messed up. "So, an hour or so in the ice cream parlor. Then what did you do on Cap Sante for two hours?" Tilda asked, crossing her arms in front of her.

"We talked about school—and football—and, you know. Stuff like that." Angie's hand was on the bathroom door. "I'm kinda tired. Okay if I go to bed now?"

Tilda remembered being sixteen like Angie. It was when she and her sister came to this country. She never missed a Swedish dance at Finnia Hall. It was true that she and the boy who took her home from the dance would stand on the doorstep a few minutes and exchange a kiss or two. But two hours! A girl could get into trouble kissing a boy for two hours!

Then, again, she had no reason not to trust her daughter. Angie went to church every Sunday and even planned to be a missionary....

"All right. You go to bed. We talk in the morning," Tilda said and watched Angie slip into the bathroom and close and lock the door.

Angie looked at herself in the mirror over the washbasin. She rinsed her face with cool water, but still her face felt hot. Her mom could probably tell she'd been necking. She wanted to tell her mom that necking was okay if you were with a boy you liked, that all the kids did it, but she and her mom didn't talk about those things.

But maybe necking wasn't right. Maybe you were supposed to save your kisses until you were engaged. Angie's Sunday school teacher said that a girl must remember that her body is the temple of the Holy Spirit, and you wouldn't want to desecrate a temple.... Still, kissing wasn't desecrating anything. She would never go all-the-way like one of the girls in her class did. That girl ended up pregnant and had to drop out of school.

Then again, if she was going to be a missionary, maybe she shouldn't be kissing boys. And certainly she was wrong in staying out so late and worrying her parents....

Still, she was sixteen years old, nearly grownup with a right to expect some freedom. Besides, adults were always saying, "Sixteen and never been kissed!" Like that was something to be ashamed of.

Angie began dampening her hair, strand by strand, and pin curling each strand. She'd be seeing Johnny tomorrow when their high-school band played at the bond rally. She was looking forward to that.

When she and her mother talked in the morning, Angie would tell her again how sorry she was that she'd worried her, and then she'd just be quiet and listen to what her mother had to say. She wasn't looking forward to that!

Angie sat down at the breakfast table. Mom and Dad had already eaten. It was ten o'clock. Mom had let her sleep in. Maybe Angie wasn't in too big a trouble for staying out late—

"I poured you some dry mush," Mom said, "and here's the milk."

"Cornflakes, Mom."

"You got another letter from your summer-camp friend," Mom said. She set the letter on the table. Angie enjoyed Lois Persons' letters. They were bubbly and fun. She tore open the envelope.

"You can read it while you eat," Mom said, and sat down across the table.

It was from Lois Persons all right, but a very different "person" this time!

Not long after the war started, Lois's cousin who was stationed in Seattle introduced her to a fellow navy corpsman, Jack Ragsdale. Jack was eighteen at the time. Lois and Jack became good friends and wrote to each other when he went overseas. Lois was concerned when she hadn't heard from him since his V Mail letter at Christmas. Now there was an article about him in the *Everett Herald*.

The newspaper reported he was wounded in June in the invasion of Saipan and was sent to the naval hospital in Oakland, California. Lois enclosed the news article in her letter.

According to Jack Ragsdale, 20, "We landed [on the beach at Saipan] about 9:30 a.m. An hour later we had run into such rough going that we had to set up makeshift aid stations and forget about our assigned position. We tried to treat the casualties as we moved along, but we weren't making much headway. Then about noon we got a direct hit on our makeshift station. My pal, Jack Bagan, a pharmacist's mate from Everett, Wash., was coming to our aid, and he was killed in his tracks.

Lois wrote that she didn't know Jack Bagan, but he was from Everett which made him a hometown boy. Somehow that made it worse. Lois wished she'd known about her friend "Rags" being in the hospital so she could have written to him. Saipan was secured three weeks later, but over 14,000 Marines were killed or wounded. Lois said she hated saying good-bye to friends and classmates who were going into the service, perhaps never to return....

Angie showed her mom the letter. Mom read it and then reached across the table, took Angie's hands in hers, and asked if she remembered Mrs. Remple, her teacher in Potlatch. And did Angie remember her older son Ainley? Of course, Angie remembered them. Ainley was in the eighth grade when Angie was in the fifth. He was good looking in a gangly way and once filled in as teacher when his mother was sick. Angie always liked him....

Then Mom said she'd heard sad news from a friend in Potlatch. Ainley was in the Air Force and had been shot down over Germany.

Angie pushed aside her uneaten breakfast. When she stood up to leave the table, her mom stood, too, and gave her a long hug. Last night's problem was no longer important.

37

HOPE
December 1944

"I still can't believe it," Charlie told Tilda as he sat down at the kitchen table. "It never happened before in this country." He'd left his work shoes in the basement but noticed he'd forgotten to brush the mill dust off his pant legs. He'd take care of that after coffee. "No President of the United States was ever elected to a third term, until Roosevelt. Last month, a fourth term! A lot of people don't think it's good to have the same man head a government that long."

"More people must think it's a good idea," Tilda said, "or they wouldn't re-elect him. He put a lot of people back to work during the Depression, you know." Tilda hesitated. "I voted for him!"

Charlie was quiet. He had driven Tilda to City Hall and waited in the car while she went in to vote. Maybe he should have applied for citizenship papers when Tilda did, so he would have a say in what was going on. He never agreed with a lot of Roosevelt's ideas for getting the country moving. The New Deal! WPA! The give-away programs during the '30s! But probably now he would have voted for Roosevelt anyway, being in the middle of a war. Better to keep the same leader—

"Coffee's coming," Tilda said as she took two cups and saucers out of the cupboard. She poured the coffee and carried it to the table.

"*Ja,* Tilda, people give Roosevelt credit for getting us out of the Depression, but you know what finally did it? It was the war that got this country moving again."

Tilda didn't answer. He knew what she was thinking, and he agreed. War was too high a price to pay for prosperity. Every day more young men were killed. Even some women. Cities in Europe were being bombed until nothing was left but shells. Hundreds of thousands of civilians were being killed. Thousands of Europeans were homeless refugees like those in Finland. America was escaping the bombings, but lives of people in this country were turned upside down, too—women leaving home to work in defense plants and kids tended by strangers or running wild in the streets.

Tilda passed Charlie the bowl of sugar lumps. Charlie put one in his mouth and sipped his coffee.

"John Westbloom came up to me on the job today and said he got a letter from Molpe, from his boy Robert."

"I've thought about his children," Tilda said. "When John worked for you in camp, he used to talk about his wife and children in the old country. Is his boy in the army?"

"No," Charlie answered. "Robert is Angie's age. Too young for the army, but old enough to write a long letter to his *pappa*, John told me. John smiled when he said that.

"John said that Robert and his younger sister Berit moved in with their grandparents when their mother died of tuberculosis. Robert wrote that the house John had built for the family had been standing vacant, so now refugees live there.

"Robert said that some refugees moved to relatives in other parts of Finland, but more refugees keep coming. Robert and other young boys and some old men in the village are working hard to fix up empty houses and barns, and even family saunas for living quarters, but most of the homeless still live with host families."

Tilda left the table to get the coffee pot. She refilled Charlie's cup.

"It's the same in Närpes," Tilda said. "Remember Ester wrote about the refugees coming to their village?" Tilda sipped her coffee. "Did you tell John about Vilhelm's letter?"

"*Ja*, I did. I told him Vilhelm wrote that a woman named Anna Kavola and her two daughters water their cows at the creek near his house. Anna told him through an interpreter that they and many others left some of their goods in storage sheds on their property in Karelia on the chance they can return like they did in 1941 at the end of Winter War. Vilhelm asked her if she thought that would happen. 'We have to hope,' the woman told him."

"Charlie, do you think they'll get back to their homes some day?" Tilda asked.

"I doubt it. It would mean going to war with Russia again, and they haven't finished this one yet."

"I guess you're thinking of Manne. Did you tell John about Vilhelm's boy Manne?"

Outside children laughed and hollered and a dog barked. Charlie pulled two slats of the venetian blinds apart to look out the window. School was out for the day. Three boys were pushing and chasing each other and a young girl skipped along the sidewalk behind them. They all looked cold with their red hands and noses, but they wouldn't be as cold as the boys fighting in Lapland.

He thought of the September armistice terms. Finland was to give Russia the Karelian Isthmus and certain other territories along the Finnish-Russian border, pay a war indemnity debt of $600 million, disarm all Germans still in their country, and drive the German army out of Lapland.

"*Ja*, I told John that Vilhelm's oldest boy Alarik came home after five years in the war, " Charlie said, "and Mauritz, his twenty-year-old son, was also discharged last month. Then I told him about Manne, the youngest son. He was with the regiment sent to Lapland and his job was to clear the land of mines."

Charlie studied the handle of his coffee cup. Not quite big enough for his finger. But it was Manne he thought about. Manne had written his parents from his hospital bed. He told them that as the Germans retreated, they blew up and burned everything—bridges, highways, power stations, whole towns, and they scorched the ground and planted mines behind them. Manne was hurt bad when a mine exploded next to him. He wrote that he tried to dig the shrapnel out of his thigh with his knife. His comrades thought he was crazy. Finally, when there was a break in the fighting, someone drove him to hospital. This was Manne's second war injury.

"Edvin was sent to Lapland, too, you know," Tilda said. "Ester hasn't heard from him. Birger was luckier, like Alarik and Mauritz. He got out of the army last month and is home now. Ester wrote that—"

The back door flew open and Angie stuck in her head. "Phyllis and I are going to the library," she said. "I'll be home before dark."

"You need to change your clothes," Tilda called.

"Aw, Mom, we're not going out to play. We're working on an assignment for school." The door shut.

Charlie watched from the kitchen window as the girls crossed the lawn to K Avenue. Phyllis was taller than Angie, but from the back they both looked like grown-up ladies. Seemed like yesterday that Angie was that little girl skipping down the sidewalk! Charlie felt Tilda's eyes studying him. "Well, what is it?" he asked.

"Charlie," Tilda said, rubbing the handle on her cup with her thumb, "I'm wondering if you plan to sign up for citizenship class this winter?"

"I think about it. I may want to vote in the next election, especially if Roosevelt runs for a fifth term!"

"Charlie, I know you're joking. You know that won't happen! The war will be over by then."

"*Ja*, the signs are good. France is freed and U.S. troops are into Germany. Also, they recaptured Guam and are moving into the Philippines. But it's not over yet."

"Well," Tilda said, "I guess we should listen to the Karelian woman who talked to Vilhelm."

"What did she say?"

"You read Vilhelm's letter. The woman said they had to hope. And that's what we have to do, Charlie. We have to hope this war's over soon."

Charlie nodded.

"And I have to hope you sign up for citizenship class," Tilda said. "Then, next spring, after you pass your test, we can celebrate with dinner at Amsberry's Café, like we did after my test last year. You know, Charlie, it's been a while since we ate out."

Tilda at Crater Lake.

Lind home, 9th and K.

Charlie, Ida's Charlie, Ida at Mt. Baker.

A gathering of Scandinavians, L to R: Charlie, ?, John Carlson, Tilda, Mr. and Mrs. West, Anna Carlson, Mrs. Norgard, Mrs. Eriks, others.

1942

Bennie saying goodbye to
Linda, age 6 months.

Thelma and Linda, age 1 year.

Angie, age 12, Causland
Memorial Park.

Joy Kamps, 10, shortly after arm casts were removed.

Kimiko (left) and Kiko Okawa dressed for parade before the war.

Mrs. Pardis (right) with a junior high class.
Angie in white (front center).

Faith with brother Bill, 1943.

Phyllis, 13, and brother Paul.

Joyce, Angie, Arloween.   Angie skating with her dad.

1944

Angie, new bike.

PART VII - 1945

38

WASPS
February

"Mom, I've decided I'm going to join the army and be a WASP!" Angie announced as she came in the back door and dropped her schoolbooks on the counter.

"*Gud I himlen*, Angie!" Tilda exclaimed. "What is that? You going to fly around and sting people?"

"No, Mom! I just want to fly. As soon as I'm out of high school, I'm going to be a Women's Air Force Service Pilot. That's what WASP stands for."

"I don't know why girls would want to join the army!"

"Because our country needs us."

"You going to go fight? I didn't know the country was that hard up!"

"We wouldn't fight! We'd take the place of men at army and air-force bases so they could fight. We had an assembly at school today, and two army officers, a man and a woman, explained to us the advantages of going into a military career. The woman recruiter told us girls about the WACs. That's Women's Army Corps. She said there are about 140,000 women in the corps now and more than 17,000 of them are working overseas."

"Don't you have to be twenty-one to do something like that?" Tilda asked.

"No. Just eighteen, and I'll be eighteen in August after graduation."

Tilda sat down. She could see Angie had more to say.

"Then the recruiter told us about WAF," Angie went on. "That means Women's Air Force. These women relieve men from their jobs at air-force bases. But listen, Mom! The best is yet to come. That was when she told us about the WASPs! WASPs are women trained to be pilots! They actually fly Army Air Force planes!"

"Then you do go into battle?" Tilda's voice came out weak.

"No, we ferry planes from one base to another. Stuff like that. When you enlist in the WASPs, they send you to Lackland Air Force Base in Texas for training, and then they station you at a base somewhere in this country or overseas. You know I always wanted to see the world, Mom."

"I thought you planned to see the world as a missionary," Tilda said. She could feel a headache coming on.

"I can do that, too. The recruiter said you can serve a short hitch of four to six years or make it a career. You can retire in just twenty years with great benefits that free you for a second career. Heck, Mom, you know I always wanted to be a pilot like Amelia Earhart."

"I wish you still wanted to be a lion tamer. It would be safer."

"Aw, Mom," Angie said and turned on her heels and marched to her room. She slammed the door behind her.

Charlie looked a little tired when he came home from work and dropped into his chair at the kitchen table. Tilda brought him his coffee and a couple *scorpa* on a plate before she told him about Angie.

"What are you saying?" Charlie exclaimed. "Angie wants to fly! She flies around here all the time! Why does she need a plane?"

"I think she's serious, Charlie." She could see he didn't think so.

Charlie dunked the *skorpa* into his coffee. "Tilda, your *skorpa* are much better for dipping than that dried toast they sell at the grocery store. *Zwieback,* I think they call it."

Whenever Tilda's coffee bread got a little stale, she sliced it, sprinkled the slices with sugar and cinnamon, and dried them in the oven. She left the sugar off this time, because the next ration stamp wasn't good for another week, but she didn't think Charlie noticed.

"I almost forgot!" Tilda said. "When Angie came home talking about joining the army, everything else flew out of my mind. Angie," she called, "I have good news. Something to show you and *Pappa*."

"I'm changing my clothes," Angie called back, but in a minute she joined them. Angie never stayed mad very long.

"We got a wedding announcement in the mail today," Tilda said. "Take a look!"

Angie picked up the announcement and read it aloud.

> Lt. Col and Mrs. Donald M. Rigby have the honor of announcing the marriage of their daughter Alice Fern to Arthur C. Carlson, Ensign, United States Naval Reserve on Friday, the fifth of January, nineteen hundred and forty-five at their home 5511 Blair Road NE, Washington, DC.

"Oh, Wow! I wish I'd been home when Art brought her here for a weekend," Angie exclaimed.

"There's a note from Alice with the announcement," Tilda said. "She writes that some of Art's navy buddies gave him their gas coupons as wedding gifts so they could go on a weekend honeymoon. They drove to Virginia, West Virginia, Maryland, and then visited Princeton, New Jersey, where Art will be going for pre-radar training."

Charlie laughed. "Leave it to Art to cover the miles, even on a short honeymoon."

Tilda went on. "Alice said she's looking forward to meeting Art's little cousin when they get back to the West Coast." Tilda gave Angie the note so she could read it herself.

"Heck, I wasn't that little when Art went in the service," Angie said, but Tilda could see Angie was pleased.

All news wasn't good. Tilda had been to sewing club at Anna Carlson's. Mrs. Anderson had shared some alarming information. The military in Japan had sent thousands of big paper balloons into the stratosphere, each carrying several thirty-pound bombs timed to explode five days after launching. The high air currents carried them across the ocean to the west coast of Canada, Washington, and Oregon. A few floated as far as Iowa and Kansas.

Most failed to go off, but some exploded, injuring several people and damaging the woods where they fell. The worst incidence took place on Mount Gearhart in Oregon. Reverend Archie Mitchell had taken his wife and five children from his church on an outing. While he was parking the car, his wife and the children searched for a campsite. On the way, they came across one of these bombs. It exploded and killed all six.

"Why hasn't any of this been in the newspaper?" Mrs. Ness asked, looking up from her knitting.

"The government is keeping it secret so the Japanese won't know if their plan was successful," Mrs. Anderson answered.

"If it's a secret, how did you hear about it?" Mrs. Haglund asked.

"Mrs. Jacobson told me. Her nephew's in the army. He had to help defuse the bombs."

And more bad news. Sally Isaacson had contracted infantile paralysis and was in an iron lung in Seattle. She was the girl that Angie said was such a beautiful ice skater. The ladies talked quietly then, sharing with each other their fears about polio. Tilda would write Telma and remind her not to take Linda out into crowds.

The worst news was from Europe. The Nazi Party in Germany had rounded up Jewish people, put them in concentration camps, and gassed them. Two places in Germany, Birkenau and Auschwitz, had killed almost two million men, women, and children. Even babies. How could a government do this, the ladies in the sewing club asked each other. Where did such evil men come from? Maybe Pastor Fosso would have some answers on Sunday. He preached a lot about evil in the world.

Everyone in the club was knitting or crocheting or doing needlework. Tilda was knitting a sweater for Angie. Bright blue. Angie's color. She'd bought enough wool yarn and four skeins extra to knit Angie a sweater when she was in third grade. When Angie outgrew that sweater, she unraveled it, added extra yarn, and knit it again. This was the second time she'd unraveled the sweater and added more yarn. Once Angie asked how it was that her sweater kept growing with her.

Tilda rested her hands in her lap and looked around at the women in the club. Probably fifteen or so. Most were a little on the heavy side. Almost everyone had tight permanents. They sat in chairs around the edge of the front room in their bright, flowered dresses, looking like a garden border of summer annuals. They chattered in a mixture of Swedish and broken English, old friends, many of them from camp days. All of them from the old country. Mrs. Carlson's living room was warm and smelled of fresh-baked coffee bread. It was hard to think that there was so much trouble in the world.

Tilda was glad for her friends and her life in Anacortes. Now if she could just get used to Angie wanting to join the Army Air Force!

39

"TOLO" DANCE
April 7, 12, 1945

"Mom, I need help!" Angie called from her bedroom.
"You told me you wouldn't need help," her mom answered through Angie's shut door.

"Well, I do. I'm having trouble zipping my dress up the back."

Angie knew her mother was standing outside her door in case she was needed. Her mom was as nervous as Angie was about her first formal dance. Her mom had never met Johnny, and her dad just knew who he was when they ice skated at the pond. They never talked or anything.

But her parents figured out that Johnny was her boyfriend the day she came home wearing his letter sweater. That took a lot of explaining! Angie told them it was a custom to wear a boy's letter sweater if she was seeing him on a regular basis. It didn't mean they were engaged or anything. Mom had said it was time she saw this boy, not just his sweater.

Sometimes after ball games or school dances, Johnny walked Angie to the front door, but he never came in. This time Johnny would have to walk up to the front door, ring the doorbell, and come right into the living room. Then Mom would meet him. Angie told her dad he didn't have to hang around, but he said he wouldn't miss it. That made Angie even more nervous.

What would her dad and Johnny talk about? Johnny's dad was a teacher and a musician. Angie's dad was a logger and a mill worker. Johnny's dad graduated from college and spoke perfect English, and her dad had gone through the fourth grade in a foreign country and talked broken English. Now Johnny would be ringing the doorbell any minute—

"Well, let me have a look at the zipper," her mom said as she came into Angie's bedroom.

Angie twisted around to watch her struggle with the zipper. "Mom! Hurry up!"

"I am hurrying, but the zipper's stuck. We pay all that money for a nice, taffeta dress and the zipper don't work!"

"We didn't pay as much for a dress as most of my friends did," Angie protested. Fortunately, Angie liked the dress anyway. It was light pink with short gathered-up sleeves and gathered bodice. The long skirt had three tiers of gathers and the taffeta made whispering sounds when she walked. She wished she had fancier shoes, but she'd polished her white summer sandals and they would do.

"Whose idea was this anyway?" her mom asked as she struggled with the zipper. "This—what did you call it—'tolo' dance? Never heard of girls asking boys out. In my day, the boys always asked the girls to the dances."

"Mom, I explained that to you already. It's a tradition. Every year Mrs. Beard and the choir sponsor a dance where the girls invite the boys." Angie couldn't see her mom behind her working on the zipper, but she knew she was probably shaking her head.

"And I guess the long dresses was the girls' idea, too, since girls do the planning."

"That's right. I was on the planning committee this year, and we all thought it would be fun to wear formals!"

Angie was tired of having to explain everything to her mother. In December, she'd had to explain Honor Society's slave auction. Boys and girls in Honor Society lined up on the stage in the big gym and were auctioned off to the highest bidder. The slave had to work for the "master" for a full day. Johnny won Angie in the auction and made her carry his books to every class and give him part of her lunch. Her mom looked shocked until Angie told her that all the money that the auction brought in, $475.80, was used to buy war bonds.

"There! Finally!" her mom said. Angie felt her dress cinch up around her waist and chest as her mother slid the zipper up the back. Angie turned around to look at herself in the mirror above the bureau. The dress fit nice and snug and the gathers across her front made her bust look bigger. Her hair reflected the ceiling light. It should! She brushed it a hundred strokes every night! Angie leaned closer to the mirror to check her eyes. Her lashes weren't long and curly like Faith's, but her mom had let her buy an eyelash curler and use a little mascara, so the lashes showed up—

"Mom, there's the doorbell!"

"I'll get the door," her dad called from the living room.

"Oh, no! Mom, you answer the door. Quick, before Dad gets there. I have to put on my lipstick."

"Come in," she heard her dad say. "Come in. Angie should be ready any time now. She's been working at it all afternoon!" She heard Johnny and her dad laugh, and then her mom introduce herself and ask him to sit down. Angie grabbed her coat and ran into the living room.

Johnny stood up when he saw her and handed her a small, white florist's box. Angie's hands shook as she took the box. Before she lifted the lid, she could smell what was inside. She was right! A snow-white gardenia with a shiny, pink bow tied to its stem.

"Joyce told me your dress was pink," Johnny said, his face suddenly turning the color of the ribbon.

"It's beautiful," Mom said. "I can smell it from here. And it matches your dress exactly. Do you want me to pin it on?"

Angie and Johnny both nodded. Angie was relieved her mom was doing the pinning, because to pin it to the dress without sticking Angie, she had to slip her fingers under the edge of the bodice.

"We better go," Angie said. "Johnny has his dad's car and we're picking up Joyce and her date."

"This was a short visit," Dad said. "I was going to ask what your father did for a living, but I guess I know. He's a music teacher. He was trying to learn Angie the clarinet. I know she practices because I hear squeaks from her room even with the door shut." He laughed. "Now, what time is the dance over?"

"Eleven o'clock," Angie answered, embarrassed by her dad's attempt at humor.

"We'll probably get something to eat afterwards, if that's all right," Johnny said.

"And then you bring her right home?" Mom asked, but it sounded more like a command. Angie knew her mom was remembering the night she'd stayed out until after one in the morning.

Johnny nodded and started to help Angie on with her coat, but she told him she'd carry it so she wouldn't smash the corsage.

"Nice meeting you," he said to her parents and started for the door.

"Wait for me," Angie said, and followed him out the door and down the walk to the car.

Joyce was on the planning and decorating committee with Angie. That afternoon they'd climbed tall ladders to hang crepe paper streamers from ceiling beams in the Big Gym. They'd placed branches of apple and cherry blossoms in large vases around the room and bunches of lilacs on the refreshment table. Now when the girls walked into the dance with their dates, they were impressed with what they'd done. It didn't even smell like a gym!

The committee had also placed folding chairs near the refreshment table for the teachers and chaperones. The students thought that most of them were too old to dance, but they were expected to be there to make sure the boys and girls didn't dance too close. The committee had asked permission to darken the room a little, but Angie noticed that all the lights in the gym were still on.

"Let's get our dance cards," Angie whispered to Joyce as they walked near a table next to the dance floor.

Dance programs were new to Angie. The little folder with the bright-blue cover and blue tassel was intended to help a girl plan her evening. Every dance was numbered with a line drawn after the number. A girl would ask a boy to sign on one of the lines and, when that number came up, they would dance together. A really popular girl would have her program filled before the music even started.

"I picked up my program this afternoon when we were decorating," Joyce said. She pulled her program out of her coat pocket and opened it. "See. I had Phil sign up for the first and last dance and a couple dances between. Now I just have to find guys to fill in the rest." Joyce tossed her coat on one of the bleacher benches. Angie did the same. Then Joyce led the way to a group of boys standing at the edge of the dance floor.

"Who'd you get?" Joyce asked Angie after a few minutes.

"Johnny signed up for the first and last dance. I got Edwin's name, and Gordy's and Swede's. Bob Fithian and Rodney and Jack Kamps. I still have more blanks to fill. How'd you do?"

"I filled my program—"

Mr. Stockman, one of their class advisors, interrupted their conversation with an announcement. "I'm your MC this evening and am fortunate that this microphone is located between the refreshment table and the phonograph. That means I won't go hungry and I have the privilege of helping choose the records. And you know, girls, when I announce the number of the dance, you find the young man who signed your program."

Mrs. Beard turned on the phonograph and placed the first record, "Sentimental Journey," on the turntable. Mr. Stockman raised his voice to be heard above the music. "Dance number one," he announced. "Find your partner."

It was a romantic number, like most of the popular songs. War meant separation and that meant longing for someone. Angie understood that, but she hoped Mrs. Beard would pick out some fast pieces, too, like "In the Mood" or "Jersey Bounce" because she liked to jitterbug, except the girls probably couldn't in their long dresses. Angie would have to settle for jitterbugging at the school sock-hops. Girls often jitterbugged together because the boys didn't know how. They waited for slower dances where they held their partners close— but not too close. The chaperones would be checking on this. In spite of the bright lights and the close supervision, the evening was a success.

On Thursday, April 12, Angie, Edna, Joyce, and Faith, as usual, found seats together in the library and continued chatting about the dance and other spring activities that had kept them and their friends so busy. They looked ahead to their class's annual picnic at Alexander Beach and wondered aloud which of the boys who signed their dance programs Saturday night would offer them a ride to the picnic.

The bell had rung, the signal for everyone to be quiet and get to work, but something was different today. Mrs. Webb hadn't stood in her usual place at the door when they came in. She wasn't there now to scold them for talking. She was standing next to the window staring out at the empty school grounds. Maybe she had spring fever. Maybe something was wrong....

Mrs. Webb walked from the window back to her desk and, without sitting down, leafed through some papers. She didn't seem to be reading them. Just shuffling them. Angie noticed other kids were watching her, too. Finally she looked up from her desk and cleared her throat.

"Boys and girls," she said, "something has happened today that is extremely sad. It could even affect the course of the war. Our President, Commander in Chief of this country's military forces, died this morning of a cerebral hemorrhage at his home in Warm Springs, Georgia. Vice President Harry Truman has been sworn in as President."

Mrs. Webb sat down at her desk. No one spoke. Forgotten was the success of their junior class play, "Don't Take My Penny," the basketball team's tournament win, the choir's superior rating at the district music festival, Saturday night's "tolo" dance.... Remembered were President Roosevelt's Fireside Chats—the calm, sure radio voice that had inspired and reassured them all.

40

A RIDERLESS HORSE
April 15, 1945

Angie sat at her parents' feet in front of their radio. The announcer told the listeners across America that the President's body was carried by train from Warm Springs, Georgia, to Washington D.C., where he lay in state in the East Room of the White House. From Washington, the train brought him to his home in Hyde Park, New York. The announcer reported that grieving crowds, many wearing black crepe or muslin, had lined both sides of the tracks at every country crossing, town and village. Men had removed their hats and held them over their hearts. Many cried. Women and children cried and clung to each other as the train crawled by.

The announcer commented that only once before in American history has there been such an outpouring of grief. "April 15, 1865, eighty years ago today, President Lincoln died from an assassin's bullet. Lincoln's funeral train, seven cars long and painted black, crept across the country to his home in Springfield, Illinois. People then, too, stood by the tracks and wept."

Lincoln, like Roosevelt, had struggled to bring to a close a major war. The Civil War had taken its toll on him, as World War II had on Roosevelt. Lincoln's face, like Roosevelt's, was drawn and his health, compromised. General Lee surrendered to General Grant at Appomattox on April 9, just days before Lincoln was assassinated. Lincoln did not live to set in motion his reconstruction program. In April, 1945, America and its Allies seemed to be winning the war, but Roosevelt did not live to see war's end.

"It's a beautiful, clear day here by the Hudson River," the announcer said, "a day that belies the gravity of this occasion. If you listen, radio audience, you'll hear above my voice a cannon firing a twenty-one-gun salute to our fallen leader. The flag-draped casket is now being carried from the train to a black-draped cart drawn by six brown horses. Waiting for the procession to begin, a riderless horse stands behind the caisson. A symbol of a lost warrior, it is hooded, its stirrups reversed. Sword and boots hang upside down from the stirrups."

The announcer described the procession as with muffled drums it wound its way up the gravel road to the rose garden in back of the Roosevelt home. There President Truman, his Cabinet, other government officials, and Mrs. Roosevelt and family watch as servicemen slowly lower the fallen warrior into his grave.

Angie turned to her parents for them to say something, but even the announcer was silent, his microphone picking up the distant sound of a bugler playing "Taps."

"This is the only President I can ever remember," Angie murmured.

"I guess that's right." Her mother spoke quietly. "Roosevelt was elected the first time in 1932 when you were only four years old."

"*Ja*, we were in Camp Two," her dad said. "We blamed Hoover for the Depression and elected Roosevelt to improve things." He hesitated. "I've had my doubts, but I'm learning in citizenship class that Roosevelt did a lot for this country."

"I'm glad you're taking the citizenship class," Angie said.

"*Ja*," Dad said, "It was time. Finnish soldiers have Germans in Lapland on the run so soon all the Finn boys will be home. I don't think they need me now," he said with a slight smile. "I'm ready to be American citizen."

Angie noticed her mom was wiping her eyes. Maybe it was because of President Roosevelt's dying, or maybe it was because her dad was finally going to get his citizenship papers. Or maybe it was because the war in Finland would soon be over.

41

V-E DAY
May 1945

Tilda dropped Thelma's letter on the table and ran to meet Charlie at the door. "Good news!" she exclaimed.

"*Ja*, I heard it on the radio on my way home," Charlie said.

Tilda was startled. "You heard on the car radio that Bennie's coming home?"

Charlie stared at her a moment, and then laughed as he put down his lunch bucket. "Maybe 'good news' like 'bad news' comes in bunches!"

"What do you mean?"

"The war in Europe is over!"

Tilda leaned on the cupboard behind her. Charlie laughed again. "Too bad we don't have any coffee to celebrate," he said, looking over at the stove.

"Oh, my! I'm sorry. Sit down. The coffee's made. There's just so much going on I can't think straight." Tilda hurried to the stove as Angie burst in the back door.

"Have you heard?" Angie shouted. "The war's over!"

"We heard!" Charlie said. "Germany surrendered! But the whole war isn't over, you know. We're still fighting the Japs."

"But Bennie's coming home!" Tilda said, holding up Thelma's letter. "Telma says he'll be stationed at a army base in this country for six months before he's discharged, and he can pick his location. Naturally he chose Fort Lewis by Tacoma. He'll be able to drive to Shelton on weekends—"

"Whoa," Charlie interrupted. "Don't count on it. You know the army." He put half a sugar lump in his mouth and sipped his coffee. "Don't forget that other good news. The Finns finally drove the Germans out of Lapland, so now Russia's satisfied and the armistice with Finland is in effect. And Vilhelm's son Mauritz is taking up seal hunting with his dad. They're probably out on the sea right now."

"*Ja*, and my nephew Edvin is home, too," Tilda put in. "Ester wrote that a thousand boys died in Lapland, so Edvin was lucky to make it home."

Angie poured herself a glass of milk and sat down at the table. "Mr. Smith said tomorrow will be designated as V-E Day," she said. "Victory in Europe. New York and Chicago and other cities are already ringing church bells, blowing whistles, and honking horns. Tomorrow people will be celebrating on every street in every city in America. People will be celebrating on Commercial Avenue in Anacortes and I want to be there!"

Tilda nodded. "But don't you have school tomorrow?"

"I do. Maybe we could go to town after school," Angie said. "Anyway, we have a school assembly in the afternoon to celebrate V-E Day. Wallie Funk is home on leave after four Pacific invasions and maybe he'll be at the assembly. His brother Jimmie made it through the Battle of Iwo Jima and might be there, too. Mr. Stephenson will read the names of those from Anacortes who died in the service and ask us to pray for the eight men who are prisoners of war in Japan."

"Well," Charlie said, pushing away his empty coffee cup, "if you ladies will excuse me, I'm going to go study my lesson for this week. May 16 is just around the corner." He turned to Angie. "Mama passed her citizenship test last year in flying colors, so I have to do good. Besides, I promised Mom a nice dinner at Amsberry's Café if I passed my test."

"So, how's your dinner?" Charlie asked Tilda.

"It couldn't be better! Amsberry's Café serves wonderful pot roast!"

"Maybe it's something else that makes it taste so good," Charlie suggested.

"Maybe so," Tilda answered. "Maybe it's because Angie and I are having dinner with a brand, new American citizen."

Charlie smiled and cut into his country-fried steak, his favorite. This was a night to splurge. He stirred the rich, brown gravy into his mashed potatoes.

Charlie's test day had arrived before they knew it. He figured time went fast because of the excitement of the war being over in Europe. The newspapers were full of pictures of V-E Day celebrations across the country and in Europe and England. Reporters wrote about the last days of the dictators, how Mussolini had been killed by Italian countrymen, and how two days later, April 30, Hitler committed suicide in Berlin.

"Tilda, did you hear the country's dimout order was lifted?" he said and took another roll from the basket in the middle of the table.

"I heard that. It's good news."

Charlie thought of all the changes. Stores would again light their display windows at night and theaters would switch on their multicolored marques. People could now turn on their porch lights if they expected company. Tilda would like that. Maybe by Christmas the war with Japan would be over and they could again display their lighted Christmas tree.

"And I know more good news!" Angie interjected. "Mrs. Trafton on Oakes Avenue heard from the Okawas, the Japanese family that lived next door to them. You remember, the family taken to internment camp in May after the war started?"

Charlie nodded. Of course he remembered. He salted his potatoes.

"They were released in January. Mrs. Trafton was told that the War Department was getting ready to close the camps."

Charlie understood. The government figured since the U.S. was winning the war in the South Pacific, the Japanese weren't a threat any more. "So, are they moving back to Anacortes?" Charlie asked. "Robinson's Fisheries closed down, you know."

"Mrs. Trafton said Frank Okawa found a job as a laborer on a ranch in Gilroy, California," Angie explained. "Close to San Jose. For now, they're living in a cabin built for migrant workers."

Charlie salted his meat and then looked at Tilda. She was always getting after him for using too much salt. She didn't say anything about it tonight.

"*Ja*," he said after a few minutes. "It looks like we're winning the war in the South Pacific, but don't throw away the blackout curtains yet."

42

CANNERY CALL
June 1945

"Angie," Tilda called, knocking on the door to Angie's room, "I need a little help cleaning house today. Would you take out the scatter rugs and shake them?"

Tilda didn't know why Angie spent so much time in her room with the door shut. Someone told her that was what young girls her age liked to do, but they didn't say why. If she at least cleaned her room while she was there, it wouldn't be so bad. And another mystery, how the scatter rugs in the hall get so dirty with just three people in the house? She'd shake them herself if it wasn't for her allergies. Doctor thought dust and lint might have something to do with her migraine headaches.

"Don't see why we have to have so many little rugs," Angie fussed as she came out of her room and began rolling the hall rugs. "You know the ends of my fingernails turn backwards when I shake them!"

"I told you to drink gelatin in water in the mornings. That will harden your nails."

"It tastes yucky!"

"Then stop fussing!"

My, oh my, Tilda thought. If it wasn't pimples on her face or hair with split ends, it was soft fingernails! And then she complained about being born with logger's hands. Tilda told her with big hands she shouldn't have any trouble shaking rugs! Well, Tilda knew what was bothering her. It was the waiting to hear from the cannery about the office job she'd applied for.

Kids her age, Angie had told her mom, didn't still pick strawberries or beans or bulbs. They found better jobs. Marivonne and Gloria

Perkins worked in the laundry at the navy base. Phyllis worked for her dad at Luvera's Market. Bonnie and Marie worked at the Polar Bear, and Faith was promoted to the meat department at Safeway. The butcher even took her with him to a farm to pick out calves for veal. Faith said she couldn't stand the idea of slaughtering those beautiful brown-eyed calves and talked him out of buying them. The butcher didn't take her on any more buying trips, but he gave her other important jobs like grinding and weighing meat, and waiting on customers.

All of Angie's friends had responsible jobs, so, when she heard Fishermen's Packing Corporation was looking for a payroll clerk, she applied. Tilda told her they wouldn't hire a sixteen-year-old girl for a hard job like that. Angie had reminded her that employers were desperate for workers, and, besides, she'd taken a couple business courses at high school. Anyway, how hard would the job be? You'd just add up the hours people worked, multiply that by their hourly wage, and write out their paychecks at the end of the week.

"Don't forget the rugs in the bedrooms and the entry," Tilda reminded her.

"This is not the better job I had in mind," Angie mumbled as she rolled up the bedroom rugs. She shook them, replaced them, and went to the entry for the last rug.

"Mom," she called, "Come and look. Mail all over the place!"

Tilda liked their mail delivery. Instead of a box out by the street or even on the porch, they had a slot in the front door and the mailman slid the mail through the slot.

"Oh, my!" Tilda exclaimed when she saw mail scattered across the entry-room floor. "We hit the jackpot today." She gathered up several bills, a letter from their life insurance company, some advertisements, and three letters.

"Nothing from the cannery," she told Angie, "but here's a letter from Telma and two from old country." Tilda slid her finger under the flap on the envelope from Thelma and pulled out the letter.

"What's she say?" Angie asked, joining her mother on the couch.

"Telma writes that the army is sending Bennie to a base in Georgia instead of Fort Lewis, like he wanted.... She's awful disappointed.... She had especially looked forward to Bennie seeing Linda. Now it would be another six months...."

Tilda finished reading the letter to herself and then handed it to Angie. Tilda understood Telma's disappointment, but she would write and remind her that at least Bennie was coming home. So many husbands and fathers weren't that lucky.

She looked at the two letters from Finland. One from Vilhelm, the other from Ester. Both sides of the family in one day! She'd wait for Charlie to get home from work so they could read them together over coffee."

"Go ahead," Charlie said as he sat down at the kitchen table. "You first. Let's hear what Ester has to say."

Tilda didn't dread opening Ester's letters now that the war was over and Birger and Edvin were safely home. She tore open the envelope and scanned the page quickly. "Oh my!" she said. "I can't believe what I'm reading."

"I can't believe it either if you don't tell me what it is," Charlie said, blowing on his coffee to cool it.

"There's going to be two weddings in Närpes this month! Both Birger and Edvin have found brides. Birger is marrying Anni Nygård on June 24 and Edvin is marrying Elvie Ollén a week later. I wish we could be there! No matter how poor people are in Finland, they know how to celebrate a wedding."

Charlie nodded at Tilda's good news and picked up his letter. He found his pocketknife in his pants pocket, cut the envelope open, and leaned back in his chair to read. Tilda watched. She noticed the letter was short and that he reread it before he laid it on the table.

"So, what does he say?" she asked.

"You can read it," he said.

Tilda set Ester's letter aside and picked up Vilhelm's. She found herself reading it twice as Charlie had done.

In May, when Vilhelm, Alarik, and Mauritz were seal hunting off the coast of Sweden, Mauritz complained of a terrible headache. Vilhelm and Alarik took him to hospital in Sweden. The doctor said they would attend to the boy and see that he got home when he was well. On May 21, when Vilhelm and Alarik were back in Molpe, they got a telegram from the doctor that Mauritz was worse. Vilhelm and Alarik drove to Sweden, but, when they got there, Mauritz was unconscious. On May 29, he died of encephalitis.

"He was twenty-one-years old," Charlie said. "Twenty-one years old!"

Tilda refolded the letter and put it back in the envelope. "To think Mauritz made it through the terrible war, just to come home and get sick and die."

Charlie got up from his chair slowly, heavily, like the world was too much for him, and walked outside. Tilda sat quietly, sipping her coffee.

"I'll get it," Angie shouted as she bolted from her room. Tilda never raced Angie to the phone because the calls were hardly ever for her.

"Yes, this is Agnes Lind," she heard her daughter say. "No, no one has called me.... Yes, I was hoping to hear from you.... When?.... Tomorrow?.... For an interview?.... Nine o'clock in the morning?.... Yes, I know where the office is.... Yes, Sir! I'll be there.... Thank you, Mr. Plancich. I'll be there. Bye."

"Ya-hoo!" Angie shouted as she put the receiver down. "Did you hear that, Mom? The cannery called me for an interview. Mr. Plancich said he was sure there'd be no problem. He'd checked with the school. Mrs. Beal, my commercial teacher, and Mrs. Beard, my English teacher, both told him they thought I could do the job!"

"Then I guess you can," Tilda said.

"Mom, I'm going to go clean my room. If there's anything else you want me to do today, just tell me. You know I always like to help with the housework."

43

PAYDAY
July 1945

Mr. Plancich strode across the office and bolted the front door. Angie peered out the window from behind her wide, time-scarred desk. People were standing in a long line waiting to pick up their week's paychecks. A man at the front of the line shook his fist at the front door of the office and shouted, "Today's payday! Where's my check?"

The year before, Fishermen's Packing Corporation in Anacortes had been named a "Nucleus Plant" by Interior Secretary Harold L. Ickes, Coordinator of Fisheries, Washington, D.C. Consolidating the five canneries bordering Guemes Channel into one significantly alleviated the critical shortage of workers. Fishermen's Pack as the sole cannery would, however, need some additional personnel in the office. Angie was hired to help out as payroll clerk.

Three weeks ago, when the office manager, John Plancich, ushered Angie into the main office, she had been nervous but excited. The room was orderly and not much larger than her living room. An oak counter, discolored from years of use, divided the room into a narrow aisle for workers and an area for office staff. Two oversized desks and a tall wooden file cabinet filled the area.

Windows on two sides of the office faced toward the street that curved past the cannery and the sidewalk that led up to the front door. Salt-sprayed windows on the third side overlooked Guemes Channel. Signs above doors in the remaining wall read "Manager" and "Exit." Angie learned that the exit door opened onto a wooden walkway to the cannery.

"Miss Helser," Mr. Plancich had said to the elderly woman seated at one of the desks, "I want you to meet Miss Lind who will be responsible for the payroll this summer."

Angie, happy with the prospect of her job, smiled at Miss Helser. Wraithlike and stern, Miss Helser rose from her chair and nodded. Angie learned that Miss Helser had been sole bookkeeper for Fishermen's Pack for many years. Now, at Mr. Plancich's request, she dutifully explained to Angie the responsibilities of a payroll clerk. Then she sat back down at her desk and returned to her ledger. Angie wondered if Miss Helser resented the idea that she needed help, especially from a high-school girl.

The bookwork at the beginning had gone well for Angie. The hourly wages for different jobs in the cannery varied, but Angie had only to fill in the employees' names and their wages in the correct columns, and then record the number of hours they'd worked and figure their salaries. Most of the cannery workers had signed on for the season and worked regular shifts, so posting this information wasn't difficult. Miss Helser did explain, however, that when people worked overtime, they got paid time-and-a-half. And then there were some deductions....

Angie thought back to that first day in the office. The smell of the oiled wood floors had made her nostalgic for her school in Potlatch. Now, with the cannery in operation, the office smelled of salmon heads and entrails and other cannery waste sloughed off into Guemes Channel. Salmon parts that were not eaten by the swooping seagulls rotted on the beach in the hot summer sun. Angie knew that living with this smell would be part of working in a fish cannery.

Then, late in July, just as she began to feel comfortable in her work, the salmon run exploded! The greatest salmon run since 1911, the newspaper said. Angie knew it was true. She could see from the office window fishing boats lined up at the end of the wharf. The boats bobbed about restlessly in the choppy water, their sides barely clearing the surface of the water as they waited to unload.

The regular cannery crew was overwhelmed. It was bad enough that five canneries had merged into one, but now to have a record salmon season! The newspaper and the local radio station announced the emergency. The cannery needed workers immediately to process what was turning out to be the largest harvest of salmon in over 30 years. Without more help on the cannery lines, salmon would spoil in the holds of the boats before they could be unloaded.

The community responded. Men and women came after working their regular jobs to put in a few hours. Mr. Wooten, the high-school football coach, called off football practice and sent his boys to the cannery. Housewives left their dishes in the sink and reported for work.

A hot spell hit Anacortes about the same time as the tremendous influx of fish. The heat in the cannery and the stench of the fish were nearly unbearable. Working conditions in the main office were not much better. The windows that faced the channel heated the room like a furnace. Miss Helser pulled down the shades, but still the temperature in the office climbed into the nineties. She opened the front and the exit doors for a cross draft, but the smell from the beach became intolerable, so she closed the doors. Angie's sweaty hands stuck to the pages of her time sheets. The penciled entries smeared and had to be rewritten.

The cannery superintendent reported more than 20,000 salmon were being unloaded on their docks every day and repeated his call for help. Angie added pages of names to her books as more and more people reported for work. Some of the new people stayed a day or two. Some, only a few hours. Those who had worked on their days off from other jobs needed to return to them, or, like Angie's mom, got sick from the heat and the smell.

Mom had really wanted to help. She'd reported to the cannery the second day of the emergency. A foreman outfitted her with a long oilskin apron, rubber boots, gloves, and arm protectors. She had to furnish her own head cover. He directed her to join the line of women at the sliming tables. The heads and tails of the salmon had been cut off and the entrails removed by machines before the fish were put onto a conveyer belt to the slimmers. The job of the slimmer was to pull a fish off the belt, wash out its cavity, and then with a knife scrape the slime off the outside of the fish. "You scrape the direction the scales lay, not against the scales," the woman standing next to Mom had instructed.

Angie's mom had cleaned fish before, but handling the big salmon was another story. The cold water from the hoses splashed against her apron and her legs, and puddled at her feet. Fish scales flew about and landed on her face and neck. She even found a scale behind her ear when she got home. At the end of the day, her arms and back hurt from handling the heavy fish and her feet ached from standing in cold water. That night she told Angie to tell the cannery foreman she wouldn't be back.

The line of people waiting for their checks had bunched up around the front door. "It's Friday night," a man shouted. "We want our paychecks!" A rumble of voices echoed the demand.

Angie turned the pages of her time book back to Monday. Maybe if she started the week over.... She looked out the front window again. There wasn't time for that! People rattled the doorknob, banged on the door, and chanted in unison, "Pay day! Pay day!" Faces filled the window in the door.

Mr. Plancich burst out of the manager's office and marched across the main office to the outside door. He pulled down the window shade and turned to Miss Helser. "No one gets paid until the checks are ready!"

"Miss Lind already wrote out the checks. They're ready—"

"Not when the books don't balance," Mr. Plancich exclaimed. "No one gets paid until the books are balanced!" He walked back into his office and slammed the door.

Big, black, lazy summer flies circled the room. A few landed on the sticky strip of flypaper that hung above the counter. People continued milling around outside the office. Angie's eyes blurred as she studied the numbers on her time sheets. Mr. Plancich had hired Angie to help Miss Helser, but now it was Angie who needed help!

"Let me see what I can do," Miss Helser said and stepped over to Angie's desk. Angie gave Miss Helser her chair and stood back to watch. Miss Helser's birdlike shoulders hunched over the desk and wisps of white hair escaped from her carefully pinned bun and stuck to the sweat on the back of her neck.

"Have you checked the adding-machine tape against the figures posted in this column?" Miss Helser asked, pointing at the open page. With her other hand she pushed her wire-rimmed glasses back in place. "Maybe you copied a number wrong."

"I've checked that," Angie said, swallowing hard to calm herself. "The figures on the tape and in the time book agree."

"How about the time-and-a-half for overtime? Did you add in the extra pay for those who worked overtime?"

"I did! It's the people who worked half a day or a day-and–a-half or two or three days who've messed up my books!" Angie exclaimed, dropping into Miss Helser's chair. "I don't know where else to look! I've added up the checks and the figure comes to more than what my books say we should pay out."

The pounding at the outside door continued.

Angie looked at the clock. The office usually closed at five. It was now six-thirty. Her mother would be worried.

"I know how impossible your job has been this last week," Miss Helser said without looking up from the time sheets. "You were doing fine and wouldn't have needed my help under ordinary circumstances." She paused. "We'll figure it out."

Angie blinked back the tears. Miss Helser had become her ally against the angry mob.

Mr. Plancich opened his office door again. Angie straightened up and swiped at her cheeks. Miss Helser looked up from the time sheets. Mr. Plancich made no comment. He walked to the front door and snapped up the shade. He looked out the window at the distressed crowd. Then he unbolted the door and turned to Angie and Miss Helser.

"Go ahead, Ladies," he said. "Hand out the checks. We'll figure it out on Monday."

44

GIANT MUSHROOMS
August 1945

Angie turned the page on her desk calendar. August 9—
Mr. Plancich burst into the front door of the office. "Did you hear the news?" he hollered. "We dropped an atomic bomb on Hiroshima! That bomb was so powerful it wiped out the whole city!"

"Have you heard?" the plant foreman shouted as he ran in the door from the cannery.

"We heard," Mr. Plancich said. The men shook hands as if they had something to do with it.

"The radio announcer said the temperature at the center of the explosion was 100 million degrees," the foreman said. "Four times the temperature at the center of the sun! A ball of fire about a mile in diameter went up and spread out like a giant mushroom."

"I heard the same news," Mr. Plancich said. "The Japs have to give up now!"

The two men darted out the exit door to the cannery to spread the news.

Miss Helser turned to Angie. "The bomb wiped out a whole city? A city full of people?"

Three days after the first atomic bomb, a second one was dropped on the city of Nagasaki. Radios and newspapers broadcast the news. Cheers went up in the cannery, in Anacortes, and across the country. Another Japanese city leveled!

Miss Helser looked at Angie. "But the women and children...." Her voice trailed off, small, apologetic.

Then, gradually, estimated statistics about Hiroshima and Nagasaki were published. In Hiroshima 70,000 men, women, and children were incinerated in the atomic blast and that many more were burned over much of their bodies. Four-and-a-half square miles of city were leveled. In Nagasaki, one-and-a-half square miles of the city were destroyed, 36,000 people vaporized, and 40,000 burned, but still alive! Miss Helser passed the newspaper on to Angie.

A doctor had been treating an ingrown wart on the bottom of Angie's foot with acid. Each application burned deeper into the ball of her foot until she couldn't sit still at her office desk. She'd press her foot hard against the floor, or she'd pace from her desk to the window and back, or she'd remove her shoe and sock and fan her foot with a folded paper. Miss Helser had sympathized with her and said she wished there was something she could do.

"Burned but alive!" Angie exclaimed as she took the newspaper from Miss Helser. The spot on the bottom of Angie's foot was the size of a dime. What would it be like to be burned over all your body? Maybe worse than dying from burns would be surviving!

Fishing boats continued to line up at the dock, waiting to unload. One-hundred thousand fish a week was the count. Angie heard talk of opening up one of the other canneries, but it didn't happen. There would be no one to work at the canning lines. Mr. Plancich told Angie to do her best with the payroll, and, even if it didn't balance exactly, go ahead and hand out the checks on time. He couldn't expect anyone to keep track of the crazy turnover of cannery workers.

Angie often ate her lunch outside on the shady side of the office to catch a little of the cool breeze off the water. Others gathered there, too, especially during the next few days. Everyone was talking about the bomb.

"Sure it was bad," one cannery worker said, "but they started it!"

The women and children started it? Angie wondered, remembering Miss Helser's words.

"It was the only way to end the war," several people said as they opened their lunch pails.

"But the war was about to end anyway," a woman responded.

"But lives of our boys were saved by ending it quick," her friend said.

"But a city full of people?" Someone echoed Miss Helser's words.

Angie looked out at the water. Across the channel, fir-covered, madrona-edged Guemes Island stretched out like a resplendant, green sea-creature absorbing the sun. At the end of Fishermen's Pack wharf, the line of boats rocked on the incoming tide. Directly below the office window, gentle waves lapped at the rocky beach. But visions of the horror of war blurred the scene. Angie watched seagulls swooping back and forth above the detritus of salmon parts, their plaintive cries suggesting that they, too, had heard about the unthinkable carnage.

Angie limped as she moved about the office. She'd tried sitting on her foot to make it go to sleep so she wouldn't feel the burning, but that hadn't worked. The acid was doing what the doctor intended, eating away at the roots of the wart. She knew she just had to tough it out.

"Next time you need something from the file cabinet, let me get it for you," Miss Helser offered.

Angie nodded her thanks. As she turned to her time sheets, Mr. Plancich flew in the front door shouting, "Here it is! What we've been waiting for!" He held up a newspaper. Angie could read the headlines from where she sat. Tall letters in bold print announced, "JAPAN SURRENDERS!"

"'Tomorrow, August 15, has been declared V-J Day,'" Mr. Plancich read aloud. "Victory in Japan Day! The whole country will celebrate like they did on V-E Day. Tomorrow night Commercial Avenue downtown will be blocked off for music and dancing!"

Mr. Plancich was out of breath but read on. "'Businesses are closing for two days, tomorrow and the next day—'"

"Us, too?" Angie asked.

Mr. Plancich thought a moment and then shook his head. "I'm afraid the salmon won't be on holiday," he said, "but we can celebrate as we work! The war is over! Our boys are coming home!"

45

STRANGER IN THE HOUSE
October 1945

Bennie received his discharge from the Army in October, but Angie was remembering May, when Bennie was allowed to go home for a short furlough. Angie and her parents had driven to Shelton to see him and to say good-bye to Thelma and Linda as they had decided to accompany Bennie to Georgia for his final six months of duty.

The first morning Bennie was home on furlough, Linda ran into the kitchen and pulled at her mother's skirt. "He's still here, Mom," she whispered, looking back toward the living room.

"I know," Thelma whispered back. "He lives here now. Go see what Grandma and Grandpa are doing. Angie and I are fixing breakfast."

The house hadn't warmed up yet on this cool spring morning in Shelton, but Linda's fine hair was stuck to her forehead from perspiration. Her round, deep-blue eyes searched her mother's face. Thelma patted her on her head. Linda hesitated, but then ran back down the hall toward the living room.

Thelma took eggs out of the refrigerator and set them on the counter by the mixing bowl. As she cracked the eggs into the bowl, she told Angie how glad she was that they had come to visit. She explained then that Linda needed reassurance because of all the changes in her young, four-year-old life. She'd been a baby when her dad left, so, to her, he was a stranger. Thelma said Linda had often slept with her on cold nights, but last night this stranger was in her mother's bed!

Thelma took the frying pan out of the stove drawer and set it on a burner. She pulled a loaf of bread out of the breadbox and plugged in the toaster. "Hey, Angie," she said, "know what I'm going to do? Just for fun, I'm going to burn Bennie's toast."

Now Angie searched her face!

"The first breakfast I fixed for Bennie as a new bride was a disaster," Thelma explained. "I kept burning his toast! I was so upset, I cried. Bennie tried to comfort me by saying he liked burnt toast best. Let's see if he still does!"

Angie had loved the conspiracy and hurried to finish setting the table.

"Mom! Mom!" Linda was back in the kitchen tugging at her mother's skirt.

"What is it, Linda?" Thelma asked, turning from the stove with a spatula in her hand. Angie wondered if the eggs would be burned too.

Linda's dimple flashed in her cheek as she worked her mouth, searching for words. "He's reading the paper now, Mom," she'd whispered.

"That's okay, Linda. He can read the newspaper if he wants," Thelma whispered back. She picked up her worried daughter and set her on the kitchen counter. "He's your daddy and we're a family again."

Linda had smiled and hugged her mother.

Mom came into the kitchen then. She said she couldn't understand the army. They'd asked Bennie where he wanted to be stationed, and when Bennie said Fort Lewis near Tacoma, they sent him to Georgia. Thelma said that was typical of the army. And now it was time to go to the table.

Bennie told Thelma the burnt toast tasted fine. He thanked Angie for all the letters she'd written him while he was overseas. She'd really kept him up to date. Then he asked how were things going for her now that she was almost a senior.

"Things are great," Angie had said. And they were, but that had been in May before her summer job at the cannery and her ingrown wart!

The fish run had been heavier than ever in September. "Greatest Fish Run Since 1911," the *American* announced, but Angie had to quit her job because school was starting. Miss Helser would be left doing the payroll along with her other work, but she hadn't complained. Angie would miss her. Miss Helser had fixed tea for them in the afternoons and, even though they didn't always have time to drink it, it smelled nice. Better than fish!

Angie and Miss Helser had gotten off to a bad start. "I don't think I tried to know her," Angie had told her mother, "because she looked so old." Her mom said maybe Miss Helser hadn't tried to know Angie because she looked so young.

Mr. Plancich had thanked Angie for her hard work and explained that next summer, with the war over, all four canneries would be open, and Miss Helser could handle the greatly reduced payroll at Fishermen's Pack.

Angie was relieved about that and happy to be back in school. Her ingrown wart was finally gone, and she'd earned enough money at the cannery to open a college savings account. She was already involved in her high-school clubs and activities. She'd been elected secretary-treasurer of her class and of choir, probably because of her office experience, and she was senior editor of the yearbook. Best of all, she, Marivonne, and Joanne Brodie had been elected song leaders for football and basketball games.

Mom had said Angie was taking on too much. Thelma said she guessed Angie could do all that because she never did anything around the house. Dad said just because gas rationing had ended, Angie didn't need to think she'd be taking the car to all those activities and ball games. Angie argued that, since the war was over, she and her friends wouldn't be spending time on paper drives and scrap metal drives, or selling war bonds. Now they had time for school activities.

The war really was over. On September 2, Japan signed a formal document of surrender aboard the *USS Missouri* in Tokyo Bay. President Truman recommended an economic recovery plan to Congress, and the United Nations was established. In the future, an international peacekeeping force would police the world.

But newspapers reminded people that effects of the war would be with them a long time. In Anacortes alone, 750 men and women had had their lives disrupted by being called into the service. Japanese Americans were released from internment, but returned to communities where there was bigotry, where they no longer had jobs, and often where their property and businesses had been unjustly taken.

It was so unfair, Angie thought. Many young Japanese American men joined the service and fought in Europe while their families were behind barbed wire. The newspaper printed a story about James Okubo, a Japanese American boy who was born in Anacortes and later moved to Bellingham to go to Western Washington College. He, along with his two brothers and two cousins, volunteered to join the Army.

While they and other Japanese Americans risked their lives in Italy evacuating and treating soldiers wounded in battle, their families were confined to Tule Lake Internment Camp. James's friend, William Nakamura from Seattle, whose family was in an internment camp in Idaho, died from an enemy bullet in Castellian, Italy, on July 4, 1944.

In September, when the war was over, ticker-tape parades in the cities had greeted the men and women who returned from overseas. Nothing that big happened in Shelton, but families, churches, and lodges welcomed their returning men and women with open arms. Bennie had been in Guadalcanal and the Philippines during the war, but he wanted to put that behind him, he told Angie at breakfast that morning in May. He just wanted to get reacquainted with his family.

Then he'd told Angie something else. He told her he still had every letter she'd written him while he was overseas, and he valued those letters more than the medal he was scheduled to receive upon his discharge from the Army.

He'd also told Angie not to tell her sister, but he really hated burnt toast!

46

"WHEN THE LIGHTS GO ON AGAIN..."
December/January 1946

"Tonight President Truman will light the Christmas tree at the White House," Angie announced at the supper table. "Mr. Smith told us about it in class today. It's the first time since 1941!" Angie helped herself to potatoes. "And we'll open our living-room blinds and show the whole world our lighted Christmas tree."

"Only if the whole world happens to be standing on ninth and K," Charlie said, but Tilda noticed he smiled as he said it.

"Did I tell you Bill Charlot is home?" Angie asked as she reached for the gravy. "Faith said when he went back to his Marine outfit after his leave, he took part in the invasion of Guam. After they took back that island, he was sent to China. That's where he was when the war ended."

"Have you seen him yet?" Tilda asked. "You spent a lot of time at Charlot's house the summer he was home on leave."

"I saw him Sunday at church. He gave me a big-brother kind of hug. Faith said he's already seeing a girl he met when he was home before. He's a lot older than me, you know."

Tilda was pleased. Angie really was growing up.

"This is going to be a happy Christmas for everyone!" Angie exclaimed.

Tilda hoped this was true. Maybe she could stop worrying about what was going on in the world now if she stopped reading the newspapers.

Eighteen-million women lost their jobs after the war. They'd liked earning money and being independent. They resented being let go and sent home to keep house. Tilda had trouble understanding this because she had never worked away from home, except for the night she slimed fish and the week she and Charlie picked potatoes. Bending over all day in the hot potato field to fill gunnysacks and then dragging the heavy sacks behind her was terrible hard work. But farmers had been desperate for help. She was happy to stay home after those experiences. Still, if millions of women were unhappy about not working, then America had a problem.

Another thing. The paper said this country needed 4,500,000 homes for the men and women coming out of the service. Families were doubling up in apartments, or living in old army barracks and Quonset huts, and a few, Tilda read, were even living in cars.

And the Department of Agriculture reported that 20,000,000 tons of food were needed to feed Europe. Like in Finland, war had destroyed farms and whole cities. People everywhere, many thousands of them refugees, needed food to survive—

"So Mom," Angie interrupted, "what did you think?"

Tilda hadn't been paying attention to the supper conversation.

"Mom, some parents are upset about our play. What did you think?"

"Your class play? *Junior Miss*? I thought it was good, especially having it on the stage at the Empire Theater. Except there was a lot of swearing in it."

"I didn't think it was that bad, but some parents called our principal."

"Well," Tilda said. "I was surprised to hear swearing in a school play."

"It wasn't in the script," Angie said, "but it just seemed to us kids that it was more real if those playing adult parts used a few swear words. You know. Like grown-ups do all the time."

"I guess it don't sound right coming from school children," Tilda said.

"Anyway," Angie said, "we made a lot of money for the Living War Memorial Athletic Field at the high school. No one can complain about that!"

That was true, Tilda thought. A living war memorial was a good thing. The young people weren't forgetting what those just a little older than them had done for their country.

"Mom," Angie said.

My, Tilda thought, Angie was talkative this evening. Sometimes she'd sit through a whole meal and not say a word. Maybe it was because Christmas was in the air.

"Mom, Dad, have you heard the popular English war song that starts out, 'When the lights go on again, all over the world'? That's what's happening, isn't it? Lights are going on at the White House and in our living room and everywhere. Maybe even Finland. This is going to be one great Christmas!"

The week before Christmas, it snowed almost every day. Tilda looked at the quiet swirls on the hedge and rooftops and was reminded of Charlie's favorite icing, her seven-minute, egg-white frosting. She hadn't made that since before the war.

Two days before Christmas, Ida and Charlie arrived. Thelma. Bennie, and Linda, the day before Christmas. Linda touched each ornament with the tip of her finger and smiled at her reflection in the shiny bulb. Chee Chee, as usual, climbed into the tree branches and swatted the tinsel, but nobody seemed to mind. The war had ended and Bennie was home.

"I wonder what kind of Christmas they have in Finland this year," Charlie said as the family sat at the dinner table on Christmas Day. His answer came the second week of January in a letter from Vilhelm.

Dear Charlie and family,

Snow is deep in Finland now and still falling. It hides for a while some of the terrible destruction of the war. We had little food or heat in our home during the holiday, but it was all right because we were together as family.

After five years in the army, Alarik was released in time for Christmas. Manne was discharged from the service December 16. His face is still terribly scarred from the machine gun accident. Finland also bears scars from the war, but, perhaps, unlike Manne's face, time will erase some of those scars.

Though we had little to give each other in material gifts, we had our Christmas traditions. Early Christmas morning, Hulda and I hung a bell from the collar of our horse, lighted torches, and, with the family and neighbors, walked to church. Anni Irene, my oldest girl, was home from Sweden. She, Nadine and Elli stayed close to their mother; Alarik and Manne walked next to me. Everyone in the parade of lights sang Christmas carols and then hymns of thanks for more than a full year of peace.

In the spring I will be back to my seal hunting. It grieves me to think of seal hunting without Mauritz. I had told Mauritz my secret for accurate shooting, and the boy had shown great promise as a seal hunter. We took flowers to Mauritz's grave on Christmas Eve.

My family sends greetings to your family. I know we share the hope that 1946 will be the first of many years of peace.

With affection,
Vilhelm

A week after Charlie heard from Vilhelm, Tilda got a letter from her sister-in-law Ester.

Ester didn't mentioned the snow, but she wrote that, in spite of the lack of food and heat, she had found much to be thankful for this Christmas. Birger had been home a little over a year now, and Edvin, six months. They, with their young wives, Anni and Elvie, came to Ester's house for Christmas dinner. Ture ran here and there gathering wood for the cook stove and helping Ester get the meal on the table. He would stop only long enough to look with admiration at his older brothers, veterans of the terrible war.

Like Finland, America had been gradually releasing its servicemen and women. Some had made it home in time for Christmas. Others still counted the days, but felt lucky to be coming home at all. Gold stars hung in the front windows of many homes in Skagit County.

Faith reminded Angie and Tilda of her brother's friend, Pat Buchanon, who had been home on medical leave the same time as Bill. He'd been offered a medical discharge but turned it down. Faith and Pat wrote to each other when he returned to the South Pacific. Now his family had received word that he was missing in action.

By the end of January, snow had melted from the streets in Anacortes, but sidewalks retained a thin sheet of ice. Tilda looked out the kitchen window and saw Angie running and sliding on the ice as she approached the house.

"Mom, I'm home," Angie called from the back door. "What's to eat?"

"Cookies in the cupboard," Tilda said, punching down a mound of lively dough that was trying to escape the bowl. "The mailman stopped at our door a while ago, but my hands were in the bread dough. Would you see what he brought us today?"

Angie munched a gingersnap on her way to the living room. "A letter from Art!" she called out as she ran into the kitchen.

"He's still in Connecticut," Tilda said, looking at the postmark on the envelope. She wiped her hands on the dishtowel, slit the envelope open with a table knife, unfolded and read the letter.

Art would be finished with submarine school and discharged from the Navy in a couple weeks. He and Alice would drive across the country by way of Florida, Texas, and California. They'd arrive at Anacortes some time in February when Art would start working at the plywood plant. The mill manager had offered him the job of developing a high-frequency edge-gluer patch machine.

"Angie, it looks like Art and Alice are moving to Anacortes," Tilda said. "But listen to this. 'Because of the shortage of housing in Anacortes, we'll be living in a government housing project. We're lucky to get even that, and with a baby coming in July—'"

"Oh, my gosh!" Angie exclaimed. "They're having a baby! And they'll be living in Anacortes, and I can see the baby every day!"

"Unless you go to that college way off in Oregon," Tilda said.

Angie sat down. Tilda could see that Angie would have to think about that.

PART VIII - 1946

47

LIBERAL ARTS
February

"Mom, look at this," Angie said, walking into the kitchen with the January 31 issue of the *American*. "'Infantile Paralysis Strikes Skagit and Whatcom Counties.' The article says that cases last July increased so fast in a few weeks that St. Joseph's Hospital in Bellingham couldn't handle them all in their regular facilities."

"So what did they do," Mom asked.

"They had to turn the nurses' meeting hall into an isolation ward for the victims, the paper says. There were two major polio epidemics last year with three deaths and it looks like this year won't be any better. Heck, Mom, it isn't even summer when people swim in the lakes."

"I guess infantile paralysis doesn't have a season after all," her mom said. "I just hope and pray that someday doctors will find a cure. Sit down now and eat your toast and dry mush."

"Cereal, Mom." Angie took her place at the kitchen table and looked out the window. "So how do we keep from getting polio?"

"Nobody knows. If we get it, it's God's will."

"I don't believe it was God's will for Joy Kamps to get polio and spend more than a year in a cast. Or for Sally Isaacson to end up in a wheel chair for the rest of her life."

"We read in the Bible that God works in mysterious ways, Angie."

"Maybe polio isn't God's work. Maybe God is there in case you get polio."

"Angie," her mom said, "your breakfast is getting cold."

"Mom, cornflakes don't get cold!" Angie poured milk on her cereal. "All I'm saying," Angie persisted, "is it's not God's fault. If I get to go to Linfield in the fall, I'll ask my religion professor why bad things like polio happen to good people like Joy and Sally. And Mrs. Hinds."

"*Ja,* that was bad, too," Mom said. "It happened a couple days after school started last fall, if I remember right. I knew Mrs. Hinds when she worked at Model Cleaners on Commercial. She came down with polio one day, and a week later she was gone. God's will."

Angie watched her mother turn away. Angie knew she was thinking about Leonard's death. She'd heard her mom say that maybe God was punishing them for something they'd done. Like too much dancing and card playing. Angie hoped they didn't still think that.

"Joy is doing well now," Angie said, wanting to tell her mom something cheerful. "She's in the middle of her first year at Mount Vernon Junior College. Marivonne said Joy is thinking of going into teaching. She'd be a really good teacher."

Angie sprinkled two teaspoons of sugar on her cornflakes to make up for doing without for three years. She glanced out the window again. "Oh, no!" she said, starting out of her chair. "Here they are and I'm not ready!"

"Who's picking you up?"

"Phyllis's mom is driving. Faith and Yvonne are with her."

"Well, invite them in. They can wait while you finish your breakfast."

"What we're doing is more important than breakfast!" Angie said, taking a quick bite of toast. She grabbed her warm coat from the back of her chair and ran out the door. "Bye," she called over her shoulder.

Mayor Joe Hagan was in charge of Anacortes's January Infantile Paralysis Drive. Everyone wanted to help. Lady Eagles and Lady

Elks and other community groups sponsored activities to raise money. The high-school Honor Society advisors, Mrs. Macready and Miss Carter, enlisted twenty high-school seniors to go door-to-door in teams of two to solicit money to fight the disease.

Kids were already standing around in front of the Big Gym when they drove up. Girls wore scarves and mittens and hugged themselves against the cold. Boys tugged knit hats down over their ears and stamped their feet to keep warm. The snow was gone, but a freezing wind bit at exposed cheeks.

Joyce and Edna waved. "Hurry up. We're about to start," Edna called.

Boys and girls waited around in groups. Angie didn't see Johnny, but Edwin was there, and Louis Grinnell. "Swede" Larson, their student body president, and Bob and Janet Fithian, stood together on the gym steps.

Joyce told the girls standing next to her that her folks had gone to the annual March of Dimes dance at Eagles Hall. "Mom said it brought in a lot of money again this year," Joyce said. "I could have gone with them if I'd wanted."

"I thought the dance was for adults only," Angie said.

"It was, but I'll be eighteen February 20. That's almost adult."

"I guess I could have gone," Faith said. "I was eighteen in November."

"Everyone over here," Mr. Smith called. He was the boys' Key Club advisor. They'd solicited money the week before.

"People know when you go to their doors that whatever they can give will help," Mr. Smith instructed. "You'll find that people are generous. Some last week contributed as much as a dollar.

"Now pick up your identification tags so people know you are legitimate money raisers. Don't forget your maps with the route marked in red. Come back here by four o'clock because it starts getting dark then. Mayflower Bakery donated cookies, and two of the mothers will see that hot chocolate is waiting for you."

Mr. Smith was right. Faith and Angie smelled the hot chocolate as they rejoined the group. They soon forgot how cold and tired they were. Two moms were handing out steaming mugs of chocolate to those already sitting on the front steps. Kids were warming their hands by wrapping them around the hot mugs. Mr. Smith collected the money from the students as they left and thanked them on behalf of Mayor Hagan and the Infantile Paralysis Committee.

"Thanks for the ride," Angie said as she got out of Luvera's car in front of her house.

"Looks like you have company," Phyllis said, pointing to a car parked in Angie's backyard.

"We're not expecting anyone. Maybe someone from the Lutheran church is here to see Mom."

"With a Connecticut license?" Faith asked.

Angie slammed the car door and ran for the back door. She flew into the kitchen!

"There she is," a familiar voice called out from the breakfast-nook table. "My lil' Cuz!" he said and stood up. Art and Alice weren't expected for another two weeks.

Angie darted across the kitchen and welcomed Art with a big hug. Art returned the hug, introduced Alice to Angie, and then held Angie at arm's length. "This isn't my lil' Cuz," he said. "This is a young lady. She must have grown up while I was gone. I'm going to have to treat her with more respect!"

Mom and Dad laughed. Alice gave Angie a shy hug. Dad offered to help Art bring in their suitcases. They'd be staying a few days until their apartment in the housing project was ready.

After supper and dishes, they all sat down in the front room. Angie told Art and Alice about the March for Dimes and all the money they collected—though she didn't know exactly how much because Mr. Smith hadn't counted it yet.

"So, Art, what did you and Alice do when you heard Japan surrendered?" Dad asked.

Art smiled at Alice. "You tell them, Dear," he said.

"Well, as you know, the President declared a two-day holiday," Alice said. "Art's classes were cancelled, and we and another couple drove to Cape Cod to celebrate. When we got there, everything was closed. Restaurants. Motels. For dinner the four of us ate cough drops, the only thing we had with us that was edible, and slept in the car. That's it," she said, a little apologetically. "Not a great story."

"Well, it was certainly memorable!" Art said and laughed.

Angie sat on the floor next to Alice's chair. Chee Chee found Angie's lap and curled up in it.

"Is that the same cat we used to tease?" Art asked. "Remember, Unc?"

Dad laughed. Mom said it sure was the same cat, and a good thing cats had nine lives or he wouldn't be here today.

"Aw, *Moster*, we weren't that hard on him."

Mom laughed then.

Art turned to Angie. "So what are your plans after graduation, lil' Cuz—I mean Angie?"

"I want to go to Linfield College in McMinnville, Oregon, but I don't know if I can get in."

"Why couldn't you get in?" Art asked. "I thought you had good grades."

"My grades are all right," Angie said, "but there may not be room. Hundreds of veterans will be enrolling on the GI Bill with the government paying for their education."

Dad said, "I'm not sure a girl needs all that education anyway. She'll just get married and then what use is it? There's a good business college in Mount Vernon. If she goes there, in two years she's almost guaranteed a job."

Angie looked around, waiting for someone to come to her defense.

Dad went on. "A private college like Linfield is expensive—"

"I'll work for my tuition!" Angie interrupted. "The Linfield catalog says students can do that. There are jobs like cleaning the library and working in the cafeteria—"

"If you learn how to cook and clean, it might be worth the price of tuition," Dad said, and grinned at Mom.

Now everyone but Alice laughed. "Angie," she said, "I think it's great you want to go to a liberal arts college. It will be a wonderful, broadening experience."

"That's one of the problems," Mom said. "She might learn ideas in a liberal school that don't fit with what she's been taught at home and in church. I've been told that liberal ideas can be dangerous."

"Heck, Mom, 'liberal arts' just means learning about the world. As a freshman I'd be taking Art and Music Appreciation, Western Civilization, World History, World Literature. I'd be studying different religions...."

The room became quiet. Chee Chee purred louder, filling the silence. Art cleared his throat.

"What do you want to be when you graduate from college?" Alice asked, easing the tension a little.

"Maybe a writer," Angie answered.

"I thought you were going to be a missionary," Mom said. Angie knew she should have shared her ideas with her mom before now.

"You can't support yourself on writing," Dad exclaimed.

"I know, I know!" Angie said, her frustration growing. "Maybe I'll be an English teacher and teach writing. Bennie said the letters I wrote him when he was overseas were worth more to him that his medal."

"Angie," her mom said, "that wasn't because of your writing. It was because they were from home. From you."

"Okay. But I may not get into Linfield anyway...."

Art cleared his throat again. "So, Unc, how are things going at the mill? I'm working my dad's share, you know, and buying it from him at the same time. In a year or so, I'll be a stockholder in my own right. I think Alice and I have a future in Anacortes."

"You and Alice and the baby." Mom smiled as she said it.

"You're right!" Art said.

"Anacortes is a good place to raise a family," Mom said.

"No question about that," Dad said and smiled at Angie.

48

GRADUATION
May 1946

A gust of wind whipped around the corner of the Big Gym. It threatened to dislodge the mortarboard hats balanced so precariously on the heads of the graduates. Angie reset the bobby pin on the back of her headpiece to hold it in place. She wondered why anyone would design such a crazy hat for a solemn occasion like graduation.

The day had been warm, but a breeze chilled the evening. Her mom had told her to wear something warm under her robe, but her mom was always telling her to wear something warm. This time she wished she'd listened. She had forgotten that the class would be lining up outside the gym for half an hour before commencement exercises began.

Angie looked down the column of graduates. Some mortarboards were askew and, as always, some of the boys were playfully pushing and shoving. Mr. Stockman pointed his finger at them and they got back in line.

Because the school colors were purple and white, the boys in graduation classes wore purple robes and the girls, white. Angie's class, the class of '46, wanted something different, perhaps because their school years had been different. Theirs was the first class in five years to graduate in peacetime. Whatever the reason, the class decided the boys would wear blue robes instead of the traditional purple. The girls would still wear white robes.

In spite of the daily distraction of war news and the time-consuming drives to sell war bonds and to collect materials needed by the army, the class had done well. The choir attended music festivals at the University of Washington and won state and national superior awards; the boys' basketball team won third in district and third in state.

Individuals in the class had been recognized for outstanding achievements. Phyllis Luvera received a plaque from the president of the Business and Professional Women's Club for her grade of "Excellent" at the District Debate Tournament. Edna served as state president of Future Homemakers of America. Others were recognized as outstanding. Not one but three students—Bob Fithian, Janet Fithian, and Dallis Perry—tied for valedictorian by earning straight A's through four years of high school. Edna, with only a fraction lower grade point, became salutatorian.

The gym they were about to enter housed a multitude of memories for Angie. P.E. classes, basketball games, dances. Once the Girls Athletic Club had a giant slumber party here and the girls made their beds on the hardwood floor. Nobody slept. Angie thought it was a very long night.

Often the Big Gym was turned magically into an auditorium. A stage located on one side of the gym became the platform for speakers for school assemblies, programs, plays, and other events. When a performance was scheduled, the janitor with student help placed rows of folding chairs on the gym floor. Tonight parents and friends of the graduates would occupy those chairs.

"Here she comes," Phyllis whispered to Angie. "Better face front."

Miss Carter, one of their two class advisors, was walking down the line of students with her clipboard. She glanced at each student as she moved along and then made a check on her list. She stopped once and rearranged two boys and a girl. "Lind, Luvera," she read as she came to Angie and Phyllis, and smiled her approval. Miss Carter was making sure students were in alphabetical order and that the girls weren't wearing saddle shoes.

Seven o'clock. The moment they'd been waiting for! As the school band began playing "Pomp and Circumstance," Mr. Stockman, their other class advisor, signaled the students to proceed. Then, like a giant blue and white caterpillar, the class marched in pairs up the stone steps, through the double doors, and into the Big Gym. Twenty-seven boys and thirty-six girls walked down the center aisle and filed into the front two rows next to the stage. When everyone was standing in place, Mr. Stockman signaled them to sit down.

Angie looked back over her shoulder as she took her seat and spotted her parents, and then Art and Alice three rows behind them. Her mom moved her hand in a tiny wave. Angie knew this was too dignified an occasion for her to wave back, though she would have liked to. She noticed that most of the bleachers and all of the chairs on the gym floor were filled.

When the band finished playing a second number, School Superintendent Clifford Duncan rose and walked from his chair on the stage to the podium to address the audience. Angie tried to concentrate on what he was saying, but her mind kept slipping back—the choir's spring concert and annual spring "tolo" dance, the class picnic, "skip day," GAC.'s annual cruise with overnight camping on one of the islands. Each organization celebrated the end of the school year with some kind of party, and then, the all-school picnic. But mostly she remembered May 2, the night of the senior ball....

Bob Fithian was general chairman of the ball. Eight committees involving most of the seniors and their class advisors worked to make this the best senior ball ever. The theme was based on Chinese culture and the decorating committee filled the town's community hall with Chinese scenes, a Buddha and shrine, and dozens of colorful Chinese lanterns.

A court of twelve gods and goddesses was chosen by the class to reign over the festive, all-school occasion. Rodney Dewar and Bea Brostrom were Zeus and Hera. Angie and Johnny were part of their royal court as Venus and Vulcan. This senior ball would be to Angie the high point of the year.

But the morning of the ball, Angie got out of bed feeling unnaturally warm. "Mom, look at my arms," she said at the breakfast table. "What are these red spots?"

Her mother examined her arms and then lifted Angie's pajama top. "Your stomach is broken out, too," she said. "I think you have measles."

Angie jumped up from the table. "I don't! I couldn't have!"

"Let me take your temperature," Mom said.

Angie held her breath while her mom read the thermometer.

"It says 102 degrees! Finish your breakfast and then you go back to bed and rest."

Angie went back to bed, but she didn't rest. She drank glass after glass of cold water and sucked on ice cubes. At four in the afternoon, her mom came again with the thermometer.

"It's down to 100. That's good, but how do you feel?"

Angie told her she felt great and maybe her rash was from something she ate. Her mom didn't think so. Angie told her that, no matter what, she was going to the ball! Her mom said not if she was sick. Angie said she wasn't sick. She just had a few spots. And what about the beautiful formal they'd bought her? Finally her mom shook her head and gave in.

The ball was spectacular! Boys in slacks, sport coats, and ties. Girls in rustling formals. The junior class had been invited to attend the ball, so, in all, 75 couples, danced to the music of Mert Perkins and his orchestra.

When the musicians put down their instruments for a break, the boys and their dates gathered around the refreshment table, sampling little sandwiches, cookies, and punch. The refreshment committee— Angie, Joyce, Faith, and Gordon Christenson—stood behind the table to refill each serving plate as it was emptied and to pour the punch.

Joyce looked up from arranging a cookie plate and stared at Angie. "Boy, your face is sure red!" she exclaimed.

Angie put her hands to her cheeks. Her face felt hot. She was hot all over. She wanted to sit down, but she was serving the punch.

"I'll do that," Joyce said and took the ladle out of her hand. Angie sat down on the bench behind the table. It was only ten o'clock. The crowning of the court was at eleven. She wasn't going to miss that!

And she didn't, but at quarter to twelve, fifteen minutes before the dance was to end, she asked Johnny to take her home.

The next morning her temperature was again 102 degrees and her entire body was covered with red spots. "I shouldn't have let you go out last night!" her mom kept saying. "Now, you stay in bed until fever's gone."

In a few days, Angie's temperature was normal. Her mom decided maybe it was the measles-type disease called roseola, not the hard measles, and now that the spots had faded, she could go back to school. But first, her mom said, handing her a letter, she should read her mail.

It was from Linfield! Angie knew they would respond—one way or the other—to her application for admission. She'd tried not to get her hopes up too much because it was a small college and returning servicemen and women should have priority. After all, four years had been taken from them, and they needed to catch up—

Angie's thoughts were interrupted. Mr. Stevenson, their principal, had been introduced at the podium. He was saying what a fine, progressive town they lived in. In fact, a petition was now circulating in the community to pave Commercial Avenue from 11th Street to 37th Street. A sign of the times—and the future of Anacortes. Now he wished to make a few comments about the future for graduates of the class of '46, but Angie's mind again wandered back into the past....

On Thursday before graduation, carloads of kids drove nearly to Bellingham for their senior banquet at a special restaurant, the Chuckanut Shell. On Sunday, Business and Professional Women hosted a breakfast for senior girls at Amsberry's Café, and Veterans of Foreign Wars served a buffet at the V.F.W. Hall for senior boys.

Sunday night, the Anacortes Ministerial Board put on the traditional Baccalaureate Service in the gym-auditorium. Betty Lunde sang "The Lord's Prayer." The main speaker, Reverend I.D. Archer, pastor of the Church of Christ, spoke on the subject, "Character, the Secret of Success Tomorrow."

Now Mr. Stevenson, still at the podium, was introducing the four honor students, each of whom would speak for three minutes on the subject of "Looking Ahead."

Angie looked ahead. After the commencement exercises, the whole class with teachers and parents who volunteered to be chaperones were going to the Fithian's home at Similk Beach for an all-night party. There'd be food and dancing, walking on the beach and swimming in the bay.

Angie looked farther ahead. To Linfield! The letter her mom handed her that day stated that her application had been accepted and she would soon be receiving a catalog of class offerings. When the catalog arrived, Angie studied the possibilities. She could major in religion and minor in education. After graduation, she would be qualified to work for a church as Director of Christian Education. Or she could major in English and minor in education to become a high school teacher. Or maybe major in literature because she loved books, and minor in writing.

Tuition was high at private schools like Linfield College, but Dad finally said that as long as she graduated in something where she could support herself, he'd find the money for her education. She'd become awful independent around the house lately, he'd noticed, and, if she kept that up, he'd be glad to help her move out! Then she saw him wink at Mom!

Angie remembered Art saying his "lil' Cuz" had grown up. She hoped that was true. She knew she'd finally learned to appreciate her parents, her dad's sense of humor, her mom's hovering, even their broken English and old-country ways that had once been an embarrassment to her. But more than that, being grown up probably meant thinking independently. Being ready to listen and examine old ideas and welcome new ideas, even in matters of religion. College would help her with all this.

The speeches were over. Mr. Duncan returned to the podium. He asked the audience to refrain from clapping until all the students had received their diplomas. He also said he hoped the graduates would be respectful of their classmates.

Mr. Stockman signaled the first row of graduates to stand and walk toward the steps leading to the stage where they would be given their diplomas, shake hands with Mr. Stevenson, and return to their seats. Boys in the class ignored Mr. Duncan's appeal and clapped for their friends as they received their diplomas. Some called out nicknames and whooped for their best buddies.

Angie worried that she'd trip crossing the stage and everyone would laugh, but she returned to her seat without incident and watched the second row stand and move toward the stage. Johnny, with the last name of "Waldorf," waited at the end of the line to receive his diploma. When it was his turn, whoops and applause followed him across the stage and all the way back to his seat. Johnny waved at his friends, but Angie could feel her face turn red.

She was remembering her conversation with Johnny the night he took her home from the senior banquet at the Chuckanut Shell. He had signed up to go into the army after graduation. Angie would be going away to college in the fall. They would each be having new experiences in new places—and meeting new people. For now, they would enjoy the graduation activities together, but after graduation they'd be going their own ways. They agreed they would probably always be friends and see each other occasionally.... The goodnight kiss was tempered with melancholy.

Commencement exercises were over. The band members picked up their instruments. Those playing clarinets and oboes sucked on their reeds to moisten them. Those with horns blew into the valves to clear the passages. Mr. Lunsford tapped his baton on his music stand to get everyone's attention. Then he lifted his baton and the recessional march began.

As the class walked back down the aisle, Angie waved to her parents and Art and Alice. Others in the class were also recognizing their families.

"Hi, Aunt Angie!" a child's voice called from the bleachers. "We come to see you 'grajate.'"

Thelma, Bennie and Linda sat in the first row of the bleachers. Angie didn't know they were coming to her graduation. She also didn't expect to get emotional, but suddenly her throat was tight.

She'd soon be going away to college, but, she reminded herself, she'd be back during vacations to see her family and friends. And maybe, fifty years from now, she'd return to Anacortes for a class reunion! She and her girlfriends would talk about the years that had gone by and show each other pictures of their children and grandchildren.

But, one step at a time. First she'd go home to change her clothes. Johnny would pick her up in an hour and they'd go to the graduation party at the beach. Tomorrow afternoon they'd come back to school to sign yearbooks. Then she'd start her summer job answering the phone and writing up classified ads at the *Anacortes American*. When she wasn't working, she'd be home letting out hems. Skirt lengths had dropped now that the war was over and material was available.

The family was already in the house when she arrived home. Dad, Art, and Bennie visited in the living room while Mom and Thelma ran back and forth from the refrigerator to the dining room table with plates of food. Alice, seven-and-a-half months pregnant, stood at the table arranging the plates.

Angie ran to her room and changed from her dress to slacks and a blouse and joined her family. "Wow! This looks like a real *smörgåsbord*," she said. "A party before the party!"

"Guess we have reason to celebrate," Dad said.

But, when Johnny rang the doorbell an hour later, she was ready to go. She called "Bye," grabbed her purse and ran out the door. Her mind spun. She was now a high-school graduate! Mature! Responsible! Independent—

"Angie," her mom called, running onto the porch after her. "Angie, you forgot your sweater! It'll be cold at the beach, so you need to wear a sweater!"

Angie and Johnny.

Angie dressed for "tolo" dance.

Angie, Lois Persons,
Faith.

Edna and Marivonne, reading the
Sunday funnies.

Skagit County Court House,
Mt. Vernon.

Naturalization
papers.

Fishing boats waiting to unload at Fisherman's Pack.
Guemes Island Ferry in background, 1945.

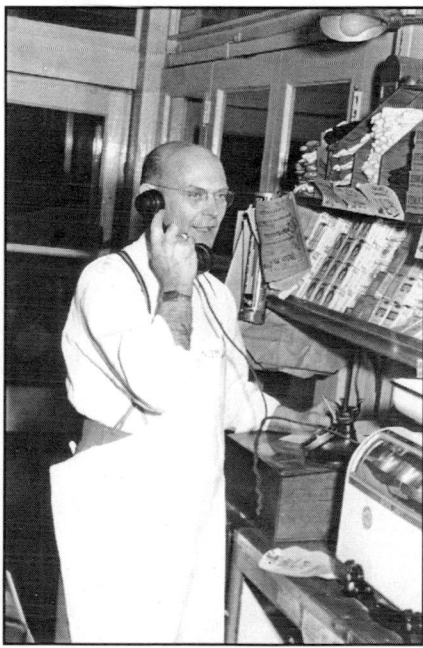

Charlie: "She's moody
sometimes..."

Paul Luvera at work.

Alice, Art (home from service), Angie, Charlie, Tilda.

1946

Art and Alice
at Mt. Baker.

Graduation breakfast: Joyce, Edna, Phyllis, Janet, Faith, Yvonne, Angie.

1946 graduates:
Faith, Edna, Angie, Joyce.

Time to relax.

Looking ahead to college: Joyce, Angie, Edna, Faith, 1946.

Joyce, Angie, Edna, Faith at class reunion, 2004.

Charlie's brother, Vilhelm Sjöroos, age 62, 1959.

Charlie's mother, Anna Lisa Sjöroos, age 80, 1943.

Närpes family from left: Edvin and Birger Häggqvist and brides,
Elvie and Annie, June 1945.

Charlie and Tilda, Finland visit, 1948.

EPILOGUE

F aith, Joyce, Edna, Phyllis, and I were among those who went on to college. Some chose employment directly out of high school. Most members of the class of 1946 married and had families. Altogether, they did very much as most high school graduates do. They found, filled, and played productive roles in society.

Joy Kamps graduated from Mount Vernon Community College and, several years later, enrolled in Bellingham Teacher's College. She was a fine student and was offered several high school teaching positions upon graduation. One week before graduation, Joy contracted Asian flu. She had a weak immune system due to polio and could not fight it off. She died at age 31. Many of her professors and teachers came to her service, one of the largest funerals ever held in Anacortes.

The polio virus was isolated in the late 1940's. Jonas Salk, in 1955, developed a safe and effective vaccine. Mothers finally relaxed. Their children could be vaccinated against the crippling and deadly disease.

Kikuko (Kiki) Okawa and her sister Kimiko graduated from high school in Gilroy, California. Kiki attended San Jose State University and, against considerable prejudice, completed a major in business administration. She went on to graduate school and studied secondary school teaching.

Kiki had difficulty finding a high-school job because of her Japanese ancestry. A few days before school started, she secured a teaching position in San Lorenzo Valley High School in Felton, California. The business teacher was moving away and the school needed someone immediately. The principal hired Kiki on the provision that the Board of Education approve. She was told that if students objected to her presence, she was to go immediately to the principal. The kids were, however, very accepting, and Kiki enjoyed her years as a high school teacher.

Kiki also taught at community colleges in the San Jose area. Her sister Kimiko worked as a legal secretary during those years. Their parents continued to live in Gilroy.

William K. Nakamura and James K. Okubo joined the 100th Battalion's 442nd Regimental Combat Team during World War II, while their families lived in internment camps. In March 2001, each man, along with 20 other veterans of Asian ancestry, was posthumously awarded the Medal of Honor, the highest award for valor. The U.S. Courthouse in Seattle was renamed the William Kenzo Nakamura Courthouse. A medical and dental clinic at Fort Lewis was named in honor of Okubo. (*The Bend Bulletin, Oregon / Northwest* March 30, 2001)

Paul Luvera spearheaded the move to bring Anacortes Veneer, Inc. to Anacortes. Born in Italy, he immigrated in 1911 and moved to Anacortes in 1918. He opened Luvera's grocery store in 1922 and managed it until retiring in 1957, at which time he became a noted carver of totem poles. Everyone's friend and dedicated to his community, he served as president of Anacortes Chamber of Commerce, chaired the Red Cross War Fund, acted on innumerable committees, and strongly supported education.

He was Washington State Senator from 1953 to 1957, long enough to initiate the reconstruction of a section of State Route 20 leading into Anacortes. This highway has been named "Paul Luvera, Sr. Memorial Highway."

In 1948, my parents, Charlie and Tilda, made their long-overdue trip to Finland. Charlie reunited with his brother Vilhelm and met Vilhelm's wife and children and their families. Tilda met her brother Ivar's widow Ester and their sons, Birger and Edvin, their wives and children, and young Ture. Tilda wrote in a letter to Angie, "People here have nothing, but they welcome us and treat us like royalty."

Tilda and Charlie enjoyed their retirement years in Anacortes—fishing the lakes, drinking coffee with friends, welcoming grandchildren on holidays.

Thelma and Bennie reared their four children in Shelton, Washington. Bennie owned a service station and later sold real estate. He exited his military career in the Army Reserve as a Lieutenant-Colonel. He died in 1985. Thelma continues to live in Shelton.

Art became superintendent of the Hardboard Plant in Anacortes in 1957. He and his family moved to the East Coast in 1962, where he continued his career in wood products. Later, Art's parents, Ida and Ida's-Charlie, joined the family in Atlanta, Georgia. Art and Alice retired in Atlanta near their three children and grandchildren.

I graduated from Linfield College in 1949 with a major in English and minor in secondary education. I taught junior and senior high-school English, speech, and writing. I married Ralph Rands, a fellow Linfield graduate, and together we reared four daughters, all of whom are now married with children of their own. Over the years, I've visited Finland five times and come to know my mother's and father's families.

In retirement, I did what retired English teachers are inclined to do: I wrote a book. *Where the Huckleberries Grow* tells the story of my parents' immigrating, meeting, and marrying, and then rearing their family in remote logging camps.

When I market the book at Scandinavian festivals, I often hear family stories from those who visit my booth. Many of the stories are far more dramatic than mine. I tell them, write it down—for your children.

From those who have read *Where the Huckleberries Grow*, I hear, "So, what happens next to the Lind family?" Thus I was motivated to write the sequel, *Even Seagulls Cry*.

Widowed in 1997, I remarried in 2000 and live with my husband, Charles Warren, at Black Butte Ranch, Sisters, Oregon.

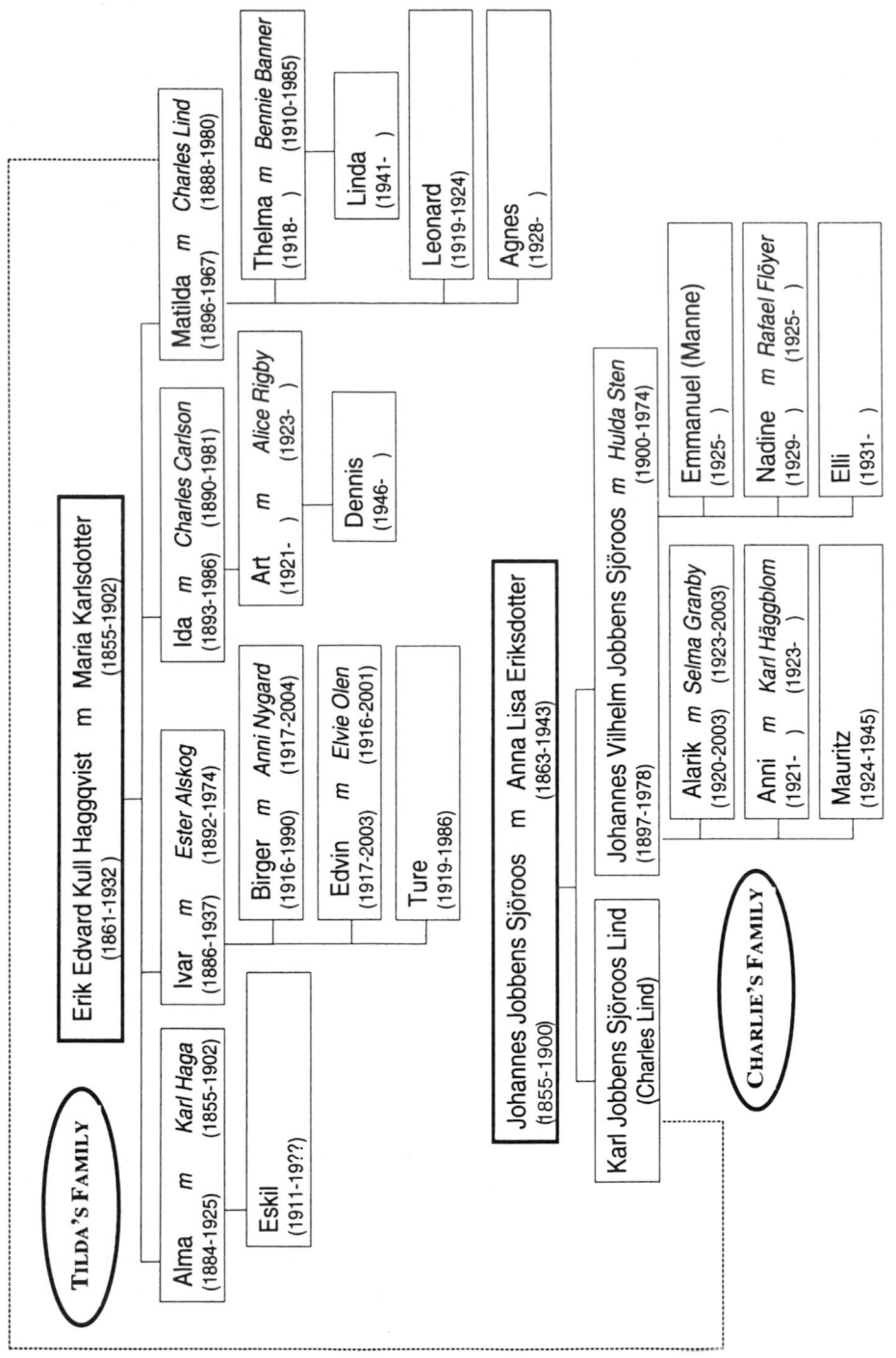

Present day boundaries of Finland shown in light gray.
Darker gray indicates areas ceded to Russia in Armistice
Agreement, September 18, 1944, and incorporated into the Paris
Peace Treaty, signed by Allied Powers, February 10, 1947.

A BRIEF OVERVIEW
OF FINNISH-RUSSIAN WARS

1939

November 29   Russia attacks Finland; Winter War begins.

1940

March 12   Winter War ends. Soviet terms in the Peace of Moscow: Finland cede to Russia southern Karelia, including Finland's second-largest city, Vyborg, and Lake Ladoga; some islands in Gulf of Finland; Petsamo area in north. Lease Finland's naval base at Hanko for 30 years. As a result, 400,000 Finns in ceded areas move into Finland.

                Those contributing to the defense of Finland during Winter War: Sweden, 8,000 volunteers; Denmark, 800; Norway, 800; Hungary, 450; Italy, 150; USA, 350. (Engle and Paananen 1992 Appendix B p. 153–156)

June   Finland enacts Rapid Emergency Resettlement Act, which acquires 330,000 hectares (~1274 square miles) of land for resettlement of farmers from Karelia.

Fall   Finland allows Germany to traverse their land and build supply bases in Lapland in exchange for military supplies.

1941

June 26	Finland participates with Germany in attacking Soviet Union. Continuation War begins.
October 10	Anthony Eden, British Foreign Secretary, declares war on Finland for entering Russian territory.
November 29	Finland responds they want only restoration of 1939 Finnish-Russian border and reclaims this border. Approximately 270,000 refugees return to their homes in Karelia. Finnish troops successfully defend this border against repeated incursions by the Russian army until June 1944.

1943

December	Finland tries to extricate itself from the war. Approaches Russia with policy of Good Neighborliness. Russia's terms in response are too extreme to be acceptable.

1944

June	Russia attacks Karelian front. Bombs Helsinki
August 4	Mannerheim elected president of Finland. Ordered peace negotiations with Russia.
September 4	Finland breaks off diplomatic relations with Germany
September 5	Armistice declared between Finland and Russia.
September 18	Finns and Russians sign Armistice Agreement. Russia's terms:

Withdraw Finnish troops to 1940 line (end of Winter War); drive German army out of Lapland; give Russians 50 year lease of Porkkala area near Helsinki; hand over Petsamo area and segment on eastern border of northern Finland; pay war indemnity $600 million over 6 years.

More than 400,000 refugees flee back into Finland.

1945

April   Finland completes expulsion of German army out of
                         Lapland, ending Continuation War.

                         Thousands of women helped in the war effort through
                         the Lotta Organization. They cooked for the troops,
                         nursed and wrote letters for the wounded, helped
                         where needed throughout the Winter War and Con-
                         tinuation War. (This organization began in 1808 dur-
                         ing the war between Russia and Sweden when a Finn-
                         ish officer took his wife Lotta with him to help at the
                         front.)

1947

February 10   Terms of Armistice Agreement between Finland and
                         Russia are incorporated into the Paris Peace Treaties
                         signed by the Allied Powers.

1948

April 6   Finland and Soviet Union sign an Agreement of
                         Friendship, Cooperation, and Mutual Assistance.

"It has been estimated that Finland lost 85,000 dead between 1939 and 1945 (2% of their total population), of whom 90% were young men between the ages of 20 and 30 years. A further 50,000 were permanently injured. This appalling total of human loss was in addition to the loss of territory and the material losses through reparations payments, the devastation of towns caused by war, the loss of productive capacity in the ceded territories. A further burden was the problem of resettling the flood of refugees, who, for the second time in four years, were forced to move out of Karelia." (Singleton 1998 p.133 A Short History of Finland)

President Mannerheim stated, "A high price has been paid for freedom." But the country had buried its dead and retained its independence. Their spirit was not compromised. By 1952, they completed payments to Russia on their $600 million war debt, and the Soviet Union became Finland's main trading partner. Finland has survived and prospered as a vital Democracy in the post war years.

A Brief Overview
of World War II

1939

September 1	Germany invades Poland.
September 3	France and Great Britain declare war on Germany.
September 17	Soviet Union invades Poland.
November 29	Russia invades Finland.

1940

March 12	Finnish-Russian War ends.
April 9	Germany invades Norway and Denmark.
May 10	Germany continues aggression in the west.
June 22	France signs armistice treaty with Germany.
July 10	Battle of Britain; blitz on London.

1941

June 22	Germany invades Russia.
December 7	Japan attacks Pearl Harbor.
December 8	U.S. declares war on Japan.
December 10	Japanese invade Philippines.
December 11	Germany and Italy declare war on U.S; U.S. declares war on Germany and Italy.
December 23	Wake Island falls to Japanese.

1942

January 2	Manila falls; U.S. withdraws to Bataan Peninsula.
January 14	Alien registration ordered by President Roosevelt.
February 13	Roosevelt signs order for internment of 110,000 Japanese Americans from the West Coast.

April 9	Bataan Peninsula falls. Death march begins.
May 30	First RAF 1000-bomber raid on Germany.
June 4	Battle of Midway begins.
November 8	Allies begin North African campaign.

1943

January 27	U.S. begins bombing raids on Germany.
February 2	German forces capitulate at Stalingrad.
February 9	U.S. Marines recapture Guadalcanal.
May 13	German forces retreat from North Africa.
September 8	Italy surrenders to Allies.

1944

January 31	U.S. forces land on Marshall Islands.
June 6	Allies land in Normandy.
June 15	U.S. begins air attacks on Japan.
August 25	Germans surrender Paris.
October 20	U.S. troops land in Philippines.

1945

February 19	U.S. forces land on Iwo Jima.
April 1	U.S. forces land on Okinawa.
April 12	Roosevelt dies; Truman becomes President.
April 25	UN conference opens in San Francisco.
April 28	Mussolini killed by partisans.
April 30	Hitler commits suicide.
May 2	Russia takes Berlin.
May 7	Germany surrenders unconditionally.
May 8	V-E Day.
August 6	Atomic bomb dropped on Hiroshima.
August 9	Atomic bomb dropped on Nagasaki.
August 14	Japan surrenders unconditionally.
August 15	V-J Day.

In 1945, at the height of WW II, U.S. military personnel numbered 12,123,455. At the end of the war, military deaths, 405,399; wounded, 670,846. (Rabinowitz, Editor 1998 p.106 *America in the Forties*)

Even more horrific statistics are cited by Emmy Werner, *Through the Eyes of Innocents*. "World War II was the first modern war in which more civilians than soldiers were killed and maimed. When it ended in August 1945, more than 39 million civilians had died as a direct result of the war and some 13 million of these were children."

At the end of the war, Europe and Japan were in ruins. In addition to the dead, an estimated 30 to 60 million people had become displaced persons, left to wander like ghosts among the tailings of what had once been a civilization.

President Roosevelt, addressing White House Correspondents' Association on February 12, 1943, said, "Unless the peace that follows recognizes that the whole world is one neighborhood and does justice to the whole human race, the germs of another world war will remain as a constant threat to mankind." (1997 p. 122 Franklin Delano Roosevelt Memorial, Washington D.C.)

Since President Roosevelt spoke those words, this country has fought in four more devastating wars: Korea, Vietnam, Gulf, and now Iraq. Sometime one nation must tell another, "I'll put away my guns and you turn back your tanks. Then let's sit down and talk it over. We are neighbors, after all."

GLOSSARY OF SWEDISH WORDS

Bark Bröd .... Bark bread

Fattigmand .... "Poor-man" cookie

Feele bunk .... Yogurt-like dish made from souring agent or "starter"

Framstugon .... Entry room to house, not sealed from weather

Goddag .... Hello, Good day

Gud i himlen .... God in heaven (mild oath)

Lillstugon .... Small house on son's property reserved for elderly parents

Lördagsvals .... "Satuday Night Waltz"

Lutfisk .... Dish made from dried fish, usually cod

Man .... Husband

Moster .... Aunt (mother's sister)

Nej .... No

På tår .... Second cup of coffee

Pappa .... Father, Dad

Scorpa .... Sliced coffee bread sprinkled with cinnamon and sugar, and then oven toasted

Småkusin .... "Small" cousin, next to first cousin

Smörgåsbord .... Buffet of heavy *hors d'oeuvres*

Spritsa, sand bakkels .... Rich butter cookies shaped for baking

Tack så mycket .... Thanks so much

Tyst, nu .... Quiet, now

Välkommen .... Welcome

Var så god .... Please, help yourself

* Today the bark-bread tradition is carried on at Kilen Museum in Sideby, Finland, where it is baked for the tourist trade. Bark meal includes important nutritional substances and contains more zinc, magnesium and iron than is found in rye and wheat and is full of fiber.

BIBLIOGRAPHY

BOOKS

Bailey, Ronald H. and Editors of *Time-Life Books. The Home Front: USA.* Time-Life Books: Alexandria, Virginia, 1978.

Barrington, Judith. *Writing the Memoir.* The Eighth Mountain Press: Portland, Oregon, 2002.

Burns, James MacGregor. *Roosevelt, The Soldier of Freedom 1940–1945.* Harcourt Brace Jovanovich, Inc.: New York, 1970.

Elting, John R. and Editors of Time-Life Books. *World War II Battles for Scandinavia.* Time-Life Books: Alexandria, Virginia, 1981.

Engle, Eloise and Paananen, Lauri. *The Winter War: The Soviet Attack on Finland 1939–1940.* Stackpole Books: Mechanicsburg, Pennsylvania, 1992.

Goldhagen, Daniel Jonah. *Hitler's Willing Executioners, Ordinary Germans and the Holocaust.* Alfred A. Knopf: New York, 1996. Pages 97–106.

Goodwin, Doris Kearns. *No Ordinary Time: Franklin & Eleanor Roosevelt, The Home Front in World War II.* A Touchstone Book, Simon & Schuster: New York, 1995.

Gordon, Lois and Gordon, Alan. *American Chronicle 1920–1989.* Crown Publishers, Inc.: New York, 1990.

Halprin, Lawrence. *The Franklin Delano Roosevelt Memorial.* Chronicle Books: San Francisco, 1997.

Heide, Robert and Gilman, John. *Home Front America.* Chronicle Books: San Francisco, 1995.

Klinge, Matti. *A Brief History of Finland.* Otova Publishing Company, Ltd.: Helsinki, Finland, 1997.

Murdock, Maureen. *Unreliable Truth: on Memoir and Memory*. Seal Press: New York, 2003.

Myhrman, Anders. *Finlandsvenskar I Amerika* (Finland Swedes in America). *Svenska Litteratursallskapet I Finland*. Helsingfors, Finland, 1972.

Otsuka, Julie. *When the Emperor Was Divine*. Alfred A. Knopf: New York, 2002.

Pensar, Margareta; Nystrand, Kajsa; and others. *Molpe Byaforskare* (Molpe Village Research) *Mera Glimtar från Gamla Molpe*. Oy Fram Ab: Vasa, Finland, 1998. p. 27–41.

Rabinowitz, Harold A. Editor. *Sentimental Journey: America in the 40's*. The Reader's Digest Association, Inc.: Pleasantville, New York/ Montreal, 1998.

Ross, Zoe, Project Editor. *Insight Guide, Finland*. Langenscheidt Publishers, Inc.: Maspeth, New York, 2000.

Sandburg, Carl. *Abraham Lincoln, One-Volume Edition*. Harcourt, Brace and Company, Inc.: New York. 1954.

Singleton, Fred. *A Short History of Finland*. Cambridge University Press: Cambridge, England, 1998.

Stolley, Richard B. *Life, Our Century in Pictures. 1940–1945 World on Fire*. Little Brown and Company: Boston, New York, London.

Tunnell, Michael O. and Chilcoat, George W. *The Children of Topaz. The Story of a Japanese-American Internment Camp*. Holiday House: New York, 1996.

Webber, Bert. *Panic at Fort Stevens: Japanese Navy Shells Fort Stevens, Oregon, in World War-II*. Webb Research Group Publishers: Medford, Oregon, 1995.

Webber, Bert. *Retaliation*. Oregon State University Press: Corvallis, Oregon, 1975.

Wenborn, Neil. *The USA, A Chronicle in Pictures*. Smithmark Publishers, Inc.: New York, 1991.

Werner, Emmy E. *Through the Eyes of Innocents: Children Witness World War II*. Westview Press, a member of Perseus Books Group: Boulder, Colorado, 2000.

PERIODICALS

Anonymous. "The Scandinavians Who Fought in the Finnish Winter War." *Scandinavian Press*. Blaine, WA. Vol. 11, Issue1, Winter 2004. p.18.

Damstrom, Gunnar. "Finland at War 1944, Interview: Walter Forsstrom, Finnish Army Veteran." *The Swedish Finn Historical Society*. Seattle WA Vol.12, Issue 3. July–August 2003.

Life, 50 Years, Special Anniversary Issue Volume 9, Number 12, Time Inc.: New York, Fall 1986.

Smedman, Lisa. "Reluctant Enemies." *Scandinavian Press*. Blaine WA. Vol. 8, Issue 2. Spring 2001. p. 21–23.

OTHER

Anacortes Museum Collection. *Anacortes American*. Selected Newspapers, 1940–1946.

**FOR ADDITIONAL COPIES OF
EVEN SEAGULLS CRY**

Write or Call:
Agnes Rands
Linden Press
P.O. Box 8249
Sisters, OR 97759
(541-595-2285)

or

E-mail: ALinden99@aol.com

Include name, address, city, state, zip
and a check for
$14.95
plus $2.00 for packaging and postage